ArtScroll Mesorah Series®

Rabbi Nosson Scherman / Rabbi Meir Zlotowitz

General Editors

הגדה של פסח
בכל דור ודור

GENERATION

The Passover Haggadah
— with its messages for our time

RABBI MOSHE GRYLAK

Translated by Rabbi Moshe Gelbein

IN EVERY

Published by
Mesorah Publications, ltd

FIRST EDITION
First Impression . . . February 2002

Published and Distributed by
MESORAH PUBLICATIONS, Ltd.
Brooklyn, New York 11232

Distributed in Europe by
LEHMANNS
Unit E, Viking Industrial Park
Rolling Mill Road
Jarrow, Tyne & Wear NE32 3DP
England

Distributed in Australia & New Zealand by
GOLDS WORLD OF JUDAICA
3-13 William Street
Balaclava, Melbourne 3183
Victoria Australia

Distributed in Israel by
SIFRIATI / A. GITLER — BOOKS
6 Hayarkon Street
Bnei Brak 51127

Distributed in South Africa by
KOLLEL BOOKSHOP
Shop 8A Norwood Hypermarket
Norwood 2196, Johannesburg, South Africa

THE ARTSCROLL MESORAH SERIES ®
IN EVERY GENERATION
© Copyright 2002, by MESORAH PUBLICATIONS, Ltd.
4401 Second Avenue / Brooklyn, N.Y. 11232 / (718) 921-9000 / www.artscroll.com
ALL RIGHTS RESERVED

ISBN:
1-57819-778-3 (hard cover)
1-57819-779-1 (paperback)

Typography by CompuScribe at ArtScroll Studios, Ltd.
4401 Second Avenue / Brooklyn, N.Y. 11232 / (718) 921-9000

➳ Table of Contents

בְּדִיקַת חָמֵץ

On the night of 14 Nissan, the night before the Pesach Seder, the search for *chametz* (leaven) is made. It should be done with a candle as soon as possible after nightfall. [When the first Seder is on Saturday night, the search is conducted on Thursday night (13 Nissan).]
Before the search is begun, the following blessing is recited.
If several people assist in the search, only one recites the blessing for all.

בָּרוּךְ אַתָּה יהוה, אֱלֹהֵינוּ מֶלֶךְ הָעוֹלָם, אֲשֶׁר קִדְּשָׁנוּ בְּמִצְוֹתָיו, וְצִוָּנוּ עַל בִּעוּר חָמֵץ.

Upon completion of the *chametz* search, the *chametz* is wrapped well and set aside to be burned the next morning, and the following declaration is made. The declaration must be understood in order to take effect; one who does not understand the Aramaic text may recite it in English, Yiddish or any other language. Any *chametz* that will be used for that evening's supper or the next day's breakfast or for any other purpose prior to the final removal of *chametz* the next morning is not included in this declaration.

כָּל חֲמִירָא וַחֲמִיעָא דְּאִכָּא בִּרְשׁוּתִי, דְּלָא חֲמִתֵּהּ וּדְלָא בְעַרְתֵּהּ וּדְלָא יְדַעְנָא לֵהּ, לִבָּטֵל וְלֶהֱוֵי הֶפְקֵר כְּעַפְרָא דְאַרְעָא.

בִּעוּר חָמֵץ

The following declaration, which includes all *chametz* without exception, is to be made after the burning of leftover *chametz*. It should be recited in a language which one understands. When Pesach begins on Motza'ei Shabbos, this declaration is made on Shabbos morning. Any *chametz* remaining from the Shabbos morning meal is flushed down the drain before the declaration is made.

כָּל חֲמִירָא וַחֲמִיעָא דְּאִכָּא בִּרְשׁוּתִי, דַּחֲזִתֵּהּ וּדְלָא חֲזִתֵּהּ, דַּחֲמִתֵּהּ וּדְלָא חֲמִתֵּהּ, דְּבִעַרְתֵּהּ וּדְלָא בִעַרְתֵּהּ, לִבָּטֵל וְלֶהֱוֵי הֶפְקֵר כְּעַפְרָא דְאַרְעָא.

THE SEARCH FOR CHAMETZ

On the night of 14 Nissan, the night before the Pesach Seder, the search for *chametz* (leaven) is made. It should be done with a candle as soon as possible after nightfall. [When the first Seder is on Saturday night, the search is conducted on Thursday night (13 Nissan).]

Before the search is begun, the following blessing is recited.

If several people assist in the search, only one recites the blessing for all.

Blessed are You, HASHEM, our God, King of the Universe, Who has sanctified us with His commandments and has commanded us concerning the removal of *chametz*.

Upon completion of the *chametz* search, the *chametz* is wrapped well and set aside to be burned the next morning, and the following declaration is made. The declaration must be understood in order to take effect; one who does not understand the Aramaic text may recite it in English, Yiddish or any other language. Any *chametz* that will be used for that evening's supper or the next day's breakfast or for any other purpose prior to the final removal of *chametz* the next morning is not included in this declaration.

Any *chametz* or leaven that is in my possession which I have not seen, have not removed and do not know about, should be nullified and be worthless and considered like dust.

BURNING THE CHAMETZ

The following declaration, which includes all *chametz* without exception, is to be made after the burning of leftover *chametz*. It should be recited in a language which one understands. When Pesach begins on Motza'ei Shabbos, this declaration is made on Shabbos morning. Any *chametz* remaining from the Shabbos morning meal is flushed down the drain before the declaration is made.

Any *chametz* or leaven that is in my possession, whether I have recognized it or not, whether I have seen it or not, whether I have removed it or not, should be nullified and be worthless and considered like dust.

עָרוּב תַּבְשִׁילִין

It is forbidden to prepare on Yom Tov for the next day even if that day is the Sabbath. If, however, Sabbath preparations were started before Yom Tov began, they may be continued on Yom Tov. *Eruv tavshilin* constitutes this preparation. A matzah and any cooked food (such as fish, meat or an egg) are set aside on the day before Yom Tov to be used on the Sabbath and the blessing is recited followed by the declaration [made in a language understood by the one making the *eruv*]. If the first days of Pesach fall on Thursday and Friday, an *eruv tavshilin* must be made on Wednesday.

[In *Eretz Yisrael,* where only one day Yom Tov is in effect, the *eruv* is omitted.]

בָּרוּךְ אַתָּה יהוה אֱלֹהֵינוּ מֶלֶךְ הָעוֹלָם, אֲשֶׁר קִדְּשָׁנוּ בְּמִצְוֹתָיו, וְצִוָּנוּ עַל מִצְוַת עֵרוּב.

בַּהֲדֵין עֵרוּבָא יְהֵא שָׁרֵא לָנָא לַאֲפוּיֵי וּלְבַשּׁוּלֵי וּלְאַצְלוּיֵי וּלְאַטְמוּנֵי וּלְאַדְלוּקֵי שְׁרָגָא וּלְתַקָּנָא וּלְמֶעְבַּד כָּל צָרְכָנָא, מִיּוֹמָא טָבָא לְשַׁבְּתָא [לָנָא וּלְכָל יִשְׂרָאֵל הַדָּרִים בָּעִיר הַזֹּאת].

הַדְלָקַת הַנֵּרוֹת

On each Yom Tov night of Pesach two blessings are recited. When Pesach coincides with the Sabbath, light the candles, then cover the eyes and recite the blessings. Uncover the eyes and gaze briefly at the candles. When Pesach falls on a weekday, some follow the above procedure, while others recite the blessings before lighting the candles. When Pesach coincides with the Sabbath, the words in brackets are added.

[It is forbidden to create a new flame — for example, by striking a match — on Yom Tov. Therefore, on the second night the candles must be lit from a flame that has been burning from before Yom Tov.]

בָּרוּךְ אַתָּה יהוה אֱלֹהֵינוּ מֶלֶךְ הָעוֹלָם, אֲשֶׁר קִדְּשָׁנוּ בְּמִצְוֹתָיו, וְצִוָּנוּ לְהַדְלִיק נֵר שֶׁל [שַׁבָּת וְשֶׁל] יוֹם טוֹב.

ERUV TAVSHILIN

It is forbidden to prepare on Yom Tov for the next day even if that day is the Sabbath. If, however, Sabbath preparations were started before Yom Tov began, they may be continued on Yom Tov. *Eruv tavshilin* constitutes this preparation. A matzah and any cooked food (such as fish, meat or an egg) are set aside on the day before Yom Tov to be used on the Sabbath and the blessing is recited followed by the declaration [made in a language understood by the one making the *eruv*]. If the first days of Pesach fall on Thursday and Friday, an *eruv tavshilin* must be made on Wednesday.

[In *Eretz Yisrael,* where only one day Yom Tov is in effect, the *eruv* is omitted.]

Blessed are You, HASHEM, our God, King of the Universe, Who has sanctified us with His commandments and has commanded us concerning the mitzvah of *eruv.*

Through this *eruv* may we be permitted to bake, cook, fry, insulate, kindle flame, prepare for, and do anything necessary on the Festival for the sake of the Shabbos [for ourselves and for all Jews who live in this city].

KINDLING LIGHTS

On each Yom Tov night of Pesach two blessings are recited. When Pesach coincides with the Sabbath, light the candles, then cover the eyes and recite the blessings. Uncover the eyes and gaze briefly at the candles. When Pesach falls on a weekday, some follow the above procedure, while others recite the blessings before lighting the candles. When Pesach coincides with the Sabbath, the words in brackets are added.

[It is forbidden to create a new flame — for example, by striking a match — on Yom Tov. Therefore, on the second night the candles must be lit from a flame that has been burning from before Yom Tov.]

Blessed are You, HASHEM, our God, King of the Universe, Who has sanctified us with His commandments, and has commanded us to kindle the light of [the Sabbath and of] the Festival.

בָּרוּךְ אַתָּה יהוה אֱלֹהֵינוּ מֶלֶךְ הָעוֹלָם,
שֶׁהֶחֱיָנוּ וְקִיְּמָנוּ וְהִגִּיעָנוּ לַזְּמַן הַזֶּה.

It is customary to recite the following prayer after the kindling.
The words in brackets are included as they apply.

יְהִי רָצוֹן לְפָנֶיךָ, יהוה אֱלֹהַי וֵאלֹהֵי אֲבוֹתַי,
שֶׁתְּחוֹנֵן אוֹתִי

[וְאֶת אִישִׁי, וְאֶת בָּנַי, וְאֶת בְּנוֹתַי,
וְאֶת אָבִי, וְאֶת אִמִּי]

וְאֶת כָּל קְרוֹבַי; וְתִתֵּן לָנוּ וּלְכָל יִשְׂרָאֵל חַיִּים
טוֹבִים וַאֲרוּכִים; וְתִזְכְּרֵנוּ בְּזִכְרוֹן טוֹבָה וּבְרָכָה;
וְתִפְקְדֵנוּ בִּפְקֻדַּת יְשׁוּעָה וְרַחֲמִים; וּתְבָרְכֵנוּ
בְּרָכוֹת גְּדוֹלוֹת; וְתַשְׁלִים בָּתֵּינוּ; וְתַשְׁכֵּן
שְׁכִינָתְךָ בֵּינֵינוּ. וְזַכֵּנִי לְגַדֵּל בָּנִים וּבְנֵי בָנִים
חֲכָמִים וּנְבוֹנִים, אוֹהֲבֵי יהוה, יִרְאֵי אֱלֹהִים,
אַנְשֵׁי אֱמֶת, זֶרַע קֹדֶשׁ, בַּיהוה דְּבֵקִים,
וּמְאִירִים אֶת הָעוֹלָם בַּתּוֹרָה וּבְמַעֲשִׂים טוֹבִים,
וּבְכָל מְלֶאכֶת עֲבוֹדַת הַבּוֹרֵא. אָנָּא שְׁמַע אֶת
תְּחִנָּתִי בָּעֵת הַזֹּאת, בִּזְכוּת שָׂרָה וְרִבְקָה וְרָחֵל
וְלֵאָה אִמּוֹתֵינוּ, וְהָאֵר נֵרֵנוּ שֶׁלֹּא יִכְבֶּה לְעוֹלָם
וָעֶד, וְהָאֵר פָּנֶיךָ וְנִוָּשֵׁעָה. אָמֵן.

Blessed are You, HASHEM, our God, King of the Universe, Who has kept us alive, sustained us, and brought us to this season.

It is customary to recite the following prayer after the kindling. The words in brackets are included as they apply.

May it be Your will, HASHEM, my God and God of my forefathers, that You show favor to me

---

[my husband, my sons, my daughters,
my father, my mother]

---

and all my relatives; and that You grant us and all Israel a good and long life; that You remember us with a beneficent memory and blessing; that You consider us with a consideration of salvation and compassion; that You bless us with great blessings; that You make our households complete; that You cause Your Presence to dwell among us. Privilege me to raise children and grandchildren who are wise and understanding, who love HASHEM and fear God, people of truth, holy offspring, attached to HASHEM, who illuminate the world with Torah and good deeds and with every labor in the service of the Creator. Please, hear my supplication at this time, in the merit of Sarah, Rebecca, Rachel, and Leah, our mothers, and cause our light to illuminate that it be not extinguished forever, and let Your countenance shine so that we are saved. Amen.

⊰ Preparing for the Seder

The Seder preparations should be made in time for the Seder to begin as soon as the synagogue services are finished. It should not begin before nightfall, however. Matzah, bitter herbs and several other items of symbolic significance are placed on the Seder plate.

Matzah — Three whole matzos are placed one atop the other, separated by a cloth or napkin. Matzah must be eaten three times during the Seder, by itself, with *maror,* and as the *afikoman.* Each time, the minimum portion of matzah for each person should equal the volume of half an egg. Where many people are present, enough matzos should be available to enable each participant to receive a proper portion.

Maror and **Chazeres** — Bitter herbs are eaten twice during the Seder, once by themselves and a second time with matzah. Each time a minimum portion, equal to the volume of half an egg, should be eaten. The Talmud lists several vegetables that qualify as *maror,* two of which are put on the Seder plate in the places marked *chazeres* and *maror.* Most people use romaine lettuce (whole leaves or stalks) for *chazeres,* and horseradish (whole or grated) for *maror,* although either may be used for the mitzvah of eating *maror* later in the Seder.

Charoses — The bitter herbs are dipped into *charoses* (a mixture of grated apples, nuts, other fruit, cinnamon and other spices, mixed with red wine). The *charoses* has the appearance of mortar to symbolize the lot of the Hebrew slaves, whose lives were embittered by hard labor with brick and mortar.

Z'roa [roasted bone] and **Beitzah** [roasted egg] — On the eve of Passover in the Holy Temple in Jerusalem, two sacrifices were offered and their meat roasted and eaten at the Seder feast. To commemorate these two sacrifices, we place a roasted bone (with some meat on it) and a roasted hard-boiled egg on the Seder plate.

The egg, a symbol of mourning, is used in place of a second piece of meat as a reminder of our mourning at the destruction of the Temple — may it be rebuilt speedily in our day.

Karpas — A vegetable (celery, parsley, boiled potato) other than bitter herbs completes the Seder plate. It will be dipped in salt water (according to the Gaon, in vinegar) and eaten. (The salt water is not put on the Seder plate, but it, too, should be prepared beforehand, and placed near the Seder plate.)

ৰঙ The Seder Plate

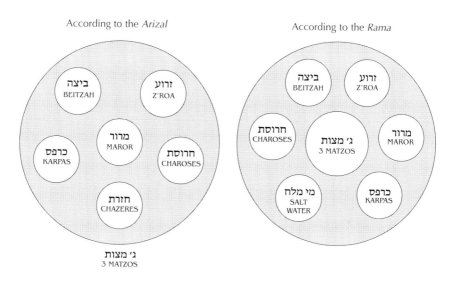

According to the *Arizal*

ביצה
BEITZAH

זרוע
Z'ROA

כרפס
KARPAS

מרור
MAROR

חרוסת
CHAROSES

חזרת
CHAZERES

ג' מצות
3 MATZOS

According to the *Rama*

ביצה
BEITZAH

זרוע
Z'ROA

חרוסת
CHAROSES

ג' מצות
3 MATZOS

מרור
MAROR

מי מלח
SALT
WATER

כרפס
KARPAS

According to the *Vilna Gaon*

חרוסת
CHAROSES

מרור
MAROR

ב' מצות
2 MATZOS

ביצה
BEITZAH

זרוע
Z'ROA

✺§ Introductory Essays

*Exploring the Meaning of Freedom,
Exile and Redemption,
and the Seder Night*

◄§ They Did Not Listen

I t makes no difference whether you are an observant Jew, a non-observant Jew, or even a non-Jew. Regardless of *who* you are, your personality, the way you view the world, and basically every aspect of your life has been in some way shaped by the extraordinary event known as the Exodus. The influence of the Exodus on the believing Jew has been direct and profound. His knowledge of Hashem's involvement, in such remarkably open fashion, with Israel's affairs in Egypt has resulted in a spiritual breakthrough. His heightened spiritual awareness causes him to view the world differently, changes his perspectives, and leads him down a new path in life.

However, it is not only the Jew who has been impacted by the Exodus. Literally the entire world (Western civilization in particular) has been touched by that very glorious event. The Exodus has served to ignite the passions of freedom fighters, has given grounds to those who promote the concept of "equal rights," and has provided a basis for countless other civil movements throughout history. In our present day and age as well, the impressions that the Exodus has left on mankind reverberate and are manifest differently in all human beings, depending on each individual's outlook and belief.

Yet let us forget the present for a moment. Let us try to imagine the way things were *then,* in Egypt, so many years ago. Let us try to imagine the way things must have looked through the eyes of the Jews in Egypt, individuals who endured so much suffering and affliction. Envision yourself for a brief moment inside the mighty empire of ancient Egypt, the "gift of the Nile," as Herodotus referred to it, whose wealth and cultural achievements were due largely in part to the toil and labor of lowly and degraded Jewish slaves. What could such a despised and depressed group of slaves hope for? What did they wish for in an apparently bottomless pit of Egyptian slavery and oppression? Perhaps they simply fantasized being granted a few moments of peace and quiet. Any small improvement in their working conditions that would help relieve some of the intense stress of slavery would certainly top their wish list . . . maybe an increase in the rations of straw that they were provided with in order to make bricks, or another such improvement. In short, they dreamed small dreams, and wished for little more than what could be considered a tiny drop in an ocean of suffering. Nothing could be farther from their minds than the prospect of redemption, which certainly did not even appear to be a glimmer on Israel's horizon. Far away were any thoughts of possible freedom. When Moses addressed the Israelites and broached the topic of an upcoming redemption, they did not listen to him *"because of shortness of breath and hard work"* (*Shemos* 6:9). His speech about the bright future that lay in store for the people of Israel was unable to affect them. His mention of Hashem's promise to redeem them, a promise so truthful that the entire world until the end of time would echo from its truth, did not penetrate their hearts. The dream of a future redemption could not rectify their bleak reality, a reality that seemed to offer little more than endless suffering. They did not hear history beckoning them, inviting them to serve as the beacon of light that could illuminate the darkness that engulfed the other nations of the world. They saw themselves as slaves, slaves indefinitely, and better off unredeemed, as they expressed to Moses after having left Egypt, *"Is this not the statement that we spoke to you in Egypt saying, 'Let us be and we will serve Egypt'?... For it is better that we should serve Egypt than that we should die in the wilderness!"* (ibid. 14:12).

We see therefore that Israel's redemption and freedom from Egypt was certainly an unexpected turn of events. They were astounded at all that was transpiring, and were certainly unaware of the magnitude and endless significance that their freedom would hold for all of mankind.

Herein lies one of the major reasons why our Seder night is of such monumental importance. It is on this night that we apply the lessons of the Exodus to our own lives, to present times. We must envision ourselves breaking free of the heavy chains that bind us in our days as well, applying the eternal message of the Exodus to a present that is often unkind to the Jewish nation. We must instill in ourselves the fervent belief that, despite the troubling times in which we find ourselves, the hope of salvation and redemption is imminent — even though we may not be expecting it. We must try to sense the hand of Divine Providence at work, just like it was in the time of the Exodus.

✺ Leavened Bread and Freedom

Please read this prayer on the eve of Passover. It is "The Prayer of *Chametz* (leavened bread)" that was composed in honor of Passover, by individuals condemned to death:

> *Father in Heaven, it is revealed and known before you that it is our will to fulfill Your will, to celebrate the holiday of Passover with the eating of matzah (unleavened bread) and the observance of the prohibitions of chametz. However, it is about the following matter that our hearts worry. Due to our subjugation we may be restricted from properly observing Your commandments, and our lives are at risk. We are therefore prepared and ready to fulfill Your commandment of "and you shall live by them (Hashem's commandments)," but not die by them. We will therefore be careful to heed Your warning: "Beware for yourself and greatly beware for your soul." It is therefore our prayer to You that You should keep us alive, sustain us, and redeem us speedily, that we should be able to observe Your commandments, do Your will, and serve You wholeheartedly. Amen.*

This prayer was composed in a concentration camp, in a time that was horrific beyond description. It serves, however, as the ideal expression of the concept we know as "freedom." A tortured Jew, subject to the greatest inhumanities known to man, lifts up the small piece of matzah that his oppressor was "kind enough" to bestow upon him. Overcome with a feeling of holiness and purity, amidst excruciating pain and suffering, he recites the aforementioned prayer prior to his blessing over the matzah. With his eyes closed and with a wailing heart, he bites into his precious piece of matzah, chewing ever so slowly, and with utmost concentration, each and every crumb. He fulfills the commandment to eat matzah on Passover, and amazingly manages to taste the sweet taste of freedom.

There are many years separating the first glorious Passover that the Jews celebrated in Egypt, and that bitter Passover spent in the Nazi concentration camp. No two Passovers could be more different. Our first Passover was a miracle-filled occasion that saw the Jews redeemed from their captivity. It was a time when Hashem granted us Divine protection, as His fire and clouds of glory accompanied us through the wilderness. The Passover of the camps, however, found the Jewish people in a time of terrible exile, helpless prey to our cruel enemies. Between these two Passovers, Passovers which represent the extremes in terms of the high and low points of Israel's existence, are Passovers of extreme variety, each one reflecting the period of time in which it was celebrated. There were the nights of Passover that shone with splendor, those years when an autonomous Jewish nation was fortunate enough to be able to worship Hashem in their Holy Temple. Then there were the nights when the Jews were forced to celebrate secretly, stricken with terror and fear, whether due to the agents of the Spanish Inquisition, or to the others who have so often sought to afflict us. Side by side they stand, the Passovers celebrated with peace of mind and tranquility, and the Passovers celebrated in fear and apprehension. The precious Passovers when we were able to celebrate openly and adhere perfectly to every single law, stand right next to the Passovers of secret celebration, the Passovers that took place in the ghettos and death camps, as Jews risked their lives in service of their Creator. Yet, all these Passovers — as different as each one might have been from the next — are essentially the same. Each one saw the Jews remembering that miraculous night on which they left Egypt. Each one was an expression of freedom.

But perhaps the greatest expression of freedom took place on that Passover spent in the cruelest of all places, that Passover which was honored by "The Prayer of *Chametz.*" In truth it defies the imagination. Does the concept of "freedom" have any place inside Auschwitz, Dachau, or Bergen-Belsen? How does one even begin to feel the slightest bit of freedom while being subjected to the horrors experienced in the Nazi concentration camps? We can start to understand only by possessing an insight into the true essence of freedom. This insight shall come from a survivor of the Auschwitz concentration camp: "Those of us who were prisoners in the concentration camps remember those individuals who used to go from bunker to bunker, trying to encourage others, even willing to share their last piece of bread with another. Perhaps such people were few, but there were enough of them in order to prove a very important point. It is possible to take everything from a man, but there is one thing that can never be taken from him, and that is his ability to choose. His ability to choose how he will respond in any situation, and which path he will take in any given circumstance, can never be taken from him" (Prof. Victor Frankl, creator of "Logotherapy," from his book, *A Man's Search for Meaning*). In other words, "freedom" is by no means a physical state, and it is completely unaffected by external factors.

"Freedom" is a spiritual state. It is the expression of man's unwavering conviction in all situations, no matter how trying or how difficult. True freedom is being able to remain true to one's values in the face of adversity, being able to decide one's actions without having to compromise one's principles or beliefs. This "freedom" cannot be affected by persecution, nor can it be taken away by constant oppression. Quite the contrary, it is precisely suffering that awakens the awareness of one's inherent spiritual freedom, and it is only through oppression that one's propensity to be a "free man" is revealed for all to see.

In truth, however, "freedom" can be understood in an even deeper context. Franz Rosenzweig, a Jewish philosopher, sheds light on Hashem's setting us free: "Hashem wanted his children to be 'free.' He therefore conceals, as it were, His true dominion over the world. For if Hashem's true powers were revealed, would the Jewish people have any choice but to serve Him? However, this alone would not be sufficient to properly guarantee the Jews' freedom. Therefore, not only does Hashem not force His children to follow Him, He even tests the Jewish people, creating room for them to err and not recognize their Creator. This allows the Jew to search out Hashem, and continuously fortify himself in his belief. This is the 'free man's' path to belief in Hashem" *(Star of Redemption)*.

We are now able to understand why that moment of a suffering Jew's composition of "The Prayer of *Chametz*" is the moment that best expresses the concept of true "freedom." Tortured Jews, starving and afflicted, confined to the horrors of a concentration camp, do not forget that that day is the eve of Passover. What's more, they offer up a prayer to Hashem apologizing for the fact that they will be forced to eat bread, in violation of the Torah's prohibitions. But why will they be forced to eat bread? Not due to the extreme hunger which weakened their bodies, nor in order to give them the strength to survive. They were forced to eat bread because this itself was the will of Hashem, as the Torah states, *"and you shall live by them* (Hashem's commandments) — and not *die* by them"! How were these Jews able to remain so firm in their devotion to Hashem, amidst the persecution that enveloped them from all sides? It was due to the feeling of freedom that permeated their very beings. On that night, while celebrating Passover in a Nazi concentration camp, those Jews experienced the glorious redemption from Egypt, the same way our forefathers did over 3,000 years ago.

The Jewish redemption from Egypt was not automatic; much had to be accomplished before it would take place. Before there was to be a physical redemption from Egypt, Israel would have to experience redemption on an individual level. Hashem required that the Jews, before being redeemed, should rid their personalities of any trace of slavery. They were not to possess the "slave mentality" that had developed under so many years of Egyptian slavery. It is for this reason that Hashem instructed the Jewish people to slaughter a lamb on the fourteenth of Nissan. The Egyptians worshiped the lamb as a deity. To publicly slaughter it was to incur the fury of the Egyptians, and put the lives of the entire Jewish people at risk. Yet, the Jews were to pay no heed to the angry faces of the Egyptians, and were to slaughter the lamb. Due to the harmful Egyptian influences, many Jews had strayed after the lamb. Slaughtering it would represent the Jewish people's dedication to ridding themselves of their Egyptian influences. For the Jews were to be a free people, neither restricted by their fear of the Egyptians, nor subject to their harmful influences. It was at that moment when the Jews slaughtered the lamb that they truly felt like a free people, even though they were still situated in the land of Egypt. At that moment the Jewish people learned a very profound lesson. One can only begin to achieve freedom when one begins to break the chains of materialism. Freeing oneself from any trace of idolatry is of utmost importance if one hopes to attain "freedom." They understood that only one who chooses to bind himself to these ideals, and stand firm in his belief, can have any hope of achieving this freedom. This is a belief that cannot be touched by the prevailing cultures nor by those who presently impose their control over us. It makes no difference whether they exert physical force on us, or whether they burden us with crushing labor; free men we remain.

From the Passover in Egypt to the Passover in the concentration camps, from the Passovers of the early generations to the Passover of present day, whenever a Jew has chosen to remain loyal to his Judaism, he has proven to be the consummate "free man." It is this loyalty that has prevailed in the periods that saw the Jewish people tested by possession of great wealth and elevated status among their gentile neighbors. It is this loyalty that has prevailed despite the periods of horrible persecution. It is this loyalty that has prevailed in each and every exile in which the Jewish people have found themselves, including our own present exile. For Egypt, as stated in the classical sources, is a representative of every form of materialism. Negative values, brutality, impurity, and falsehood are all represented by the land of Egypt. Leaving Egypt connotes, therefore, an elevation in man's character. It represents a dedication to morality and principled behavior, and recognition of the Creator. These are all qualities that were represented by the pure Jews eating *chametz* in the horrors of the Nazi concentration camp.

הגדה של פסח / 22

⊰ To Delve Into One's Innermost Soul

*I*f one observes the traditional Passover Seder, he is bound to notice something quite fascinating. There is an endless array of details that comprise the Passover Seder. Upon entering a Jewish home on Passover night, one is immediately aware of a festive atmosphere, albeit a calm and serene one. The house has been cleaned immaculately and it exudes the pleasant aroma of festival delicacies. The members of the family as well as their guests are all seated around the table, Haggadahs in hand. They read from their Haggadahs and tell over the story of the Exodus, as they have done numerous times before. The eating is performed while leaning to one's left side (the bitter herbs, however, are specifically eaten while in an upright position), as is the drinking of the four cups of wine.

There are many more laws and customs that make up the Seder night, each one adding to the night's holiness. Yet, despite all of the laws, despite all of the customs, there appears to be something missing. Nowhere over the course of this very special night — special not only because of the glorious event that transpired on this night, but also for the message that it sends to the future generations — do we find one law, custom, or action that is specifically targeted at evoking a feeling of extreme joyfulness. We are not commanded at any point to perform an act that will result in spontaneous celebration in commemoration of the Jewish nation leaving Egypt. It is incumbent upon us to understand: Why is this so? This is a question that was asked by one of the foremost teachers of ethics in modern times, Rabbi Joseph Yehudah Bloch: "On the surface it would seem to be more useful to the Jewish people if Passover were celebrated somewhat differently. We should celebrate by staging huge festivities in each and every city, singing songs of praise, and speaking publicly in honor of the day. We should arrange plays and performances depicting the glorious events of the Exodus, as well as making the most of all our technological capabilities to add splendor and excitement to the event. There is little doubt that such a celebration would evoke feelings of extreme happiness, infusing one with a deep appreciation for all that Hashem performed for the people of Israel. It would ensure our remembering the Exodus, and would certainly inspire us a lot more than the bitter taste of the *maror* (bitter herbs), the leaning while eating and drinking, and the other practices we perform at the Passover Seder. So why do we not celebrate in this fashion?'' (*Shiurei Da'as*, *Ma'amar "Nishmas HaTorah"*). The question is a striking one. Why in fact do we not celebrate Passover in the same way that the nations of the world celebrate their days of independence? Why do we not allow our joy to flow freely, expressing ourselves in song and dance? Should we not illuminate the night with sparkling fireworks, filling the sky with a dazzling array of vivid colors? Or perhaps a presentation of sorts, one that would appeal to the younger generation as well as the old? Rabbi Bloch is so correct, for wouldn't these methods serve to stimulate us more than the reading of the Haggadah or the eating of matzah?

The answer to the question is a resounding "no." However, in order to properly understand the answer we must probe the recesses of the soul and try, to the best of our ability, to understand its mechanics. Rabbi Bloch explains as follows: "In truth, it's exactly the opposite of what we would normally think. We imagine that in order for Passover to penetrate and leave its imprint on the heart, we would be best off celebrating in a way that results in tremendous fervor and excitement. Yet, just the opposite is the case. It is specifically the seemingly minor actions, actions that leave but a small imprint on the heart, that are able to reach even the farthest corners of the soul and serve to inspire it. For when one celebrates in a manner that is resonant and visible, it may certainly appear that he is in fact affected by the amazing display, but this is not so. The openness of the celebration, and its external nature, serve to activate only the lowest levels of a person's soul, but the highest levels remain uninspired. However, it is precisely those higher levels that we are required to reach."

Perhaps we can attempt to probe the depths of Rabbi Bloch's words and come to a greater level of understanding. Hashem desires that the eternal message of the Exodus penetrate the innermost sanctum of one's heart. It must make its way into the very essence of his being. Once nestled in his subconscious, the message will refine his character and add a new dimension to his soul, thereby uplifting him and making him a better Jew.

A loud and demonstrative celebration, despite all the excitement it causes, is unable to delve into the soul's deepest depths. It only serves to tap into man's more "external" potentials, generating within him a very superficial excitement. He may shout out in gay adulation, his heart may even pound with feelings of joy, yet only the outermost layers of his soul are affected. His inspiration is comparable to the very fireworks he sends flying through the dark night. While they are momentarily able to illuminate the darkness, once they have faded, the darkness resumes. The inspiration that results from such celebrations is very much the same. While he may feel quite uplifted by the songs and dance, the idea of redemption is quickly forgotten. The performances and plays he observes are likely to generate much excitement within him, as do the beautifully drawn artistry and technological effects. Yet, the main point of the entire celebration fades from memory. Very little remains embedded in the subconscious, and the soul remains unaffected.

Smaller actions, however, actions that would appear almost insignificant to the unlearned eye, are able to reach the deepest depths of the soul. It is specifically due to the fact that we have such a difficult time feeling the effects of these actions that they are able to have their effect. As we focus less emotional energy on each action, the action is able to bypass the barriers of the conscience and make its way, unnoticed, into our subconscious. Since we are unable to immediately sense the aftereffect of our acts, we make it possible for them to exert a long-term influence on our souls. Anyone who has ever studied the subject of "hypnotic suggestion" will immediately recognize and validate all that was stated above. The drinking of the four cups of wine in order to signify the four statements of redemption; eating matzah in memory of the "poor man's bread" that we ate in Egypt; the eating of *maror;* and the recital of the Haggadah — are able to instill within us a feeling of redemption and memory of the Exodus that all the external, technological effects would never be able to do.

The truth of our above statements is self-evident, as the Jewish people, now more than 3,000 years removed from the redemption, are still performing their Seders with an ever-apparent newness and excitement. There are no fireworks, no musical instruments, only matzah and *maror.* Yet the Passovers remain fresh, vibrant, and ever influential on the Jewish soul.

◆§ Counting the Days That Lie Ahead

O n the second night of Passover we begin the great count forward. As the Torah tells us, *"You shall count for yourselves — from the morrow of the rest day . . . Until the morrow of the seventh week you shall count, fifty days"* (*Vayikra* 23:15-16). From the second night of Passover until Shavuos eve, the Jewish people fulfill the commandment of "Counting the *Omer."* (The *Omer* [lit. "sheaves"] refers to an offering brought by the Jewish people on the second day of Passover. It was an offering that consisted of barley, and its being offered entitled the Jewish people to eat from the new crop.) After the evening prayer, a Jew is commanded to recite a blessing and then count the corresponding day and week.

For example: On the first night of the *sefirah* count, we recite a blessing and say, "Today is one day of the *Omer."* When the days begin to form weeks, we add to our declaration. For example, on the thirteenth day of the *Omer* we say, "Today is thirteen days, which are one week and six days, of the *Omer."* This is the way we count day after day, until day forty-nine, when seven full weeks have been counted.

That is the technical aspect of *Sefiras HaOmer,* incumbent on each and every Jew. We must try, however, to understand the deeper meaning behind the *sefirah* count and grasp its hidden message.

On Passover the Jews left Egypt after hundreds of years of crushing labor and constant oppression. For the first time, they tasted the sweet taste of freedom. With the taste of freedom still on their palates, the Jewish people were given a new commandment, a commandment to begin counting toward a new plateau. The Jewish people were to realize that there was more to be accomplished; the true goal had not yet been reached. To simply enjoy their newfound freedom without continuing to grow would be tragic, as the Jewish people would fall short of actualizing their true potential. Freedom from slavery was by no means an end in itself; rather it was the means to a very magnificent end. It was the first step toward Mount Sinai, where the nation of Israel would receive the holy Torah and achieve spiritual freedom. This was the lofty purpose of counting, to set Israel's sights toward the future and keep the Jewish people from lethargy, from complacency. It implanted within them a desire to continue growing, without settling for minimal accomplishments.

It is during this period of counting that we focus on our spiritual development and the refinement of our character. Only through such endeavors will we be worthy of receiving the gift of eternal value — the Torah. We see, therefore, that the *sefirah* count serves as a prelude to the acceptance of the Torah. This prelude was not intended only for the generation of the Exodus, but applies to ensuing generations as well. By counting we exhibit "our great desire for that distinguished day for which our hearts long, like a slave who yearns for (the evening) shade and counts the moments until this time will arrive. For counting shows about a person that all his hope and desire is to reach that appointed time" (*Sefer HaChinuch, Mitzvah* 306: *Sefiras HaOmer*). Like a prisoner who yearns for his day of freedom, so too did the Jewish people yearn for the giving of the Torah. Their counting was able to transform Passover from a day of redemption to a harbinger of the upcoming Shavuos festival.

The days of *Sefiras HaOmer* bridge the festivals of Passover and Shavuos. By connecting the two festivals we are made aware of the fact that it is impossible to separate the physical redemption from the spiritual one. A physical redemption simply cannot last, if not followed by a spiritual one. There have been countless nations and governments that have toppled after achieving independence, simply due to the fact that they aspired to no more than overthrowing their former oppressors. Such a physical redemption, not backed by anything spiritual, will be hard pressed to attain any longevity. While the physical redemption is certainly vital, it is only a means, the first step to achieving a spiritual redemption. This is the message of *Sefiras HaOmer.*

But why do we count ahead? Why do we not count backwards? For example, in Cape Canaveral, when N.A.S.A. sends up a space shuttle, they count *down* to the launching! When the count reaches "zero," the space shuttle is sent up into orbit. Why do we not count the same way? The answer is that in Cape Canaveral the "launch" is the goal. The counting is simply an incidental prelude to the goal. It has no real significance; rather, its entire purpose is to lead up to the launching of the space shuttle. The counting that leads up to the day on which we received the Torah, however, is an entirely different type of counting. It is a counting that is imbued with tremendous meaning, as each day that we count instills in us the burning desire to receive Hashem's Torah. Each and every day that we count, we continually focus on the upcoming festival of Shavuos, our anticipation of this great day growing and growing. It is our counting that lays the basis for a successful acceptance of the Torah. We therefore count forward, adding one day to the next. It is not a count that will end up at "zero," but rather at forty-nine days, and seven full weeks, each one of which was an essential means of preparation for the acceptance of our holy Torah.

∽§ The Donkey of Redemption

The concept of "redemption" is one that can be understood on many different levels. In order to grasp and fully understand a deeper aspect of the redemption from Egypt and the concept of "redemption" in general, we must consider a most unlikely candidate — the donkey. The donkey is connected to a commandment that is not directly related to the festival of Passover. Yet, despite the fact that this commandment does not directly relate to Passover, it constantly appears in close proximity to the verses that deal with the festival of Passover. For example, the Torah tells us, "You shall observe the Festival of Matzos: For a seven-day period you shall eat matzos — for in the month of spring you went forth from Egypt" (Shemos 34:18), and the very next verse states, "Every first issue of a womb is Mine; as well as any of your livestock that produces a male, the first issue of an ox or a sheep. The first issue of a donkey you shall redeem with a lamb or kid, and if you do not redeem it you shall axe the back of its neck" (ibid. vs. 19-21).

As stated above, there is no direct relationship between the commandment to observe the laws of Passover and that of sanctifying the firstborn of an animal. The commandment to redeem the firstborn of an animal is a requirement that goes into effect on the thirtieth day after the birth of the firstborn. This is a requirement that was applicable every day of the year, in the era that saw the Holy Temple still standing. Even in present times, while we are no longer required to actually sanctify the firstborn of an animal, we are still not permitted to use the firstborn as we see fit. A quick glance at the above verse will reveal that there is a significant difference between the law of the ox and sheep and that of the donkey. While the firstborn of the ox and sheep are indeed sanctified, the firstborn of the donkey is not. It is redeemed for a sheep, which in turn will be given to the Kohen, and if it is not redeemed, it is put to death. The question is, of course, "Why?" Why is the donkey treated differently from the ox and sheep? Why specifically does the Torah choose a donkey for this distinction? Why not a horse or some other animal? How are we to understand this commandment? What is its deeper meaning?

In order to begin to understand we must focus our attention on what appears to be the focal point of this commandment — the firstborn. There is a clear connection between this commandment, which revolves around the firstborn of an animal, and the "Plague of the Firstborn," the tenth and final plague that afflicted Egypt, which saw Hashem personally smite the entire population of firstborns in the land of Egypt. The Torah itself alludes to this connection, "*And it shall be when your son will ask you tomorrow, 'What is this?' you shall say to him, 'With a strong hand Hashem took us out of Egypt . . . It happened when Pharaoh stubbornly refused to send us out, that Hashem killed all the firstborn in the land of Egypt, from the firstborn of man to the firstborn of beast. Therefore . . . I shall redeem all the firstborn of my sons'*" (ibid. 13:14-15). We see clearly the intrinsic connection between the act of redeeming a firstborn and the killing of the firstborns in Egypt. It is incumbent upon every Jew to always remember how Hashem smote the firstborns in Egypt. We actively engrave this miraculous feat in our memories, secure this historical wonder in our minds, when we perform the commandment of redeeming a firstborn. Redeeming a firstborn creates a physical representation of the wonders that occurred in Egypt, and of our subsequent redemption.

There is, however, a question that must be addressed. Why did Hashem specifically choose to smite the firstborns? Would the desired effect not have been achieved had Hashem chosen to kill, for argument's sake, the youngest child of every Egyptian family? Would it have been any less of a miracle? The answer is "no." Certainly it was no greater miracle to kill the firstborn than it would have been to kill the youngest of every family. It is also rather safe to assume that Pharaoh would have relented and allowed the Jewish people to leave after witnessing such a national debacle. Yet, there is something inherently different about the firstborn, something that prompted Hashem to choose them specifically to be the recipients of Divine punishment. Let us attempt to understand exactly what the significance of the firstborn was in the eyes of the Egyptians.

In ancient times a firstborn was not simply the first son born to a family. A firstborn represented something much, much greater. Besides being a source of tremendous pride to the Egyptian parent, seeing the firstborn that "they" were responsible for creating (which represents the first step towards idolatry, not recognizing the Providence of Hashem, and viewing oneself as being independent, refusing to acknowledge Him), they also viewed the firstborn as a physical manifestation of Divine power. He was looked upon as a near-God, and was accorded unlimited honor, if not actually worshiped.

It is not difficult to understand, therefore, why the killing of the firstborn was such a national calamity. Their demise served to achieve the effect, to send the message that Hashem wanted to impart, namely, *"In order for Egypt to know that I am Hashem."* It was the desire of Hashem that the Egyptians come to the realization that there is only one true power in the world. It is Hashem, and only Hashem, Who has dominion over the world, and is able to exert control over the forces of nature. The death of the firstborns, who were held on such a lofty plane, served to confound the outlooks of the Egyptians, who thought it worthless to live a life confined to the statutes of Hashem.

The purpose of the commandment to sanctify a firstborn is for the Jewish people to absorb and integrate within themselves the important message that Hashem sent upon killing the firstborns. The Torah intends for us to accomplish this by its adding an extra dimension of spirituality to the Jewish family. Through the sanctity vested in the firstborn the entire family is uplifted. "The firstborn son is the 'representative' of Hashem, he carries the banner of Hashem. He fosters as well as fights for the fulfillment of Hashem's desire, within each and every family" (*Rabbi Samson Raphael Hirsch, Shemos* 13:2). The words of Rabbi Hirsch do much to illustrate to us the Torah outlook on family and on life in general. An individual's family is very much responsible for his values and moral sensitivities. It is the family that infuses a person with priorities — what is to be considered important, what is not. The firstborn son of every family being sanctified, his being endowed with a special holiness, sends a very significant message to the entire family, namely, that the main focus of one's life has to be the spiritual. Unlike the Kohen, who is very much disassociated from the physical world due to his constant involvement in completely spiritual matters, the firstborn is very much involved in the physical world. He teaches the family and, on a larger scale, the entire Jewish people, that living in a physical world does not restrict one to being only a physical being, confined to a mundane and rather insignificant existence. Quite the contrary, for the physical world is no more than a means to grow spiritually. It is our job to sanctify the physical world and to utilize it in our pursuit of spirituality, holiness, and the perfection of our character traits. This is the vital lesson that the firstborn imparts to each and every family. The physical world is ours to sanctify and to uplift in our pursuit of the service of Hashem, which is ultimately our top priority.

When the Jewish nation sinned with the Golden Calf, the firstborns were demoted from the elevated status they had previously held. No longer would the firstborns be engaged in singing songs of praise to Hashem, no longer would it be their responsibility to be involved in the spiritual dealings of the Jewish people. They would no longer send the lofty message of physical sanctification as they once did; instead, that responsibility, as well as many others, now belonged to the Levites. The Levites did not receive an inheritance along with the rest of the Jewish people; the nation gave them cities in which to live. The nation supported them by giving them tithes from their own produce. By sustaining the Levites and enabling them to continue in their Divine service, the Jewish people integrated and continued to exemplify the concept that we mentioned above, namely, that it is spirituality which must be our main focus, while the physical must be used to further spiritual goals. This is the lesson of the firstborn and of the Levites that followed them. By supporting those who wish to study Hashem's Torah and grow spiritually, we can apply the valuable lesson of the firstborn to our own lives, sanctifying our existence.

The question remains, however: Why is the firstborn of the donkey not sanctified as well? Why are we commanded to either redeem it with a sheep or to break its neck? In the *Tanach,* a donkey (*chamor* in Hebrew) symbolizes the Egyptian nation. The Hebrew word *"chamor"* stems from the same root as the word *"chumrius,"* which means "materialism." The essence of Egypt is exactly that, materialism in its most mundane form, devoid of all spirituality. Egypt represents a life of indulgence, of hedonistic pleasure-seeking. This is a lifestyle that runs contrary to the desires of Hashem; as opposed to uplifting and sanctifying the spiritual, the physical is the main focus and the spiritual is shunned. The Torah is teaching us that the donkey, which represents Egypt and a lifestyle of materialism, must be exchanged for the sheep, which represents the nation of Israel and a life of holiness. The donkey itself cannot be sanctified; it is the essence of materialism and it must be exchanged. If we simply cannot exchange this donkey we must break its neck, as it represents a lifestyle unworthy of existence. This is the lesson that a donkey has been chosen to teach us, that true freedom is achieved only when it is a spiritual freedom.

To Drink From the Wines of Eternity

On the Seder night we are obligated to drink four cups of wine in commemoration of having been granted the status of a "free nation" over 3,000 years ago. We celebrate the remembrance of our redemption, and renew in our conscience the fundamental meanings embodied by several significant concepts, namely, redemption, freedom, and Divine Providence.

The four cups of wine represent four different aspects, four different levels of "freedom." These four levels are alluded to in the four different expressions the Torah uses to refer to the redemption, which Hashem performed for the Jewish people in Egypt. It is in commemoration of these four expressions that our Sages enacted that we drink four cups of wine at the Passover Seder. The four expressions of redemption are as follows: *"I shall take you out from the burdens of Egypt"; "I shall rescue you from their service"; "I shall redeem you with an outstretched arm and great judgments"; "I shall take you to Me for a people"* (*Shemos* 6:6-7).

The end of the above verse is also very meaningful. It states, *"and I shall be a God to you."*

When we lift up the first cup of wine, recite a blessing, and drink the measurement required by our Sages, we imbed in our consciousness the aspect of freedom that the verse, *"I shall take you out from the burdens of Egypt,"* alludes to. It is important to note that the verse speaks of "burdens" and *not* "hard labor," for "burdens" refers to something altogether different from the crushing labor that the Jewish people endured in Egypt. "The burdens of Egypt," refers to the denigrated and lowly status that the Jews held in Egypt. They were not fortunate enough to have a "Geneva Convention," which would entitle them to the "fair" treatment to which prisoners of war today are entitled. Rather they were accorded the lowest possible status, worthy only of oppression and slave labor. The problem was, however, that after so many years of degradation and persecution it was not only the Egyptians who viewed the Jewish people as being a lower form of man; even the Jewish people themselves had come to view themselves in this light.

The freedom that Hashem provided served to free the Jewish nation from this "slave mentality." No longer did they view themselves as undeserving of respect and the honorable stature accorded every decent human being. They once again achieved a status of respectability, never to return to the lowly level on which they had previously been. No matter where exile would find the Jewish people, they would never again experience the degradation or feel as little sense of worth as they felt in Egypt. Whether experiencing the tortures of the Spanish Inquisition, or languishing in the death camps of Stalin and Hitler, there always remained that spark of redemption lying deep within the hearts of the Jewish people. It is in honor of this redemption that we drink the first cup of wine on Passover night.

By drinking the second cup of wine, we commemorate the fact that Hashem saved us from the brutal physical labor inflicted upon us by the Egyptians. Besides the actual physical trauma that such labor induces, it also gave the Egyptians a vehicle through which to actualize their prejudiced philosophies. Theirs was a society of extreme inequality where there existed a dominant social group and a dominated social group. It was a society that saw the oppressive treatment of a lower class sanctioned by the government and established as the law of the land. Master and slave — this was the hierarchy of the land of Egypt.

In a very real sense, it was not only the Jewish people who were redeemed on that historical night 3,000 years ago, but the entire concept of what it means to be a human being was "redeemed" as well. The Exodus forever nullified the right for one social class to impose its will upon another social class. It established the precedent that all are worthy of equality and fair treatment, as all have been created in the image of Hashem. All subsequent movements to abolish slavery, from Spartacus until the days of Lincoln, drew their strength and inspiration from the Exodus. It is in honor of this ideal that we drink the second cup of wine.

The third cup corresponds to the verse, *"I shall redeem you with an outstretched arm and great judgments."* The word "redemption" does not simply mean the act of freeing from slavery; it also connotes the act of acquiring, the transferal of ownership from one to another. The third cup alludes to the metaphysical aspect of our redemption, to the fact that Hashem and only Hashem enacted it. The redemption from Egypt did not come about through the might of the Jewish nation, by their taking the initiative and freeing themselves from their cruel captors; it was the Divine hand of Hashem that was responsible for all that transpired. The Exodus, therefore, has a much more profound significance than, for example, freedom from "colonialism," for the Jewish people were not merely freed, but were the recipients of Divine kindness as Hashem acquired them to be His nation. As Moses said in the Name of Hashem, *"Send away My nation and they will serve Me"* (ibid 7:16). The Jewish people were not simply freed, but transferred to a new ownership, one that demands spiritual, as opposed to physical, labor.

The fourth cup is in commemoration of the Jewish people becoming a nation. The verse says, *"I shall take you to Me for a people."* This redemption was not merely the act of leaving Egypt. It was a redemption which shaped the Jewish nation. They became a nation shaped by oppression, a nation shaped by the promise Hashem made to our forefather Abraham. They were a nation that had the distinction of being chosen to be redeemed by Hashem, and a nation that would never forget the miraculous events that were wrought for their benefit. They became a nation that would carry the message of the Exodus to the entire world for generations to come.

By drinking the fourth cup we proudly proclaim to our mighty Redeemer that we are forever faithful to the eternal message of the Exodus, and we will continue to drink from the "wines of eternity" until the end of time.

סִימָנֵי הַסֵּדֶר
The Order of the Seder

kaddesh	Sanctify the day with the recitation of Kiddush.	קדש
urechatz	**Wash** the hands before eating Karpas.	ורחץ
karpas	Eat a **vegetable** dipped in salt water.	כרפס
yachatz	**Break** the middle matzah. Put away larger half for Afikoman	יחץ
maggid	**Narrate** the story of the Exodus from Egypt.	מגיד
rachtzah	**Wash** the hands prior to the meal.	רחצה
motzi	Recite the blessing, **Who brings forth,** over matzah as a food.	מוציא
matzah	Recite the blessing over **Matzah.**	מצה
maror	Recite the blessing for the eating of the **bitter herbs.**	מרור
korech	Eat the **sandwich** of matzah and bitter herbs	כורך
shulchan orech	The **table prepared** with the festive meal.	שלחן עורך
tzafun	Eat the afikoman which had been **hidden** all during the Seder.	צפון
barech	Recite Bircas Hamazon, the **blessings** after the meal.	ברך
hallel	Recite the **Hallel** Psalms of praise.	הלל
nirtzah	Pray that God **accept** our observance and speedily send the Messiah.	נרצה

קַדֵּשׁ

Kiddush should be recited and the Seder begun as soon after synagogue services as possible — however, not before nightfall. Each participant's cup should be poured by someone else to symbolize the majesty of the evening, as though each participant had a servant. Some recite the following before *Kiddush*:

הֲרֵינִי מוּכָן וּמְזוּמָן לְקַדֵּשׁ עַל הַיַּיִן, וּלְקַיֵּם מִצְוַת כּוֹס רִאשׁוֹן מֵאַרְבַּע כּוֹסוֹת. לְשֵׁם יִחוּד קֻדְשָׁא בְּרִיךְ הוּא וּשְׁכִינְתֵּיהּ, עַל יְדֵי הַהוּא טָמִיר וְנֶעְלָם, בְּשֵׁם כָּל יִשְׂרָאֵל. וִיהִי נְעַם אֲדֹנָי אֱלֹהֵינוּ עָלֵינוּ, וּמַעֲשֵׂה יָדֵינוּ כּוֹנְנָה עָלֵינוּ, וּמַעֲשֵׂה יָדֵינוּ כּוֹנְנֵהוּ.¹

On Shabbos begin here:

(וַיְהִי עֶרֶב וַיְהִי בֹקֶר)

יוֹם הַשִּׁשִּׁי: וַיְכֻלּוּ הַשָּׁמַיִם וְהָאָרֶץ וְכָל צְבָאָם. וַיְכַל אֱלֹהִים בַּיּוֹם הַשְּׁבִיעִי מְלַאכְתּוֹ אֲשֶׁר עָשָׂה, וַיִּשְׁבֹּת בַּיּוֹם הַשְּׁבִיעִי מִכָּל מְלַאכְתּוֹ אֲשֶׁר עָשָׂה. וַיְבָרֶךְ אֱלֹהִים אֶת יוֹם הַשְּׁבִיעִי וַיְקַדֵּשׁ אֹתוֹ, כִּי בוֹ שָׁבַת מִכָּל מְלַאכְתּוֹ אֲשֶׁר בָּרָא אֱלֹהִים לַעֲשׂוֹת.²

KIDDUSH CONTINUES ON THE NEXT PAGE.

קַדֵּשׁ – Kaddesh

❧ What Is ''Kiddush''?

Kiddush *is the "sign" which severs our ties to our mundane existence. It is similar to the horn blown at wartime, which signifies the end of a period of danger and serves to restore feelings of tranquility. It is as though the* Kiddush *lifts us to an entirely different planet — the planet of Shabbos or Yom Tov.*

The "all clear" following an air raid announces that danger has passed and restores tranquility. In fact, the simple sounding of this horn immediately causes tension to dissolve and the pressure — which had weighed so heavily during those hours of terror — to suddenly dissipate. This horn brightens the gloom and allows those imprisoned in their bomb shelters to come out for a breath of the fresh air. Smiles reappear on the faces of those

KADDESH

Kiddush should be recited and the Seder begun as soon after synagogue services as possible — however, not before nightfall. Each participant's cup should be poured by someone else to symbolize the majesty of the evening, as though each participant had a servant. Some recite the following before Kiddush:

Behold, I am prepared and ready to recite the *Kiddush* over wine, and to fulfill the mitzvah of the first of the Four Cups. For the sake of unification of the Holy One, Blessed is He, and His Presence, through Him Who is hidden and inscrutable — [I pray] in the name of all Israel. May the pleasantness of my Lord, our God, be upon us — may He establish our handiwork for us; our handiwork may He establish.[1]

On Shabbos begin here:

(And there was evening and there was morning)

The sixth day. And the heavens and the earth and all their array were completed. And God completed on the seventh day His work which He had done. And He rested on the seventh day from all His work which He had done. And God blessed the seventh day and sanctified it, for on it He rested from all His work which God created to make.[2]

KIDDUSH CONTINUES ON THE NEXT PAGE.

(1) *Tehillim* 90:17. (2) *Bereishis* 1:31-2:3.

---

who had been worried, and a feeling of calm prevails.

Kiddush, too, is a signal. *Kiddush* releases an individual from the "clutches of the enemy," from the burdens and pressures of making a livelihood which pursue him all week long. It ushers in the serenity of Shabbos or Yom Tov and serves to separate him from the mundane days of the week. It focuses his mind on the upcoming day and instills a feeling of sanctity in his soul, as his soul begins to anticipate the ensuing twenty-four hours of existence on a different planet. On this planet he will experience new senses, have different desires, and breathe the air of an exciting new world, a world whose quality far surpasses our own. These will be twenty-four hours of pure spiritual existence, a lighthouse in an ocean of mundane physicality.

On the Seder night, not only does the *Kiddush* create a divider between the mundane and the sanctified, it also enables us to lift our heads out of the present and set our gaze toward eternity, an eternity whose glory is contained within the memories of a past filled with splendor. At the moment we make *Kiddush* we are swept away from our Seder of the present and taken in

סַבְרִי מָרָנָן וְרַבָּנָן וְרַבּוֹתַי:

בָּרוּךְ אַתָּה יהוה אֱלֹהֵינוּ מֶלֶךְ הָעוֹלָם, בּוֹרֵא פְּרִי הַגָּפֶן:

בָּרוּךְ אַתָּה יהוה אֱלֹהֵינוּ מֶלֶךְ הָעוֹלָם, אֲשֶׁר בָּחַר בָּנוּ מִכָּל עָם, וְרוֹמְמָנוּ מִכָּל לָשׁוֹן, וְקִדְּשָׁנוּ בְּמִצְוֹתָיו. וַתִּתֶּן לָנוּ יהוה אֱלֹהֵינוּ בְּאַהֲבָה (שַׁבָּתוֹת לִמְנוּחָה וּ)מוֹעֲדִים לְשִׂמְחָה, חַגִּים וּזְמַנִּים לְשָׂשׂוֹן, אֶת יוֹם (הַשַּׁבָּת הַזֶּה וְאֶת יוֹם) חַג הַמַּצּוֹת הַזֶּה, זְמַן חֵרוּתֵנוּ (בְּאַהֲבָה) מִקְרָא קֹדֶשׁ, זֵכֶר לִיצִיאַת מִצְרָיִם, כִּי בָנוּ בָחַרְתָּ וְאוֹתָנוּ קִדַּשְׁתָּ מִכָּל הָעַמִּים, (וְשַׁבָּת) וּמוֹעֲדֵי קָדְשֶׁךָ (בְּאַהֲבָה וּבְרָצוֹן) בְּשִׂמְחָה וּבְשָׂשׂוֹן הִנְחַלְתָּנוּ. בָּרוּךְ אַתָּה יהוה, מְקַדֵּשׁ (הַשַּׁבָּת וְ)יִשְׂרָאֵל וְהַזְּמַנִּים.

בָּרוּךְ אַתָּה יהוה אֱלֹהֵינוּ מֶלֶךְ הָעוֹלָם, בּוֹרֵא מְאוֹרֵי הָאֵשׁ.

to be guests at the glorious Seders that have comprised the history of the Jewish people. We are taken back to ancient Egypt where we relive, step by step, our experiences that led up to our eventual redemption. We recount the inhumane suffering that we were forced to endure. We hear the sharp crack of the whip as it scarred our backs, and sigh along with our brethren who were treated so brutally. Our hearts flow with waves of joy when the Jewish people come to a clear realization that they are destined to be free men, and we feel the awesome anticipation of redemption that was so prevalent in Egypt during the hours preceding the Exodus. On this night, feelings such as these pervade the atmosphere as the evening takes on an aura quite reminiscent of the aura that filled the air on that fateful night in Egypt. We fulfill the dictum of our Sages, ''In every generation one is obligated to see himself as though *he personally* had gone out of Egypt.''

On all nights other than Friday, begin here;
on Friday night include all passages in parentheses.

By your leave, my masters and teachers:

Blessed are You, HASHEM, our God, King of the Universe, Who creates the fruit of the vine.

Blessed are You, HASHEM, our God, King of the Universe, Who has chosen us from among all peoples, raised us above all languages, and sanctified us with His commandments. And You have given us, HASHEM, our God, lovingly, (Shabbasos for rest, and) appointed times for gladness, festivals and holidays for rejoicing, this day of (Shabbos and this day of) the Festival of Matzos, the time of our freedom, (lovingly,) a holy convocation, in commemoration of the Exodus from Egypt. For You have chosen us and sanctified us from among all peoples and (Shabbos and) Your sacred holidays (with love and goodwill) with gladness and joy You have granted us as a heritage. Blessed are You, HASHEM, Who sanctifies (the Shabbos and) Yisrael and the Festivals.

On Saturday night, add the following two paragraphs:

Blessed are You, HASHEM, our God, King of the Universe, Who creates the lights of the fire.

Kiddush is performed on a cup of wine. Wine has the unique ability to change and impact upon the mood of an individual. Its uniqueness also extends to its ability to enable an individual to transcend the world of senses, thoughts, and experiences and ascend to a spiritual plateau. When drunk haphazardly, with reckless abandon, wine only serves to lower a person and ultimately bring about a humiliating drunkenness. However, when drunk with a spiritual goal in mind, responsibly, and with clear intention, that same wine which had the power to cause so much destruction, can now be the cause of a heightened spiritual experience. Happiness and not foolishness will accompany him on his spiritual journey, as he discovers the true meaning of King David's words, *"Wine makes glad the heart of man"* (*Tehillim* 104:15).

Now attempt to listen closely to the words of *Kiddush* and let its blessing enter your heart.

בָּרוּךְ אַתָּה יהוה אֱלֹהֵינוּ מֶלֶךְ הָעוֹלָם, הַמַּבְדִּיל בֵּין קֹדֶשׁ לְחוֹל, בֵּין אוֹר לְחֹשֶׁךְ, בֵּין יִשְׂרָאֵל לָעַמִּים, בֵּין יוֹם הַשְּׁבִיעִי לְשֵׁשֶׁת יְמֵי הַמַּעֲשֶׂה. בֵּין קְדֻשַּׁת שַׁבָּת לִקְדֻשַּׁת יוֹם טוֹב הִבְדַּלְתָּ, וְאֶת יוֹם הַשְּׁבִיעִי מִשֵּׁשֶׁת יְמֵי הַמַּעֲשֶׂה קִדַּשְׁתָּ, הִבְדַּלְתָּ וְקִדַּשְׁתָּ אֶת עַמְּךָ יִשְׂרָאֵל בִּקְדֻשָּׁתֶךָ. בָּרוּךְ אַתָּה יהוה, הַמַּבְדִּיל בֵּין קֹדֶשׁ לְקֹדֶשׁ.

On all nights conclude here:

בָּרוּךְ אַתָּה יהוה אֱלֹהֵינוּ מֶלֶךְ הָעוֹלָם, שֶׁהֶחֱיָנוּ וְקִיְּמָנוּ וְהִגִּיעָנוּ לַזְּמַן הַזֶּה.

The wine should be drunk without delay, while reclining on the left side. It is preferable to drink the entire cup, but at the very least, most of the cup should be drained.

וּרְחַץ

The head of the household washes his hands as if to eat bread (pouring water from a cup, twice on the right hand and twice on the left hand), but without reciting a blessing.

כַּרְפַּס

All participants take a vegetable other than *maror* and dip it into salt water. A piece smaller in volume than olive size should be used. The following blessing is recited (with the intention that it also apply to the *maror* which will be eaten during the meal) before the vegetable is eaten.

בָּרוּךְ אַתָּה יהוה אֱלֹהֵינוּ מֶלֶךְ הָעוֹלָם, בּוֹרֵא פְּרִי הָאֲדָמָה.

יַחַץ

The head of the household breaks the middle matzah in two. He puts the smaller part back between the two whole matzos, and wraps up the larger part for later use as the *afikoman*. Some briefly place the *afikoman* portion on their shoulders, in accordance with the Biblical verse (*Shemos* 12:34) recounting that Israel left Egypt carrying their matzos on their shoulders, and say, בְּבֶהָלוּ יָצָאנוּ מִמִּצְרָיִם, "In haste we went out of Egypt."

Blessed are You, HASHEM, our God, King of the Universe, Who distinguishes between the sacred and the profane, between light and darkness, between Yisrael and the other peoples, between the seventh day and the six days of labor. You have made a distinction between the sanctity of Shabbos and the sanctity of a holiday, and sanctified the seventh day over the six days of labor. You have separated and sanctified Your people Yisrael with Your holiness. Blessed are You, HASHEM, Who distinguishes between one sanctity and another.

On all nights conclude here:

Blessed are You, HASHEM, our God, King of the Universe, Who has kept us alive, and maintained us and enabled us to reach this time.

The wine should be drunk without delay, while reclining on the left side. It is preferable to drink the entire cup, but at the very least, most of the cup should be drained.

URECHATZ

The head of the household washes his hands as if to eat bread (pouring water from a cup, twice on the right hand and twice on the left hand), but without reciting a blessing.

KARPAS

All participants take a vegetable other than *maror* and dip it into salt water. A piece smaller in volume than olive size should be used. The following blessing is recited (with the intention that it also apply to the *maror* which will be eaten during the meal) before the vegetable is eaten.

Blessed are You, HASHEM, our God, King of the Universe, Who creates the fruit of the soil.

YACHATZ

The head of the household breaks the middle matzah in two. He puts the smaller part back between the two whole matzos, and wraps up the larger part for later use as the *afikoman*. Some briefly place the *afikoman* portion on their shoulders, in accordance with the Biblical verse (*Shemos* 12:34) recounting that Israel left Egypt carrying their matzos on their shoulders, and say, בְּהִלּוּ יָצָאנוּ מִמִּצְרַיִם, "In haste we went out of Egypt."

מגיד

Some recite the following before *Maggid:*

הִנְנִי מוּכָן וּמְזוּמָן לְקַיֵּם הַמִּצְוָה לְסַפֵּר בִּיצִיאַת מִצְרַיִם. לְשֵׁם
יִחוּד קֻדְשָׁא בְּרִיךְ הוּא וּשְׁכִינְתֵּיה, עַל יְדֵי הַהוּא טָמִיר
וְנֶעְלָם, בְּשֵׁם כָּל יִשְׂרָאֵל. וִיהִי נֹעַם אֲדֹנָי אֱלֹהֵינוּ עָלֵינוּ, וּמַעֲשֵׂה
יָדֵינוּ כּוֹנְנָה עָלֵינוּ, וּמַעֲשֵׂה יָדֵינוּ כּוֹנְנֵהוּ:

The head of the household lifts the broken matzah for all to see,
and recites the following brief explanation of the proceedings.

הָא לַחְמָא עַנְיָא דִי אֲכָלוּ אַבְהָתָנָא בְּאַרְעָא
דְמִצְרָיִם. כָּל דִכְפִין יֵיתֵי וְיֵיכוֹל, כָּל דִצְרִיךְ
יֵיתֵי וְיִפְסַח. הָשַׁתָּא הָכָא, לְשָׁנָה הַבָּאָה בְּאַרְעָא
דְיִשְׂרָאֵל. הָשַׁתָּא עַבְדֵי, לְשָׁנָה הַבָּאָה בְּנֵי חוֹרִין.

הָא לַחְמָא עַנְיָא — **This is the bread of affliction**

◄§ The Statement of the Matzah

This is the declaration with which we begin our festive Seder night. It is a declaration which recalls the suffering of our regal ancestors; it is an invitation to the poor, as we open our hearts and homes to the suffering Jews of the present; it is a declaration which affirms our belief and hope for a future redemption. It is a declaration which connects the past, present, and future of the Jewish nation.

With this declaration we open the Seder night. It is a declaration that is said in Aramaic, for reasons that are irrelevant at the present moment. Let us first grasp the meaning of this declaration, and attempt to understand each and every word: "This is the bread of affliction (the matzah) that our fathers ate in the land of Egypt. Whoever is hungry — let him come and eat! [Whoever is hungry is invited to join us on this Seder night!] Now we are here; next year we will be in the land of Israel. Now we are slaves; next year we will be free men!"

These are the statements declared by the leader of the Seder. These statements teach us much about the educational goals that characterize this very special family gathering. They lend our night direction and focus us toward creating a spiritual atmosphere in the home.

MAGGID

Some recite the following before *Maggid:*

Behold, I am prepared and ready to fulfill the mitzvah of telling of the Exodus from Egypt. For the sake of the unification of the Holy One, Blessed is He, and His presence, through Him Who is hidden and inscrutable — [I pray] in the name of all Israel. May the pleasantness of my Lord, our God, be upon us — may He establish our handiwork for us; our handiwork may He establish.

The head of the household lifts the broken matzah for all to see, and recites the following brief explanation of the proceedings.

This is the bread of affliction that our fathers ate in the land of Egypt. Whoever is hungry — let him come and eat. Whoever is needy — let him come and make Pesach. Now we are here; next year we will be in the land of Israel. Now we are slaves; next year we will be free men.

Our declaration is comprised of three parts. When viewed as three separate and distinct statements, each statement is significant and meaningful. Yet when viewed together as three parts of a whole, this declaration paints a picture of the universal Jew, whose beliefs and qualities are heavily focused upon during the course of this meaningful night.

The purpose of the first statement ("This is the bread of affliction...") is to awaken the hearts of those seated around the table (the younger generation in particular) to feel a connection with the Jews of Egypt, the Jews of so many years ago, and with that great day when they became a free people, a nation that would spread the word of Hashem throughout the world. By awakening the hearts of our young and by helping them feel connected to the glorious days of the Exodus, we enable them to view themselves as links in the chain of Jewish history, connected to all past and future generations. This is a chain not easily broken.

How are we to achieve such an effect?

The father, the leader of the Seder, lifts the matzah for all to see. He declares that this is the bread which our forefathers ate in Egypt. The eyes of the Seder participants gaze at the elevated matzah, their minds immediately conjuring up thoughts of the horrible years of Jewish sojourning in Egypt. At this moment, the past of the Jewish people comes to life for all those seated around the table. Bringing the past to life is the first step toward educating our children.

The Seder plate is removed and the second of the four cups of wine is poured. The youngest present asks the reasons for the unusual proceedings of the evening.

מַה נִּשְׁתַּנָּה הַלַּיְלָה הַזֶּה מִכָּל הַלֵּילוֹת?

The second statement of the declaration focuses on the present, on the actual Seder itself. It is a statement which teaches us volumes about what the character of the Jewish home should be. This is a festive night, a night to be happy! The table is beautifully set and the joyful feeling of freedom fills the air. Yet our joy is not complete. The knowledge of fellow Jews, perhaps not as fortunate as we, hungry and without a family with whom to share Passover, detracts from our own happiness as well. True joy cannot be experienced if a member of our people is without food. We therefore open our doors to the poor and unfortunate and invite them to our Seder. By offering an invitation to the poor we accomplish much more than simply bestowing a kindness upon another individual. We call to mind the fact that unity among the Jewish people in Egypt was very instrumental in protecting them from ultimate destruction. Their ability to view each other as equals and to achieve a great level of national unity, all this amidst a sea of suffering, helped ensure their survival and usher in the redemption.

We therefore open our doors and hearts to the poor of our nation. We exhibit the great character traits of mercy and hospitality, serving as role models to our children and giving them a lesson about the qualities a Jewish home should contain. These are qualities that include feeling mercy for another, greeting him with an exuberant countenance, and making it our utmost concern that he is happy in our home, and jubilant on this very joyous festival.

The third statement of our declaration deals with the fostering of our hopes for the magnificent future in store for the Jewish nation. As we tell over the story of the Exodus and of all the miracles that Hashem wrought for the Jewish people, we soberly remind ourselves that there was a long and arduous road that led to our eventual redemption. We open our statement with the expression of hope that has enabled the Jewish nation to survive those long and arduous roads. Many nations have come and gone, their existence ending at the moment they decided that there was no longer anything left to accomplish, or any way to embellish their earthly existence. Yet the Jewish people stand the test of time and continue to outlive them all. We do not settle for worldly accomplishments and limited achievements. The hope toward the future forever burns within us as we dream and yearn for the great day when the Jewish people, as well as the world, will reach its perfected state in the future world. It is this hope that has kept the Jewish

The Seder plate is removed and the second of the four cups of wine is poured. The youngest present asks the reasons for the unusual proceedings of the evening.

Why is this night different from all other nights?

spirit high throughout history, and has enabled the Jewish people to bear the long road that leads to redemption.

This idea has been accurately elucidated by a sociologist from Holland, S.L. Falk (a non-Jew) in his book entitled *The Past Is the Future.* "How is it possible," he asks, "that this 'Bedouin tribe,' one of many different tribes, has achieved such prominence throughout history?" He answers, "From the strength that has resulted from anticipating a future of unlimited quality."

The image of a perfected future world is an image that has never left the minds of the Jewish people. It is a vision that the Jew continues to yearn for, no matter what predicament he finds himself in, and it is that vision which has sustained him until this very day. It lends us a deeper understanding of the present day in which we live, and it enables us to deal with the difficulties that may come our way.

On the Seder night we bring our glorious past to life in order to help shape the present, all for the sake of a much-anticipated future.

מַה נִּשְׁתַּנָּה הַלַּיְלָה . . . ? — Why is this night different . . . ?

ৰ্জ And Now the Son Asks . . .

The attempt to lessen the generation gap begins at this moment. We encourage the son to ask questions. His asking connects him to all that is taking place. His questions will ultimately be responsible for his developing an identity.

After Kiddush proclaims the commencement of this festive night, after the introduction of "This is the bread of affliction," which teaches us about the character of the Jewish nation and the Jewish home, the Seder proceeds with a series of questions.

All eyes focus on the youngest son in the family, as he is encouraged to ask, "Why is this night different?" With this question, this Jewish child has *truly* commenced the Passover Seder. Everything that subsequently follows over the course of the evening is simply an answer to the son's questions.

The question must be raised, however: Why did the author of the Haggadah choose specifically the "question and answer" format with which to

שֶׁבְּכָל הַלֵּילוֹת אָנוּ אוֹכְלִין חָמֵץ וּמַצָּה,
הַלַּיְלָה הַזֶּה – כֻּלוֹ מַצָּה.
שֶׁבְּכָל הַלֵּילוֹת אָנוּ אוֹכְלִין שְׁאָר יְרָקוֹת,
הַלַּיְלָה הַזֶּה – מָרוֹר.
שֶׁבְּכָל הַלֵּילוֹת אֵין אָנוּ מַטְבִּילִין אֲפִילוּ פַּעַם אֶחָת,
הַלַּיְלָה הַזֶּה – שְׁתֵּי פְעָמִים.
שֶׁבְּכָל הַלֵּילוֹת אָנוּ אוֹכְלִין בֵּין יוֹשְׁבִין וּבֵין מְסֻבִּין,
הַלַּיְלָה הַזֶּה – כֻּלָּנוּ מְסֻבִּין.

write the Haggadah? The answer is a simple one. Through posing a question the child becomes an active participant in the Seder! He relinquishes his role as simply an outside observer, and becomes a partaker in the night's events. For when the child asks a question it signifies that he is curious. If he pays attention to the evening's festivities, and appears amazed at all of our "strange" actions, which seem to be so different from our normal day-to-day behavior, then it is a sign that curiosity has been awakened within him. This is quite an important moment, as curiosity is the mother of all knowledge, and it provides us with a basis on which we will be able to establish a connection with the child.

This is the first occasion of the evening when we serve to lessen the generation gap, which weighs so heavily in today's day and age. It is at the very moment that the son asks his questions that a common ground is created. The son is prepared to listen to his father and expresses interest in what he has to say, ready to accept the message his father wishes to transmit to him on this night.

◆§ This is the night on which the generation gap is diminished.

That and much more. The desire to question is also the beginning of self-identification. We place very much importance on the asking of these questions at the Passover Seder. This is clearly evidenced by the way many families are accustomed to have each and every child, from youngest to oldest, recite the questions. The importance of asking the questions can also be illustrated by the Sages' requirement for even the individual celebrating Passover without family, sitting alone at his own Seder, to ask *himself* the questions! For only when one is forced to grapple with a question is he really interested in the answer.

To the Jewish nation the importance that lies within the asking of these

1. On all other nights we eat *chametz* and matzah. On this night — only matzah.

2. On all other nights we eat all kinds of vegetables. On this night — *maror.*

3. On all other nights we do not dip even once. On this night — twice.

4. On all other nights we eat either sitting straight or reclining. On this night we all recline.

---

questions is immeasurable. We are very interested in seeing the torch of freedom that was concealed within the redemption from Egypt passed from generation to generation. It is through questions and answers that a dialogue is created between father and son, linking the chains between the generations.

The questions serve an additional purpose as well. It is the nature of a child — unduly enhanced by a present-day society, which intensively aids and abets this nature — to scorn the older generation, the generation to which his parents belong. He refuses to be taught by this generation how to live, what to think, and how to act. Therefore, at the moment the son turns to his father and asks him a question, a small amount of humility enters his heart. He realizes and understands that his father, older and richer in life experience than he, is able to disseminate wisdom and guide him down the proper path in life.

There is yet another blessing hidden within the dialogue between father and son, and that is the renewal and strengthening of the family bond. This is a bond that was weakened during the years of slavery. It is on this night that we emphasize and stress this connection, in order to prove to all of our enemies who plotted and schemed against us that the Jewish family is, thank God, still strong and intact. It is on the Seder night that the family bonds that have fallen victim to society's craving for rebellion and disrespect, experience a strengthening and renewal.

◄§ **Within the "questioning" son lies the hope for the future of the Jewish people.**

Now let us discuss the actual questions themselves:

There are four questions in all, four questions that revolve around four practices performed at the Seder that appear to be somewhat abnormal. The practices are as follows: 1) the eating of matzah, as opposed to *chametz;* 2) the requirement to eat *maror;* 3) eating that is done while leaning to the left; 4) the dipping of foods into a variety of different dips.

At first glance, it would appear as if there were several other practices that

The Seder plate is returned. The matzos are kept uncovered as the Haggadah is recited in unison. The Haggadah should be translated if necessary, and the story of the Exodus should be amplified upon.

עֲבָדִים הָיִינוּ לְפַרְעֹה בְּמִצְרָיִם, וַיּוֹצִיאֵנוּ יהוה אֱלֹהֵינוּ מִשָּׁם בְּיָד חֲזָקָה

we perform at the Seder that would be worthy of explanation as well. For example: 1) Why do we drink four cups of wine? 2) Why do we wash our hands twice over the course of the Seder, while during a regular meal we only wash our hands once? 3) Why is it that during the period in which the Holy Temple stood, Passover was the only festival where the family gathered together at night in order to eat from the sacrificial offering, which on this night was the Pesach Lamb? Why is it that in regard to these very irregular practices the son does not ask, "Why is this night different?"

Rabbi Don Isaac Abarbanel (a noted Torah commentator who was among the giants of Spanish Jewry; he was also an official of the Royal Treaury of Portugal) enlightens us with the following passage from his commentary on the Haggadah:

> The idea behind the questioning is for the one posing the question to observe our actions which connote a state of freedom. He sees us performing actions which portray our status as free men, children of royalty, and advisers to the world. He is then to notice our actions which seem to connote exactly the opposite, an existence of lowly and degraded slaves.

In other words, the son isn't asking four separate questions; he is asking only one. He is questioning the paradoxical nature of this evening, that on one hand we recall the unbelievable miracles and redemption that Hashem performed for us, yet on the other hand we recall the horrible suffering we endured as slaves.

On this night we eat only matzah and not *chametz,* in order to call to mind memories of our dreary lives as slaves, when not a crust of bread found its way into our mouths. This is precisely the reason why the matzah is called "bread of our affliction," in order to recall that dismal period for the Jewish people. On this night we eat only those vegetables which symbolize the bitterness which so characterized our sojourn in Egypt, again a reminder of slavery and oppression. Yet, on the other hand, our Seder is conducted with a feeling of royalty and freedom, illustrated by our sitting in a leaning position, "which portray(s) our status as free men... We eat while leaning in positions of great honor." Likewise, our Sages also required us "to dip into it two times... which portray(s) our status as free men, as we eat in a manner

The Seder plate is returned. The matzos are kept uncovered as the Haggadah is recited in unison. The Haggadah should be translated if necessary, and the story of the Exodus should be amplified upon.

We were slaves to Pharaoh in Egypt, and HASHEM, our God, took us out of there with a strong hand

---

similar to the officers of high prestige who indulge in delicacies" (*Abarbanel*).

Therefore, the son questions why it is necessary to mention both our suffering and our redemption in the same breath. If we have already noted our glorious redemption, why must we bring to mind memories of trauma?

עֲבָדִים הָיִינוּ לְפַרְעֹה — We were slaves to Pharaoh

⧉ The Exile of Many Faces

The father begins to answer his son's questions. This is a golden opportunity to transmit the message of the Jewish faith. It is the father's opportunity to explain in detail the essence of exile and redemption, and how a physical oppression is simply the inevitable result of a spiritual oppression, a spiritual exile that finds the soul drowning in a sea of idolatry and materialism.

The father, the leader of the Seder, listens to his son's questions and now prepares to answer them properly. His answer can be divided into two parts. The first part of his answer begins with the paragraph, "We were slaves to Pharaoh." The second part of his answer begins with the paragraph, "At first our ancestors were idol worshipers."

In the first paragraph we recollect the physical oppression that we were forced to endure, and our subsequent rescue from that oppression. The second paragraph, however, delves even deeper, as it returns to yet earlier points in history. It depicts a time of spiritual exile, a time that saw all of humanity following idolatrous practices. This was a malaise which would affect the Jewish people as well, as they would fall under the influence of misguided neighbors who lured them into idol worship. Yet despite all of the strong influences emanating from his society, our forefather Abraham was able to separate himself and completely purify himself from their harmful effects.

This will be the answer to the son's questions. There are two forms of exile and two forms of redemption, one exile being directly responsible for the other and one redemption being directly responsible for the other. Our

וּבִזְרֹעַ נְטוּיָה. וְאִלּוּ לֹא הוֹצִיא הַקָּדוֹשׁ בָּרוּךְ הוּא
אֶת אֲבוֹתֵינוּ מִמִּצְרַיִם, הֲרֵי אָנוּ וּבָנֵינוּ וּבְנֵי בָנֵינוּ

---

physical exile is intrinsically linked to spiritual "exile," while our miraculous physical redemption from Egyptian bondage redeemed us spiritually as well, as we were able to clearly see the worthlessness of idolatry and the truth of the faith which had been propagated by Abraham. This is the lesson the author of the Haggadah teaches us by placing these two paragraphs in close proximity.

As the Haggadah begins to answer, it opens with a vivid description, depicting with utmost clarity the horrible suffering and frightening oppression that embodied our lives as slaves in Egypt. However, the memory of our anguish-filled existence in Egypt does not detract in the slightest from our feelings of joy associated with our salvation and redemption, as the questioner would have thought. Quite the contrary, they only serve to enhance our happiness. The memories of our suffering deepen our everlasting appreciation of the redemption, and enable us to truly experience the feeling of redemption. For only one who has experienced the darkness is truly capable of understanding the real meaning of light. What appears as a paradox in the eyes of the son is, in fact, perfectly logical, and enables us to properly perceive the inestimable value of our redemption.

It is only by knowing and remembering what we endured in that bitter exile, only by developing an understanding of the extent of our slavery, of the strength of the Egyptian empire, and of the strong influence their degenerative culture had upon society — that we will be able to fully grasp just how greatly our lives were changed by the Exodus. We will then be able to feel real excitement over the miracle that took place in Egypt, without simply "going through the motions."

We see an example of this phenomenon in our present day-lives. In recent years, groups of young students from all over the world (Israel included) have begun traveling to the Nazi death camps and concentration camps and then to Israel. Facing the Western Wall after facing the "valley of death" which is Auschwitz, teaches these young men and women something about the essence of being a Jew and of the value of being able to live in Israel. It is a lesson their teachers have been unable to fully transmit to them. It is truly incredible that specifically through contrasting that which took place in those years of destruction and our present-day situation, a deeper understanding of the meaning of that contrast develops.

This is the answer of the father.

Now for the details.

and an outstretched arm. If the Holy One, Blessed is He, had not taken our forefathers out of Egypt, we and our children and our children's children would

---

⊰§ "The Hawk"

The house of Egyptian bondage was in the model of Auschwitz, a most frightening and horrible model indeed. Yet it was specifically in the Egyptian concentration camp that a multitude of Jewish slaves were transformed into a Jewish nation. How could such a transformation take place under such circumstances, and why did it have to occur in such a fashion?

The house of bondage in Egypt was quite similar to the concentration camp. Through examining the unethical and immoral characteristics of Egypt we find ourselves faced with the distorted image of Auschwitz. Despite the fact that thousands of years separate the two calamities, the two are in fact one. Different surroundings and different circumstances, yet the same abusive mentality and cruelty.

⊰§ **From the lowest point on earth is born a new nation** — *specifically from there.*

"For what purpose," asks Professor Andre Nahar, "did Pharaoh refuse to supply the Jewish people with straw, without which they would be unable to form bricks? Furthermore, he demanded that each day the Jews produce the same quota of bricks that they had made the day before. Why?"

Clearly, we are not dealing here with demands that will ensure more productivity. "The forced labor was for the express purpose of oppressing those who performed it"; (*"In order to afflict the nation"*... says the Torah; *Shemos* 1:11, and *Rashi* ad loc.). Therefore, "We are entering into the dark and grim realm of the concentration camps."

The analogy is both horrible and frightening. "The drowning of the male infants awakens with utmost clarity the terrible parallel of the genocide that pursued the Jewish people in the Holocaust... The demeaning labor was but a show. The victims were the performers, and the oppressors played the roles of the entertained spectators... as it was in Egypt so too in Auschwitz — the whip was the sign of dominance, and it enabled the spectator to participate in the amusing entertainment of the victim" (A. Nahar, *Moses*, p. 104).

מִשְׁעְבָּדִים הָיִינוּ לְפַרְעֹה בְּמִצְרָיִם. וַאֲפִילוּ כֻּלָּנוּ
חֲכָמִים, כֻּלָּנוּ נְבוֹנִים, כֻּלָּנוּ זְקֵנִים, כֻּלָּנוּ יוֹדְעִים אֶת
הַתּוֹרָה, מִצְוָה עָלֵינוּ לְסַפֵּר בִּיצִיאַת מִצְרָיִם.

Yet it is specifically in this Egyptian Auschwitz, in the depths of humanity and in the most trying times, that a beaten and broken Jewish people became an exalted nation, as the verse states, *"I shall take you to Me for a people and I shall be a God to you"* (Shemos 6:7).

For this is the perfect moment for the birth of a nation that is unlike any other nation in the world. "A nation untied to those conditions that have determined the course of mankind up until this point in time," in the words of Rabbi Samson Raphael Hirsch (*Commentary on the Torah*).

A nation that is born in such circumstances, in such a predicament, distinguishes itself from all other nations. It is a nation that is clearly above and beyond the laws of nature that prevail in our day-to-day lives and have prevailed throughout history. This is the result of being the recipients of Divine freedom, freedom bestowed upon us by Hashem, the Creator and Controller of all laws of nature. It is not coincidental that the commentators on the section of the Torah dealing with the Exodus compare the creation of the Jewish nation to the creation of the world.

"The emergence of the nation of Abraham," explains Rabbi Hirsch, "reawakens within our conscience the concept of freedom, and releases humanity from its chains." Within these words lies life's eternal truth. They are the explanation of all that we have endured from then on: The essence of the unusual birth which brought about this nation — and all we have gone through as a people — forms and develops the character of our nation.

In Scripture, the Jewish nation is likened to a dove. It is interesting to note that the non-Jewish writer Saint-Ives Daleydreit finds us similar to a hawk. After pondering and reflecting on the uniqueness of the Jewish people, he had this to say:

> Like the hawk that soars through the clouds, that is not truly awakened until it is caught in the winds of a storm strong enough to rock mighty ships, so too is this tiny nation (the Jewish nation). The hawk simply spreads its wings and infuses itself with renewed strength, vigor, and motivation, restoring its original form. It glides through the strong gusts of wind, while the bodies of powerful politicians sink to the depths of the sea in futility. So too are the Jewish people. What serves to destroy every other nation or group that exists, only serves to give additional life to the Jewish people, restoring them to their initial glorious form.

still be enslaved to Pharaoh in Egypt. Even if all of us were men of wisdom, understanding, experience, and knowledge of the Torah, it would still be an obligation upon us to tell about the Exodus from Egypt.

These words are appropriate for every generation, including our own. As the verse states, "And Hashem our Lord brought us out from *there...*"; from every single "*there,*" and in every generation, we look toward Hashem for salvation.

מִצְוָה עָלֵינוּ לְסַפֵּר בִּיצִיאַת מִצְרַיִם —
An obligation upon us to tell about the Exodus from Egypt

⇜ "To Tell and Tell ..."

The dialogue that takes place among the family members, between the father and son, is the secret to the night's success. Relating the story of the Exodus with excitement, many details, and much lively embellishment is the key to transmitting our heritage from generation to generation. The one who relates the story benefits greatly as well. Even the greatest scholar ...

O n this night we are obligated to tell over a story. It is only by retelling the story of the Exodus that we fulfill the night's purpose, as prescribed by the Torah in four different verses. The Torah commands us that every year, on the anniversary night of the miraculous Exodus, we are to speak with the future generation. We are to relate exactly what transpired on this night, and encourage him to participate in the discussion, so that he establish a personal spiritual connection to the event.

Three of the verses are written in *Parashas Bo,* the portion of the Torah that describes the redemption from Egypt, while the fourth verse is found in the book of *Devarim.* The verses are as follows:

❏ "And it shall be that when your children will say to you, 'What is this work to you?' You shall say, 'It is a Pesach feast-offering to Hashem ...' " (*Shemos* 12:26-27).

❏ "And you shall tell your son on that day, saying, 'It is because of this that Hashem did so for me when I went out of Egypt' " (ibid. 13:8).

וְכָל הַמַּרְבֶּה לְסַפֵּר בִּיצִיאַת מִצְרַיִם, הֲרֵי זֶה מְשֻׁבָּח.

מַעֲשֶׂה בְּרַבִּי אֱלִיעֶזֶר וְרַבִּי יְהוֹשֻׁעַ וְרַבִּי אֶלְעָזָר בֶּן עֲזַרְיָה וְרַבִּי עֲקִיבָא וְרַבִּי טַרְפוֹן שֶׁהָיוּ מְסֻבִּין בִּבְנֵי בְרַק, וְהָיוּ מְסַפְּרִים בִּיצִיאַת מִצְרַיִם כָּל אוֹתוֹ הַלַּיְלָה. עַד שֶׁבָּאוּ תַלְמִידֵיהֶם וְאָמְרוּ

❏ "And it shall be when your son will ask you tomorrow, 'What is this?' you shall say to him, 'With a strong hand Hashem took us out of Egypt from the house of bondage' " (ibid. v. 14).

❏ "When your son will ask you tomorrow, saying, 'What are the testimonies, the decrees, and the laws that Hashem, our God, has commanded you?' You shall say to your child, 'We were slaves to Pharaoh in Egypt, and Hashem took us out of Egypt with a strong hand' " (*Devarim* 6:20-21).

The Torah is imparting to us a fundamental lesson: namely, that the message of the Exodus was not meant simply for the generation which was redeemed from Egypt. The Torah intends for us to transmit this experience and its eternal lesson to future generations, until the end of time. It therefore has commanded us to engage in discussion on the Seder night, and for the father to relate the story of the Exodus to his children as a means of accomplishing this feat.

We do not sit separately on the Seder night, each individual reading the story of the Exodus to himself. Nor do we converse privately about the redemption from Egypt, limiting ourselves to one-on-one conversation. Children do not engage in their own celebration and adults in another. Rather, the entire family celebrates together, as the father inspiringly brings the story of the Exodus to life for all to hear. Is it any wonder that throughout the generations the Jewish home has been able to withstand the damaging effects of the ever-widening generation gap and society's "winds of change"?

On the Seder night the son feels important in the eyes of his father (as opposed to the prevailing fatherly attitude of "take the money and go do with it what you want"). It is only natural therefore that the son will in turn pay attention to the father and listen to what he has to say. He will be more receptive, identifying with all that is taking place. Perhaps he will even deem it worthy to act in a similar fashion with his own children.

The story of the Exodus, told in an exuberant and lively manner, is the focal

The more one tells about the Exodus, the more he is praiseworthy.

An incident took place in which Rabbi Eliezer, Rabbi Yehoshua, Rabbi Elazar ben Azaryah, Rabbi Akiva, and Rabbi Tarfon were reclining in Bnei Brak and recounting the tale of the Exodus from Egypt all that night, until their students came and told

---

point of the evening. It creates a link in the chain that connects generation to generation, forming an unbreakable bond. The relating of the story of the Exodus is so important that our Sages have commanded even one who does not have members of the future generation seated alongside him, to nonetheless discuss and delve into the story of the redemption of the Jews from Egypt. Even if one does not have a son he is still required to relate to himself the story and profound messages of the Exodus. It is thus stated in the Haggadah, "Even if all of us were men of wisdom, understanding, experience, and knowledge of the Torah, it would still be an obligation upon us to tell about the Exodus from Egypt. The more one tells about the Exodus, the more he is praiseworthy."

> *An incident took place in which Rabbi Eliezer, Rabbi Yehoshua, Rabbi Elazar ben Azaryah, Rabbi Akiva, and Rabbi Tarfon were reclining in Bnei Brak and recounting the tale of the Exodus from Egypt all that night . . .*

In our generation we have been witnesses to historic events. However, we seem to be satisfied with simply retaining such monumental events in our memory banks. While we will occasionally experience moments of nostalgia, we do very little to actually transform these historical milestones into living, exciting events that evoke much enthusiasm and meaning for future generations. The memories slowly fade and are soon forgotten.

The story of the redemption of the Jewish people from Egypt is entirely different however.

Try for a moment to imagine that Passover Seder in Bnei Brak: the greatest Sages reclining together at a joint Seder, engaged the entire night in discussion, all the conversation centered on one topic — the Exodus. Had it not been for the students who had come to observe their teachers — entirely absorbed in the topic at hand, up until the point where they did not realize that dawn was approaching — these Sages would have continued to discuss the redemption and the miracles that Hashem wrought for the Jewish people.

לָהֶם, רַבּוֹתֵינוּ הִגִּיעַ זְמַן קְרִיאַת שְׁמַע שֶׁל שַׁחֲרִית.

אָמַר רַבִּי אֶלְעָזָר בֶּן עֲזַרְיָה, הֲרֵי אֲנִי כְּבֶן שִׁבְעִים שָׁנָה, וְלֹא זָכִיתִי שֶׁתֵּאָמֵר יְצִיאַת מִצְרַיִם בַּלֵּילוֹת, עַד שֶׁדְּרָשָׁהּ בֶּן זוֹמָא, שֶׁנֶּאֱמַר, לְמַעַן תִּזְכֹּר אֶת יוֹם צֵאתְךָ מֵאֶרֶץ מִצְרַיִם כֹּל יְמֵי חַיֶּיךָ.[1] יְמֵי חַיֶּיךָ הַיָּמִים, כֹּל יְמֵי חַיֶּיךָ הַלֵּילוֹת. וַחֲכָמִים אוֹמְרִים, יְמֵי חַיֶּיךָ הָעוֹלָם הַזֶּה, כֹּל יְמֵי חַיֶּיךָ לְהָבִיא לִימוֹת הַמָּשִׁיחַ.

בָּרוּךְ הַמָּקוֹם, בָּרוּךְ הוּא. בָּרוּךְ שֶׁנָּתַן תּוֹרָה לְעַמּוֹ יִשְׂרָאֵל, בָּרוּךְ הוּא. כְּנֶגֶד אַרְבָּעָה בָנִים דִּבְּרָה תוֹרָה: אֶחָד **חָכָם**, וְאֶחָד **רָשָׁע**, וְאֶחָד **תָּם**, וְאֶחָד **שֶׁאֵינוֹ יוֹדֵעַ לִשְׁאוֹל.**

Why did they have to engage in such a lengthy discussion?

Clearly, these Sages were not simply telling a story. They identified with every single word they spoke and felt connected to every minute detail that comprised their profound discussion. They were not simply dusting off old and rarely recalled memories, but were personally reliving each and every aspect of the glorious Exodus from Egypt.

This is the reason why the author of the Haggadah tells us about this special Seder in Bnei Brak. It impresses upon us how even the greatest scholars in our history took it upon themselves to discuss and relate to one another the story of the Exodus as well as the messages and lessons of faith that are derived from it. Through imitating them, and their ability to relive every aspect of the redemption, we will be able to ensure the transmittal of our glorious past to future generations.

It is through telling over and reliving what transpired, speaking about the miracles Hashem wrought for us, and enabling the future generations to connect with all that is being related, that we guarantee the Exodus will live on in our hearts forever.

them: "Our Rabbis! The time for the recitation of the morning *Shema* has arrived."

Rabbi Elazar ben Azaryah said: Behold, I am like a seventy-year-old man, yet I have never been privileged to show that the Exodus from Egypt must be said at night until Ben Zoma explained it. It says: "So that you will remember the day of your departure from Egypt all the days of your life."[1] "The days of your life" indicates the days. "All the days of your life" indicates the nights. The other Sages say, "The days of your life" indicates the world in its present state. "All the days of your life" includes the days of Mashiach.

Blessed is the Omnipresent. Blessed is He. Blessed is He Who gave the Torah to His people, Israel. Blessed is He. Concerning four sons does the Torah speak — one is wise, one is wicked, one is simple, and one is unable to ask.

---

(1) *Devarim* 16:3.

כְּנֶגֶד אַרְבָּעָה בָנִים דִּבְּרָה תוֹרָה —
Concerning four sons does the Torah speak

◄§ The Four Sons

The four sons of the Haggadah represent four different approaches in relating to the world. Among the four sons we find four unique personalities and outlooks. The Torah communicates with each son on his own level and in his own language.

At the Passover Seder we are joined by four sons, each with his own unique personality, character traits, and approach to life. These four sons correspond to the four different types of individuals that comprise every society in mankind's existence. In other words, these four sons are each and every one of us.

The author of the Haggadah categorizes the sons into four different cate-

חָכָם מָה הוּא אוֹמֵר? מָה הָעֵדֹת וְהַחֻקִּים
וְהַמִּשְׁפָּטִים אֲשֶׁר צִוָּה יהוה אֱלֹהֵינוּ
אֶתְכֶם?[1] וְאַף אַתָּה אֱמָר לוֹ כְּהִלְכוֹת הַפֶּסַח, אֵין
מַפְטִירִין אַחַר הַפֶּסַח אֲפִיקוֹמָן.

---

gories: the wise son; the wicked son; the simple son; and the son who is unable to ask. Illustrators of various Haggadahs have often chosen to depict the wise son as an elderly scholarly Jew, similar in appearance to a rabbinical figure of many generations ago, while the wicked son is often depicted as a derelict, a good-for-nothing. These images are not necessarily accurate. The wicked son portrayed by the Haggadah can be a wise man as well, perhaps even wiser than the wise son. He may exhibit proper manners and social graces when interacting socially. Yet when measured on a scale of Jewish values, such an individual may still be considered wicked. For it is on this scale alone that an individual is measured, according to his connection with his heritage, and the eternal inheritance of the Jewish nation — the Torah.

Let us examine the four sons based on this criterion. A quick glance will reveal that the four sons represent four different types of personalities and four different approaches to interacting within a social order. The personalities are as follows:

1) A self-identified personality who constantly wishes to broaden his understanding (the wise son).

2) A negative personality, diametrically opposed to just about everything (the wicked son).

3) A personality characterized by simplistic curiosity (the simple son).

4) A personality characterized by indifference (the son who is unable to ask).

(In truth, these four approaches are general categories, which apply to the way one views any issue. The following paragraphs deal exclusively with these approaches in a framework of how each one relates to his Jewish heritage, but the sensitive reader will recognize their relevance to all issues.)

According to the Torah's guidelines, the author of the Haggadah attempts to open a dialogue with each son, each one according to his level in a language he will be able to understand. The father is speaking in the name of the Torah, in other words in the name of Hashem. He is well aware that in order to instill within the future generations a sense of uniqueness and

What does the wise son say? "What are the testimonies, the decrees, and the laws that HASHEM, our God, has commanded you?"[1] And you, too, should tell him the laws of Pesach: "It is forbidden to eat anything after the Pesach sacrifice."

---

(1) *Devarim* 6:20.

---

responsibility for fulfilling their intended purpose, he must pave a path that leads to the heart of each and every son, as different as they may be.

The wise son has a very strong sense of identity. He views himself as part of the Jewish nation, connected to his Jewish heritage and to Jewish history. In short, he sees the purpose of the Jewish nation as *his* purpose, their role as *his* role, and he acts accordingly. However, he still wishes to know more, to broaden his understanding, and to strengthen his connection to Judaism. His question therefore is, "What are the testimonies, decrees, and laws?"

We respond accordingly. In order for us to understand why we are required in today's day and age to fulfill Hashem's commandments, we must return to our redemption from Egypt. As we were preparing to leave Egypt, we were given the commandment to slaughter a lamb and offer it to Hashem as a Passover offering. As we will soon explain, the slaughtering of the lamb was a part of the Jewish people's struggle to eradicate any trace of idolatry remaining in their hearts. This struggle is far from finished. Idolatry is alive and well, having shaken its pagan and primitive form of yesteryear, and disguising itself in a more modernized and sophisticated ensemble. Only the "testimonies, decrees, and laws" that make up the Torah can offer protection from the forces of idolatry that so wish to dominate our hearts.

The father therefore remarks to the wise son, "One may not eat dessert after the final taste of the Passover offering." After eating the Passover offering it is forbidden to taste anything, even those desserts which are customarily eaten after a meal (in the period when our Sages lived, this dessert was called *afikoman*). The reason for this was so that at the conclusion of the Passover Seder, no taste would be left in one's mouth besides the taste of the Passover offering. The taste of the meat of the Passover lamb would linger in every individual's mouth for hours after the Seder. So, too, in our present day; if one has the desire to investigate and broaden his understanding of his own Judaism and his own Jewish roots he need not "taste" anything after "tasting" the ideas and

רָשָׁע מָה הוּא אוֹמֵר? מָה הָעֲבֹדָה הַזֹּאת לָכֶם?[1] לָכֶם וְלֹא לוֹ, וּלְפִי שֶׁהוֹצִיא אֶת עַצְמוֹ מִן הַכְּלָל, כָּפַר בְּעִקָּר – וְאַף אַתָּה הַקְהֵה אֶת שִׁנָּיו וֶאֱמָר לוֹ, בַּעֲבוּר זֶה עָשָׂה יהוה לִי בְּצֵאתִי מִמִּצְרָיִם.[2] לִי וְלֹא לוֹ, אִלּוּ הָיָה שָׁם לֹא הָיָה נִגְאָל.

concepts of Passover, for therein lie the foundations upon which our nation is built and from there extend our obligations to learn the Torah and fulfill Hashem's commandments. The taste of the Passover offering must accompany us wherever we may turn, as therein are hidden the secrets of the Jewish people's existence, both on a national level as well as on a personal level.

The wicked son, on the other hand, represents a personality that tends to alienate itself and is a proponent of extremely negative views, diametrically opposed to just about any ideal. The words spoken at the Seder simply do not penetrate his heart, as he almost instinctively pushes their meaning aside. He finds the memories of Jewish history burdensome, and they weigh upon him like a heavy load. He sees only the present day and places his belief in nothing else. He finds little value in the lessons and messages his father is trying to impart. "Don't you realize that the times have changed?" he asks his father. "What was relevant in the past has little bearing in today's world!" All the values and concepts of the father are archaic; they have no place in today's "advanced" society. He doesn't realize that his father's values will only enhance the present, helping to lay the foundations of the present on the lofty values of the past. Such a realization is simply not possible in his pursuit of the ideal present. In his mind, Jewish heritage and ritual are unnecessary and detrimental, and it is incumbent upon him to struggle against this oppressive approach that wishes to restrict his choice of lifestyle.

Through his question we are able to clearly see where the wicked son stands in terms of his connection with his nation and their Torah.

"Of what purpose is this work to you?"

Could it be any clearer? As opposed to the wise son, he is entirely uninterested in the details and differences of Judaism. In his eyes, the entire Torah can be summed up in one term — a heavy and unnecessary burden. When he uses the word "work" in his question, it refers to his entire concept of

What does the wicked son say? "Of what purpose is this work to you?"[1] "To you," but not to himself. Since he excludes himself from the group, he denies that which is fundamental. You, too, should blunt his teeth, and say to him: "It is because of this that HASHEM did so for me when I went out of Egypt."[2] "For me," but not for him. Had he been there he would not have been redeemed.

(1) *Shemos* 12:26. (2) 13:8.

Judaism as a whole. He chooses to specifically use this word in response to the words of his father, "The Egyptians subjugated the Children of Israel with hard work." In other words, what is the difference between the hard work inflicted upon us by the Egyptians and the "hard work" inflicted upon us by the Torah? This is the question of the wicked son. This is precisely the way the *Talmud Yerushalmi* (Tractate *Pesachim,* Chapter 1, *Halachah* 4) understands the question as well: *"What is this burdensome work that you burden us with every single year?"*

His question is, in fact, an answer. It is a clear demonstration of his lack of reverence for the Jewish heritage.

It is now the father's turn to respond. Yet he faces a major dilemma. The derisiveness vested in the words of his son is liable to have a profoundly negative impact on the night's atmosphere. What is also of utmost concern is that certain participants at the Seder, those of weaker character strength, are very likely to be influenced by the wicked son's remarks.

The father, therefore, "blunt(s) his teeth." This is not to imply, God forbid, that the father is to inflict physical harm upon the child, actually blunting his teeth. Rather it means that the father should respond to the wicked son by removing the "sting" from his words, and counter any effect his statements might have had. In response to the son's attempt to diminish the importance of Judaism, and his outward disregard for the purpose and inestimable value of the Passover Seder, the father, in turn, shatters his son's illusion of his own inestimable worth. His father reveals him for what he truly is — an individual who senselessly tries to uproot age-old roots without having even the slightest understanding of that which he is trying so hard to uproot. Should he choose to participate in the night's recounting of Jewish redemption from Egypt he would gain a keen insight into his flawed personality, flaws so severe that they would have prevented him from tasting the sweet taste of redemption.

תָּם מָה הוּא אוֹמֵר? מַה זֹּאת? וְאָמַרְתָּ אֵלָיו,
בְּחֹזֶק יָד הוֹצִיאָנוּ יהוה מִמִּצְרַיִם מִבֵּית
עֲבָדִים.[1]

וְשֶׁאֵינוֹ יוֹדֵעַ לִשְׁאוֹל, אַתְּ פְּתַח לוֹ. שֶׁנֶּאֱמַר,
וְהִגַּדְתָּ לְבִנְךָ בַּיּוֹם הַהוּא לֵאמֹר,
בַּעֲבוּר זֶה עָשָׂה יהוה לִי בְּצֵאתִי מִמִּצְרַיִם.[2]

"Had he been there, he would not have been redeemed."

It appears to the wicked son — who undoubtedly believes himself to be correct — that he does not need the recollections of the Passover Seder nor the plethora of memories of great events that the Jewish religion has to offer. He is convinced that he can retain his Jewishness without them. It would be wise to inform him otherwise. For it is not only in *our* generation that he and his offspring stand the chance of assimilating and ultimately getting lost among the nations of the world, but they would have most likely assimilated in Egypt as well, losing their chance at redemption.

The ultimate purpose of such a harsh response is in order to save the wicked son. It is an attempt to instill in him a bit of humility. Perhaps he will realize that he is alienating himself from the Jewish nation, and from a purely historical standpoint this leads to a road of extinction. Perhaps this will be enough to set him along the correct path in life.

The simple son depicted in the Haggadah is not unintelligent; rather he is lacking a deep-rooted spiritual connection to Judaism. He is filled with curiosity, but unfortunately it is the type of curiosity that characterizes the inquisitive bystander who observes from the sidelines. He doesn't actually feel himself to be a part of that about which he is inquiring. While the defiance of the wicked son, to a certain degree, connotes somewhat of a connection (albeit a negative one) to the framework of Judaism, the simple son is altogether different. His desire to know and to understand stems from a purely intellectual motivation. He is well versed in the many facts and facets that depict the life of penguins in the South Pole; he can rattle off the average height of the members of the Busman tribe in central Africa; so to know exactly what transpired in the Jewish redemption from Egypt certainly won't do him any harm. Obviously he is inquiring from a purely academic standpoint, shedding light on his lack of a spiritual connection to Judaism. The words the father has spoken at the Seder, while they serve to penetrate

What does the simple son say? "What is this?" Say to him: "With a strong hand HASHEM took us out of Egypt, from the house of bondage."[1]

And regarding the one who is unable to ask, you open a conversation with him, as it says: "And you shall tell your son on that day, saying, 'It is because of this that HASHEM did so for me when I went out of Egypt.'"[2]

---

(1) *Shemos* 13:14. (2) 13:8.

---

his mind, are a long way from penetrating his heart. After satisfying his thirst for knowledge he will simply turn to an alternative source to gain intellectual satisfaction, storing his newfound knowledge in the corrals of his mind, never permitting them to influence his life in any way.

In response to his question, the father responds, "With a strong hand Hashem took us out of Egypt, from the house of bondage." Our aims must be to remove the simple son from his purely intellectual outlook, and to connect him spiritually. The father's response is an attempt to instill a feeling of wonder and amazement within his son. It is intended to relay to him an idea of just how special and amazing the Exodus really was. He is also told about the miracles that took place by the Red Sea, and of the Divine revelation that occurred there. If the father is successful in properly relating this message, he will have transformed the Seder night into much more than just another lesson in history. It will become an intensely personal experience that is simply beyond description.

The son who is unable to ask is characteristic of one who is simply indifferent and not in touch with much that is taking place around him. He is completely detached from the topics being discussed at the Seder. He is not even drawn intellectually to the matters at hand, that they should stir within him the desire to find what to say. The legacy bestowed upon us by our forefathers is completely beyond his frame of interest. His interest is piqued by more "exciting" things. Instead of journeying through the past, he journeys to faraway lands. The pagodas in India, the tropical jungles in South America, or the mountain peaks in the Himalayas speak to his heart more than the story of the Exodus and all its lessons do.

Yet the Torah does not disregard such a person. The Torah speaks, or better yet, attempts to speak, even to such an individual. "You must initiate the subject for him," says the Haggadah. In other words, the father must make an effort to delve through those barriers that are responsible for the

יָכוֹל מֵרֹאשׁ חֹדֶשׁ, תַּלְמוּד לוֹמַר בַּיּוֹם הַהוּא. אִי בַּיּוֹם הַהוּא, יָכוֹל מִבְּעוֹד יוֹם, תַּלְמוּד לוֹמַר בַּעֲבוּר זֶה. בַּעֲבוּר זֶה לֹא אָמַרְתִּי אֶלָּא בְּשָׁעָה שֶׁיֵּשׁ מַצָּה וּמָרוֹר מֻנָּחִים לְפָנֶיךָ.

מִתְּחִלָּה, עוֹבְדֵי עֲבוֹדָה זָרָה הָיוּ אֲבוֹתֵינוּ, וְעַכְשָׁו קֵרְבָנוּ הַמָּקוֹם לַעֲבוֹדָתוֹ.

---

son's lack of interest and subsequent lack of knowledge. Perhaps he will find an undiscovered point hidden within his son that can be activated in order to draw him closer to the treasures of Judaism.

Interestingly enough, we offer the son who is unable to ask the same verse that was offered to the wicked son ("It is because of this that Hashem did so for me when I went out of Egypt"). Here however, it sends a message altogether different from the one it sent to the wicked son. This verse — due to its generality — is the perfect "warning sign" to help awaken this uninterested child. It informs him that his lack of interest will only serve to harm his spiritual standing, inevitably causing him a drastic spiritual decline. He will fall so far that he will eventually develop feelings of scorn and cynicism. These feelings will ultimately evolve into open hostility and opposition to Judaism and everything else, character traits that very much resemble those of his wicked brother. Despite his disinterest in Judaism, we can safely assume that the spiritual baseness of his wicked brother is one level to which he has little interest in declining. It can be safely assumed that he wishes to retain his connection to the Jewish nation.

There is one glaring truth which the above verse wishes us to hear. Our unbreakable connection with the Exodus is ultimately tied in with the concept of what it means to be a Jew. "It is because of this that Hashem did so for me..." means that all that comprises one's existence ultimately stems from the fact that Hashem took us out of Egypt! Without this concept firm in our belief, there is no possibility to apply the term "Jew," no matter how watered down and lame our assimilated brethren wish this term to be. Therefore, if it is one's desire to maintain his connection with his Jewish heritage, let him research the topic known as the Exodus, keeping an open mind and, most importantly, ridding himself of all preconceived notions.

We might have held from the first of the month, but the Torah tells us: "On that day." Since it says "on that day," we might have held that we should begin while it is still day. But the Torah says: "Because of *this*." I only say "because of *this*" at a time when matzah and *maror* are placed before you.

At first our ancestors were idol worshipers, but now the Omnipresent has brought us close to His service,

---

מִתְּחִלָּה, עוֹבְדֵי עֲבוֹדָה זָרָה הָיוּ אֲבוֹתֵינוּ,
וְעַכְשָׁו קֵרְבָנוּ הַמָּקוֹם לַעֲבוֹדָתוֹ. —

**At first our ancestors were idol worshipers,
but now the Omnipresent has brought us close to His service**

◄ঙ *One Is Abraham*

At the young age of three began the spiritual quest of our forefather Abraham. It was an unbelievable quest that led him to recognize the existence of the Creator. His war against idolatry and its falsehoods was a war waged by a single individual against the entire world. It was a war waged for the sake of truth, without giving a moment's thought to the perils that might confront him.

In truth, the Haggadah begins here. Our attempts to grasp the metamorphosis experienced by the Jewish nation as a result of the Exodus forces us to dig deeper into our ancient history, back to the roots of the Jewish nation. At the core of all our searching lies one individual — "one" in every sense of the word — the father of the Jewish people, Abraham.

In order that we obtain a proper perception of this most historical individual, the Haggadah begins with words of "disgrace," as our Sages put it. The author of the Haggadah informs us that several generations preceding the Jewish people's sojourn in Egypt, there was a period of time when all the nations of the world worshiped idols and did not recognize the Supreme Ruler, Creator of heaven and earth.

Who was Abraham?

Abraham was a man whose entire being surged with freedom. He was

שֶׁנֶּאֱמַר, וַיֹּאמֶר יְהוֹשֻׁעַ אֶל כָּל הָעָם, כֹּה אָמַר יהוה אֱלֹהֵי יִשְׂרָאֵל, בְּעֵבֶר הַנָּהָר יָשְׁבוּ אֲבוֹתֵיכֶם מֵעוֹלָם, תֶּרַח אֲבִי אַבְרָהָם וַאֲבִי נָחוֹר, וַיַּעַבְדוּ אֱלֹהִים אֲחֵרִים. וָאֶקַּח אֶת אֲבִיכֶם אֶת אַבְרָהָם

---

courageous and the living definition of a non-conformist, refusing to yield to the ideals of the powerful dictator Nimrod, whose idolatrous views dominated the world in his lifetime. Nimrod's dictatorship knew no bounds and all were required to be faithful to and worship the false gods that "prevailed" at that time, namely, the sun, the moon, the stars, and other elements that demonstrated their "powers" before the eyes of the people.

Abraham, however, was not satisfied with the accepted dogmas of the world at large and began to search:

> He began to contemplate when he was yet young. He began to ponder day and night and he was filled with wonder: How is it possible that this sphere (the universe) functions constantly and is without an overseer? Who rotates it? For it is impossible that it should rotate on its own (Rambam; Mishneh Torah, Hilchos Avodah Zarah, Chapter 1).

He alone had such thoughts, a lone individual amidst an entire world:

> And he was without a teacher nor one who made him aware of this. Rather, he was entrenched in Ur Casdim amidst foolish idol worshipers, with both his father and mother and the entire nation worshiping idols; and he too worshiped with them. His mind contemplated and understood until he grasped the true path (ibid.).

At the age of three, according to the Midrash, began the spiritual journey of Abraham. It was a journey that involved much mental anguish as well as physical suffering and torment. It was a journey filled with questions and internal struggles that would continue until Abraham reached the age of 40. At that point, Abraham's outlook on life materialized and he arrived at faith in one Being. His exalted character was able to absorb the concept of the existence of a Supreme Being, He being the unseen Creator Who has no equal, from Whose essence stems all. Abraham was able to break through a wall of disharmony and strife that so characterized the people of his generation and succeed in "connecting that which had been torn," in the words of the Midrash. He forged the image of a world vested with the

as it says: "And Joshua said to all of the people: So says HASHEM the God of Israel: Of old, your forefathers dwelt beyond the river — Terah, the father of Abraham and the father of Nahor, and they worshiped other gods. And I took your father Abraham from

---

potential to achieve ultimate perfection, a world that could return to the harmony of Divine service and unity.

It was then that Abraham displayed enormous courage:

He began presenting his ideas in public forum, ignoring very real threats of danger simply for the sake of truth. Despite a national government whose beliefs ran directly contrary to his, Abraham did not stop proclaiming his beliefs. He publicly stated his difficulties with the idolatrous practices of the time, and posed irrefutable questions that baffled the masses. He shattered the myths and ideologies that were fabricated by the generations that had preceded him, by those who had distanced themselves from the traditions of Noah.

Nimrod sensed the challenge that Abraham posed to his dictatorship. The "Refuseniks" who followed so faithfully in the ways of Abraham threatened to disturb the "religious" stability that permeated the kingdom of Ur Casdim. Abraham was therefore sentenced to be burned alive, only to be saved by means of a miracle. Abraham fled to Charan, eventually to journey to the land of Canaan. This is a short summary of a remarkable story. These are events that transpired in the life of an extraordinary thinker who was willing to give up his life for that which he believed. It is an incredible biography of the individual who laid the foundations of the Jewish faith. This was the beginning of the Jewish faith, a faith that saw the Exodus add to it a new dimension, as we will soon explain.

וָאֶקַּח אֶת אֲבִיכֶם אֶת אַבְרָהָם מֵעֵבֶר הַנָּהָר —
And I took your father Abraham from beyond the river

⁄₅ You Have Chosen Us From All the Nations

At the moment Hashem commanded Abraham, "Go for yourself from your land," the concept of a "chosen nation" was born. This concept, which has aroused the

מֵעֵבֶר הַנָּהָר, וָאוֹלֵךְ אוֹתוֹ בְּכָל אֶרֶץ כְּנָעַן,
וָאַרְבֶּה אֶת זַרְעוֹ, וָאֶתֵּן לוֹ אֶת יִצְחָק. וָאֶתֵּן
לְיִצְחָק אֶת יַעֲקֹב וְאֶת עֵשָׂו, וָאֶתֵּן לְעֵשָׂו אֶת
הַר שֵׂעִיר לָרֶשֶׁת אוֹתוֹ, וְיַעֲקֹב וּבָנָיו יָרְדוּ
מִצְרָיְמָה.[1]

---

nations of the world to inflict an untold amount of suffering on the Jewish people, has even been shunned by
many of the Jewish nation who deem themselves unworthy of such a lofty title. It is incumbent upon us to understand why it was Abraham and his descendants who were
specifically chosen by Hashem.

Despite all that we have mentioned above, the "official" biography of
our forefather Abraham begins at the moment he heard the commandment of Hashem, "Go for yourself..." At that moment a new Abraham was
born. This was no longer the Abraham who had brought himself closer and
closer to Hashem through the use of his own potentials and abilities, but
rather an Abraham who had begun to be drawn closer to Hashem by none
other than Hashem himself. It was an Abraham who had been called upon
by Hashem in order to bring to fruition the exalted purpose which Hashem
had in store for mankind.

Up until this point, Abraham had exemplified the absolute peak of
human understanding. He was a renowned philosopher who recognized
the Creator of the World and acknowledged His message to mankind.
He was esteemed in the eyes of the people, and his influence upon their
lives was readily apparent. Yet now he was transformed into an individual who had been privileged to be touched by the hand of the Master
of the world, an experience far beyond the human intellect. Any action that
he would perform from that point on would take on a completely new
meaning. He now faced an entirely new life, to be accompanied by entirely
new challenges. He had now been designated a messenger of Hashem;
Abraham had now been "chosen." At this point began the concept of the
Jewish people's being chosen by Hashem. This concept, which has aroused
the nations of the world to inflict an untold amount of suffering on the
Jewish people, has even been shunned by members of the Jewish nation

beyond the river, and I led him throughout all the land of Canaan, and I multiplied his seed, and I gave Isaac unto him, and I gave Jacob and Esau unto Isaac, and I gave unto Esau Mount Seir to inherit, but Jacob and his sons went down to Egypt."[1]

---

(1) *Yehoshua* 24:2-4.

---

who deem themselves unworthy of such a lofty title. Yet the truth remains that the children of Abraham are an exalted nation, recipients of favorable discrimination.

The "You have chosen us" of our forefather Abraham is for the sake of all mankind.

Therefore we must understand: Why did Hashem specifically choose Abraham? Was this choice the planting of the seed of discrimination and racism against the Jewish nation?

To properly understand the above questions, it is worthwhile to examine with the utmost simplicity the verses that deal with the chosenness of the Jewish nation. Then perhaps we will begin to comprehend the significance of the pact between Hashem and the Jewish people known as "You have chosen us."

The verse states (*Bereishis* 12:1-3):

> Hashem said to Avram, "Go for yourself from your land, from your relatives, and from your father's house to the land that I will show you. And I will make of you a great nation; I will bless you, and I will make your name great, and you will be a blessing . . . and all the families of the earth will be blessed through you."

What we are in fact dealing with here is a demand for Abraham to turn his back on the prevailing culture of his generation. He is to break family ties and distance himself from the land and life of his youth in order to set up a new life in a new land. All of this was required for a very special purpose. After Hashem would produce from the children of Abraham a great nation, they were to bestow blessing to the entire world, as the Torah states (ibid.), "... and all the families of the earth will be blessed through you." This verse represents the elevated purpose that required Abraham's separation from his homeland.

In other words, man, who chose to serve Hashem, was in turn chosen by Hashem with the explicit purpose of bringing Hashem's message to

בָּרוּךְ שׁוֹמֵר הַבְטָחָתוֹ לְיִשְׂרָאֵל, בָּרוּךְ הוּא.
שֶׁהַקָּדוֹשׁ בָּרוּךְ הוּא חִשַּׁב אֶת הַקֵּץ,
לַעֲשׂוֹת כְּמָה שֶׁאָמַר לְאַבְרָהָם אָבִינוּ בִּבְרִית
בֵּין הַבְּתָרִים, שֶׁנֶּאֱמַר, וַיֹּאמֶר לְאַבְרָם, יָדֹעַ תֵּדַע
כִּי גֵר יִהְיֶה זַרְעֲךָ בְּאֶרֶץ לֹא לָהֶם, וַעֲבָדוּם
וְעִנּוּ אֹתָם, אַרְבַּע מֵאוֹת שָׁנָה. וְגַם אֶת הַגּוֹי אֲשֶׁר

---

humanity.

Man accomplishes this by observing His commandments and by serving as an example of how to live one's life as a believer in Hashem. He is to stand opposite the ways of the rest of the world — for the world's own sake. Hashem would certainly never turn his back, as it were, on the rest of mankind as a first course of action. Quite the contrary, in fact, for Hashem in His great mercy has constantly turned to mankind, waiting for mankind's favorable response, yet the response has not come. Mankind's lack of response has been depicted in the following Midrash:

> "We would have healed Bavel, but she was not healed; forsake her and let us go every one to his own land" (Yirmiyah 51:9). "We would have healed Bavel," (this refers to) the generation of Enosh (the first generation to engage in idol worship). "But she was not healed" in the generation of the Flood. "Forsake her," in the generation of Disunion. "And let us go every one to his own land," (this is) "Hashem said to Avram, 'Go for yourself from your land'" (Bereishis Rabbah 39:5).

The Midrash is teaching us that only after 2,000 years of failure on the part of the world to absorb Hashem's message was a single individual finally chosen to stand opposite the entire world — for the sake of mankind.

It is quite interesting to note how the matter at hand appeared in the eyes of one of the world's most well-known historians, an individual who not only lacked any feelings of warmth for the Jewish nation but actually despised them. It is almost exhilarating to read how such an individual in perhaps a moment of grace would view the Jewish nation and their purpose in the annals of history:

Blessed is He Who keeps His promise to Israel. Blessed is He. For the Holy One, Blessed is He, calculated the end [of the exile], to do as He said to Abraham our father at the Covenant Between the Parts, as it is said, "And He said to Abram: Know that your offspring will be a stranger in a land not theirs, and they will serve them and they will torment them for four hundred years. But also the nation whom

---

I have the nerve to say that it is the destiny of Judaism to bring unique tidings to the world. For it is rather odd how twice in mankind's history did the Jewish people witness how individuals from outside the framework of Judaism took hold of their religion and spread it throughout the world. I am referring to Christianity and Islam. Is it simply coincidental that these strangers took hold of some of the most basic tenets of Judaism and clothed them in their own religious beliefs? Is Judaism not one day destined to spread its Torah in its true form, "True Judaism" — if one can use such a term — throughout the entire world without being clothed in the garments of Christianity and Islam? After all has been said and done, is not Judaism a more refined form of monotheism than is Christianity and Islam? Will this not be the Jewish people's gift to the world in the future?

He finishes with a statement of great significance:

And does the solution to the problem that exists in the relationship between the Jews and the nations of the world not lie in this very point? (the words of Professor Arnold Toynbee; printed in the French newspaper "La Rosh," June 1959).

Within these words lies a deep understanding of the huge complexities that comprise the relationship between the Jewish people and the nations of the world. These are complexities that have existed from the time that Hashem chose our forefather Abraham, and appointed him to be His messenger to carry His word to all of mankind.

These are words that are relevant to our present-day relationship with the nations of the world, and will continue to be relevant until the truth of Abraham's message becomes revealed to all.

יַעֲבְדוּ דָן אָנֹכִי, וְאַחֲרֵי כֵן יֵצְאוּ בִּרְכֻשׁ גָּדוֹל.[1]

וְאַחֲרֵי כֵן יֵצְאוּ בִּרְכֻשׁ גָּדוֹל —
And afterwards they will go out with great possessions

⇜§ Paying the Price

Before the Children of Israel left Egypt they took gold and silver vessels from the Egyptian homes. From the verses written in the Torah it would appear that Hashem commanded the Jewish people to borrow these vessels from their Egyptian neighbors. It goes without saying that when one lends an item to someone else, he expects to have the item returned to him. Yet Hashem commanded the Jewish people to ask the Egyptians for their vessels despite the fact that they would never be returned to them. "Would Hashem permit deception?"

At midnight, on the 14th of Nissan, all the Egyptian firstborns died at the same time (*Shemos* 12:29). Piercing cries and horrible screams erupted from each and every Egyptian home (ibid. v. 30). Pharaoh urged Moses and pleaded with him, *"Rise up, go out from among my people"* (ibid. v. 31). Even the Egyptians themselves implored the Jews to leave Egypt (ibid. v. 33).

While the Jewish people certainly left Egypt, it was not before they did *"according to the word of Moses; they requested from the Egyptians silver vessels, gold vessels, and garments. Hashem granted the people favor in the eyes of the Egyptians and they lent them — so they emptied Egypt"* (ibid. vs. 35-36).

Is it possible that at the Jewish people's moment of redemption, as a new life of freedom awaited them, they could actually be interested in gold and silver, in amassing the spoils of the Egyptians? Was this an act of revenge on the part of a long oppressed nation, being carried out on their cruel oppressors?

Certainly not.

The Jewish people's requesting of the Egyptian vessels was part of a Divine plan that had been conspired, as it were, long before the process of the redemption from Egypt had begun. The moment of redemption was simply the time chosen by Hashem to deliver His commandment, as the

they will serve I will judge. And afterwards they will go out with great possessions."[1]

---

(1) *Bereishis* 15:13-14.

---

verse states, *"Please speak in the ears of the people: Let each man request of his fellow and each woman from her fellow silver vessels and gold vessels"* (ibid. 11:2).

The Jewish people, therefore, went and fulfilled the words of Hashem exactly as He had commanded them, solely for the sake of following Hashem's orders. For the verse states that Hashem used the expression, *"Please speak,"* perhaps connoting a request on the part of Hashem, urging the Jewish people to perform an act which they themselves had absolutely no desire to do.

We must understand, however, the exact nature of this commandment. Is it conceivable that Hashem would command the Jewish people to ask the Egyptians to loan them their vessels on condition never to return them? As one of the classical commentators remarks, *"God forbid that Hashem should permit an act of deception"* (*Rabbeinu Bachya,* in his commentary on the Torah).

In front of us we have a striking example of what can result in the misinterpretation of a single word of the Torah. In our modern-day dialect, the word *"sha'al"* (request) connotes the act of borrowing an item with the intention of returning it. Such a meaning is found in the Torah but once: *"When a man will borrow (yish'al) from his fellow..."* (ibid. 23:13). However, every other time this word appears in the Torah it means simply to "request" without any implication of borrowing and subsequent return. There is a general rule that we can apply: Whenever the word *"sha'al"* appears next to the word *"me'im"* ("from"), it connotes an act of borrowing. However, any time it is paired with another word, it simply means "to request," without any implication of repayment. Therefore, when the Torah states, *"They requested (sha'al) from the Egyptians"; "Let each man request (vi'yishalu) of his fellow,"* the Torah is referring to the simple act of requesting an item from another, without any obligation to return that which he has been given.

We see, therefore, that the act of the Jewish people's taking the Egyptian silver and gold vessels was not, Heaven forbid, a fraudulent act. It was a request on the part of the Jewish people for the Egyptians to bestow a portion of their assets upon a nation leaving their land. Divine justice certainly required that the Egyptian slave-masters offer at least minimum compensation for the hundreds of years of slavery they imposed upon the Jews.

The matzos are covered and the cups lifted as the following paragraph is proclaimed joyously. Upon its conclusion, the cups are put down and the matzos are uncovered.

וְהִיא שֶׁעָמְדָה לַאֲבוֹתֵינוּ וְלָנוּ, שֶׁלֹא אֶחָד בִּלְבַד עָמַד עָלֵינוּ לְכַלוֹתֵנוּ. אֶלָּא שֶׁבְּכָל דּוֹר וָדוֹר עוֹמְדִים עָלֵינוּ לְכַלוֹתֵנוּ,

The Jews were certainly entitled to at least minimum reparations for the damages incurred by the Egyptians. It also served the purpose of teaching the Egyptians that one is forbidden to profit from the exploitation and oppression of another, and that one should never receive the fruits of another man's labor without due payment.

שֶׁלֹא אֶחָד בִּלְבַד עָמַד עָלֵינוּ לְכַלוֹתֵנוּ. —
For not only one has risen against us to annihilate us

ᴥ§ The Predicted Phenomenon

The miracle of the Jewish people's continued survival is one that amazes both Jew and non-Jew. The fact that we are still in existence defies every historical "rule" and theory. "The continued existence of the Jewish nation is an amazing phenomenon that testifies that the life of this nation continues to be driven by the force of an ancient decree. (It is a decree) that is far beyond any of the laws of adaptation." — These are the words of a secular historian. What meaning do these words have for us in our present day?

This paragraph in the Haggadah is a summary of history's most amazing phenomenon. It is a phenomenon that has impressed all those who are aware of it, regardless of religious affiliation. This is the phenomenon of the continued existence of the Jewish nation, which has scorned all the hardships that history has thrown its way. What is most interesting, however, is that all of this — both the hardships and the survival — have been stated and predicted from the very beginning. Let us attempt to understand by examining several facts that comprise the history of our nation:

The matzos are covered and the cups lifted as the following paragraph is proclaimed joyously. Upon its conclusion, the cups are put down and the matzos are uncovered.

It [the Covenant Between the Parts] has stood firm for our fathers and for us. For not only one has risen against us to annihilate us, but in every generation there are those who stand against us to annihilate

---

1) **We have been scattered among the nations of the world:** We are a "cosmopolitan" nation. We speak every language that is spoken across the globe. There is not a country in the world — from China in the Far East, to the darkest corners of Africa — that has not been host, at some point in time, to our people on their journey through exile. The Jews have left their mark — sometimes for better, sometimes for worse — in every corner of the globe.

   The "wandering Jew" is an international concept.

   Where has this been predicted in the Torah?

   "Hashem will scatter you among all the peoples, from the end of the earth to the end of the earth" (Devarim 28:64).

2) **We have been subject to anti-Semitism:** Anti-Semitism is one of the frightening secrets about the nature of mankind. The greatest philosophers have long sought to decipher the mystery of anti-Semitism. They have tried to understand from where it stems, to discover its source. Yet all their thought has ultimately been fruitless. For anti-Semitism defies all logic. What can be the cause of anti-Semitism in one country ("They separate themselves from society, that is the reason the Jews are hated") can be exactly the opposite in another country ("They stick their noses into everyone's business. They occupy all the best jobs"). Therefore, despite all the analysis, there has yet to be found a satisfying answer. However, let us see the prognosis:

   "You will be for astonishment, for a parable, and for a topic of conversation, among all the peoples where Hashem will lead you" (ibid. v. 37).

3) **We have been persecuted:** We are not strangers when it comes to this issue. Words such as *Tach V'Tat;* the Inquisition; Cantonists; border confinement; ghettos; yellow stars; the Spanish Expulsion; Siberia; and the Holocaust are sufficient to enable us to recall the painful memories that are associated with them.

   The verse states: *"And among those nations you will not be tranquil, there will be no rest for the sole of your foot; there Hashem will*

וְהַקָּדוֹשׁ בָּרוּךְ הוּא מַצִּילֵנוּ מִיָּדָם.

---

give you a trembling heart, longing of eyes, and suffering of the soul. Your life will hang opposite you, and you will be frightened night and day, and you will not be certain of your life. In the morning you will say, 'If only it would be evening!' And in the evening you will say, 'If only it would be morning!' — for the fright of your heart that you will fear and the sight of your eyes that you will see" (ibid. vs. 65-67).

4) **Yet we continue to survive:** Mankind will be unable to destroy us. The nations of the world will have defeated us on numerous occasions, but in the long run they will have lost — for we continue to exist. Thousands of years of suffering, harsh decrees, oppression, and degrees of persecution that have vanquished powerful nations from the face of the earth have been unable to destroy us. This phenomenon has left philosophers — primarily non-Jewish philosophers — in utter amazement:

> *In the days of my youth I attempted to validate historical theory through presenting the fates met by the nations of the world. Yet the entire theory has been shattered by the Jew, whose fate, according to the theory, should have been decidedly negative. According to the criterion of the theory this nation should have passed from the world long ago. Its continued existence is an amazing phenomenon that testifies that its life continues to be driven by the force of an ancient decree. (It is a decree) that is far beyond any of the laws of adaptation, which fuel the historical theory. The continued existence of the Jewish people, their rebellion against the forces of destruction, their living according to specific principles and conditions, and the role which they have played in society... All of these items point to their mysterious and most unique fate (Nicholas Bardive).*

Consider these words of the French philosopher Jean Paul Sartre:

> *I am unable to judge the Jewish nation according to history's accepted principles. The Jewish nation is beyond time and I am therefore unable to pass judgment on the dilemma that relations with the Jewish nation represents, without taking this factor into account.*

Once again the Torah has foreseen such a phenomenon:

> *But despite all this, while they are in the land of their enemies, I will not have been abhorred by them nor will I have rejected them to*

us. But the Holy One, Blessed is He, rescues us from their hand.

---

obliterate them, to annul My covenant with them — for I am Hashem their God" (Vayikra 26:44).

We have enumerated several historical observations and have shown how each one has already been predicted in the Torah. Each observation is the model of utmost absurdity from a historical standpoint, for the fate of no other nation in world history has mirrored that of the Jewish nation. The events foretold in the verses of the Torah, however, mirror with exactitude all that has transpired and continues to transpire until the end of time. Reality may be painful and difficult to understand; yet within it all there lies an element of consolation. Our reality points to a purpose, to a pre-ordained plan that operates under the all-encompassing hand, as it were, of Divine providence. It points to the fact that the many generations of Jewish history are not simply a collection of chance events, but rather steps, each one bringing us closer to the rectification of all mankind, which is the ultimate goal of the future.

וְהַקָּדוֹשׁ בָּרוּךְ הוּא מַצִּילֵנוּ מִיָּדָם — But the Holy One, Blessed is He, rescues us from their hand

---

⋖ Blessing From the Depths of a Curse

There is a surprising paradox that is embodied within the many generations of Jewish history. Hidden within the prophecies which foresaw the destruction of the Holy Temple lay the seeds of eventual salvation for the Jewish people. Beneath the punishment lies the salvation. Anti-Semitism is a blessing in disguise. The Jewish people being scattered across the world contributes more to our survival than any other factor. Simply amazing.

One of the astonishing lessons fashioned by Judaism is represented by the fact that hidden within the prophecies that depict the destruction of the Holy Temple (*Vayikra* 25; *Devarim* 28), lie the seeds of eventual salvation and continuous survival for the Jewish people. This would seem to be the ultimate paradox, but in fact is not the case. The receiving of Divine

צֵא וּלְמַד מַה בִּקֵּשׁ לָבָן הָאֲרַמִּי לַעֲשׂוֹת לְיַעֲקֹב
אָבִינוּ, שֶׁפַּרְעֹה לֹא גָזַר אֶלָּא עַל הַזְּכָרִים,
וְלָבָן בִּקֵּשׁ לַעֲקוֹר אֶת הַכֹּל. שֶׁנֶּאֱמַר:
אֲרַמִּי אֹבֵד אָבִי, וַיֵּרֶד מִצְרַיְמָה וַיָּגָר שָׁם בִּמְתֵי
מְעָט, וַיְהִי שָׁם לְגוֹי, גָּדוֹל עָצוּם וָרָב.[1]

---

prophecy is proof of the fact that Hashem is all-powerful without any limitations whatsoever (which of course is the main message to be transmitted on
this night). It proves without an iota of doubt that Hashem has the ability to
wrap both devastation and salvation in the same package.

Let us present several examples of this idea:

❏ In the book of *Vayikra*, the Torah relates to us a prophecy regarding the
matter of the Jewish people's future exile from the land of Israel, and the
land's subsequent desolation during that time period.

*"I will make the land desolate; and your foes who dwell upon it will be
desolate"* (*Vayikra* 26:32). Hidden in the apparent negativity of the verse's
depiction is a blessing in disguise. As the Midrash states when referring to the
aforementioned verse, "This is a good measure. In order that Israel should
not say, 'Since we have been exiled from our land, our enemies will now
come (settle the land) and experience gratification upon it. Therefore (the
verse states) *'Your foes who dwell upon it will be desolate,'* so that they
should not experience gratification" (*Sifra, Vayikra*).

Our generation has been witness to the benevolence vested in this "good
measure." We, the generation that was privileged to return to the land of our
forefathers, had the good fortune to find the land empty and desolate with
few inhabitants. If the land of Israel had been settled by another nation (as has
been the case in practically every instance when a land has been either
conquered or evacuated), our dream of resettling it would not have been able
to materialize. The land of Israel's desolation, which is a curse, is also a
tremendous blessing.

This idea can also be illustrated by analyzing the rest of Hashem's words
of rebuke that appear in the Torah. For example:

❏ *The curse of our being scattered amongst the nations:* "This is a harsh
measure, because at a time when the inhabitants of a country are exiled to
one place, they see one another and are consoled" (*Rashi*, quoting a
Midrash). In other words, "togetherness" is a major source of comfort in
times of hardship The lack of "togetherness" contributes to the curse of
being scattered among the nations.

Go and ascertain what Laban the Aramean intended to do to Jacob our father, for Pharaoh decreed destruction only for the males, but Laban intended to eradicate everything. As it is said:

An Aramean would destroy my father, and he went down to Egypt, and he sojourned there with few people, and there he became a nation, great, mighty, and numerous.[1]

------
(1) *Devarim* 26:5.

Despite the severity of such a curse, it nonetheless carries with it an important blessing: *"Hashem performed an act of charity (with the Jewish people) by scattering them among the nations,"* says the Midrash. If not for this "scattering," the Jewish people would have been destroyed long ago. If the Jewish people had not been scattered, but rather concentrated into one area, it is likely that a calamity would have occurred. Over the course of many generations it is highly probable that a tyrant would come to rule the area in which the Jews would be concentrated, and one day fulfill his great anti-Semitic fantasy of wiping out the entire Jewish race.

Wandering from country to country has helped ensure our survival.

Our wandering from country to country and land to land has helped ensure our survival among the nations of the world. It is impossible to fathom a situation in which every single leader of the world will unanimously decide to exterminate the Jewish nation wherever they may dwell. Conflicts of interests that would inevitably arise between nations would simply not permit this to happen. Our being scattered is an enormous miracle that has been at the root of our survival until the present day. The wandering of Jewish immigrants in the past century — from Europe to America, South America, and South Africa — enabled the Jewish people to establish new communities and congregations even in the midst of the Holocaust.

❏ Even the curse of anti-Semitism is not simply a tragic curse void of all blessing. This curse, mentioned by Moses *("You will be for astonishment, for a parable, and for a topic of conversation"),* and from which has sprouted all the derision and scorn that has been the lot of the Jewish people, also contains within it seeds of blessing. All the pain and suffering that the Jewish people have felt throughout the generations has served to keep us an individual nation, separate and distinct from the other nations of the world. Every land that has expressed tolerance of the Jewish people, has inevitably been a haven of assimilation, resulting in a "Silent Holocaust" that has wiped out

וַיֵּרֶד מִצְרַיְמָה – אָנוּס עַל פִּי הַדִּבּוּר.

hundreds of Jewish communities.

Thus have these three curses established an unbreakable covenant. It is a covenant whose purpose has been to guard the Jewish people over the course of thousands of years, and never to allow them to compromise on their eventual return to their "desolate" land.

In addition, the phenomenon of reality conforming with exactitude to the Torah's eternal verses is relevant in our present day as well. Read the final chapter of Moses' address to the Jewish nation. It has been designated specifically to impart that which will occur in the distant future. This chapter, Chapter 30 in *Devarim*, has been called "The *Parashah* (Torah portion) of Redemption." It is a clear prophecy depicting the order in which the future redemption will come about *(Haamek Davar)*.

The chapter begins as follows: *"It will be that when all these things come upon you — the blessing and the curse that I have presented before you — then you will take it to your heart among all the nations where Hashem, your God, has dispersed you"* (ibid. v. 1).

The central idea in this chapter is that the redemption will arrive following a chain of events and after there has been an ingathering of the exiles from all four corners of the world.

"And he will gather you in from all the peoples to where Hashem, your God, has scattered you. If your dispersed will be at the ends of the heavens, from there Hashem, your God, will gather you in and from there He will take you. Hashem, your God, will bring you to the land of which your forefathers took possession" (ibid. vs. 3-5).

The ingathering of exiles will be a gradual process, occurring in stages. It will be a process that will eventually see the Jewish people return to their roots — namely, the Torah and our ancient heritage *("And you will return unto Hashem, your God, and listen to His voice... You shall return and listen to the voice of Hashem"*; ibid. vs. 2,8). It is a process we have begun to witness in our times as well.

In his final address to the Jewish people, Moses decries a fatalistic approach as opposed to an optimistic one. The initial notice of the Jewish people's eventual redemption was meant to awaken one's awareness of his Creator, Who controls each and every event that transpires throughout history. As the verse states, *"It will be that when all these things come upon you — the blessing and the curse... you will take it to your heart"* (ibid. v. 1).

Pondering the history of our nation, a nation that has seen simultaneous curses and blessing, leads to such awareness, from which will stem the

And he went down to Egypt — compelled by Divine decree.

---

eventual redemption. This is a lesson that becomes readily apparent upon viewing historical events and realizing that they correspond with that which has been stated in the final chapters of the Torah, within which are contained all the secrets of the coming days.

אָנוּס עַל פִּי הַדִּבּוּר — Compelled by Divine decree

⇜ A Nation Born Outside Its Homeland

If not for Joseph, the beloved son of our forefather Jacob, Jacob would never have journeyed down to Egypt, for he feared leaving the land of Israel. Hashem, however, told Jacob that it was only in Egypt that his descendants would become a nation. Why?

Jacob journeyed down to Egypt "compelled by Divine decree." Hashem drew Jacob and his family to Egypt, as they followed Joseph who had been sent there by Hashem.

Upon his departure to Egypt, Jacob had already been made aware of the fact that Joseph was alive. The brothers, upon returning from Egypt with food to sustain the family, had brought this good tiding to their father. Jacob's eyes lit up when he heard the news about the beloved son he had long thought to be dead, and felt as if he had been granted a new lease on life. After twenty-two years of suffering, mourning, and depression, an elderly Jacob heard what he never dreamed he would — that Joseph was alive and living in Egypt. This was a true gift from Hashem, greater than anything Jacob could have hoped for in his lifetime.

Jacob's heart yearned to see his beloved son: *"I shall go and see him (Joseph) before I die"* (Bereishis 45:28).

Thus, the family of Jacob journeyed down to Egypt. They went to Egypt with a good frame of mind eager to have their family reunited. They all shared in the profound joy of their elderly father, who had finally found his beloved son.

Despite all the happiness, a dark cloud of apprehension hung over Jacob. It was an apprehension that was certainly not noticeable to the outside observer. Yet deep within the great heart of the father of the Jewish nation lay

וַיָּגָר שָׁם – מְלַמֵּד שֶׁלֹּא יָרַד יַעֲקֹב אָבִינוּ
לְהִשְׁתַּקֵּעַ בְּמִצְרַיִם, אֶלָּא לָגוּר שָׁם. שֶׁנֶּאֱמַר,

fear over the uncertainty that lay ahead. We are only aware of this fear because of Hashem's revelation to Jacob on the border of the land of Israel. In a vision that occurs at night, Hashem beseeches Jacob not to be afraid: *"Do not be afraid of descending to Egypt"* (ibid. 46:3).

We see therefore that Jacob was afraid. He knew quite well that his descent to Egypt would signify the beginning of exile for the Jewish people, the exile that had been decreed upon Abraham and his descendants in the "Covenant between the Parts." Jacob understood that although he personally would experience much happiness in Egypt, living out the final years of his life with the utmost tranquility, his family's sojourn in Egypt was to have far-reaching consequences. The consequences would be quite dramatic, culminating in the frightening words that Hashem spoke to our forefather Abraham: *"Know with certainty that your offspring shall be sojourners in a land not their own, they will enslave them, and they will oppress them"* (ibid. 15:13). Jacob's personal joy was diminished by his knowledge of the grief that lay in store for his descendants.

The thought of sojourning in Egypt frightened Jacob. It was not only the knowledge that the Egyptians would one day afflict his descendants, which disturbed Jacob. His main concern was the danger of possible assimilation. He feared the lure of the culture that prevailed in the "Land of the Nile," and was worried lest his descendants become involved in idolatry and immoral practices, which were so rampant in Egypt. Would his children always re-member their homeland in Canaan, or would the memory eventually begin to fade, resulting in a Jewish nation who were "Jews at heart," but not in practice?

This was Jacob's fear.

From the viewpoint of Divine providence, however, the Jewish presence in Egypt would result in something quite positive. This is what Hashem said to Jacob: *"Do not be afraid of descending to Egypt, for I shall establish you as a great nation there"* (ibid. 46:3).

> *It is I, who am saying to you, "Do not be afraid of descending to Egypt, for I shall establish you as a great nation there." For indeed, if your children would remain here (in the land of Canaan), they would marry Canaanites (as opposed to Jews), and assimilate with them. In Egypt, however, this will not occur. For the Egyptians could not bear to eat bread with the Hebrews (Sforno).*

> **He sojourned there** — This teaches us that
> our father Jacob did not descend to Egypt to set-
> tle, but only to sojourn there temporarily, as it says,

In other words, Hashem is telling Jacob that things are not the way they appear to be. His descendants will be formed into a nation. They will be a nation that will be guided by that which has been transmitted by their forefathers, Abraham, Isaac, and Jacob. Such a nation could never have been formed in the land of Canaan. Specifically in that land, which was designated to be the Jewish homeland, they would be subject to the dangers of assimilation. In Canaan, Jacob's descendants would grow up in an environment that offered total and absolute freedom — including complete freedom of worship — but would eventually blend into the Canaanite society and succumb to the lure of the prevailing culture. Eventually they would assimilate completely and would be lost. Only in Egypt would the Jewish nation be guarded from assimilation and only there could they form a nation with its own unique identity. There in Egypt, a flourishing land, would the Jewish nation be afforded the "spiritual isolation" desired by Hashem. The inhabitants of the land would distance themselves from the Jewish people. They would denigrate them and alienate them from society (in other words, the anti-Semitism in Egypt was necessary in order to build the Jewish nation and form their identity and was not simply a means of inflicting harm). Only after the many years of suffering in Egypt — suffering that in fact molded the Jewish nation — and the receiving of the holy Torah would the Jewish nation be worthy of returning to the land of their forefathers, complete with a new identity and culture. Theirs would be a culture that stemmed from Sinai, a culture that would influence the entire world. Upon hearing Hashem's next guarantee," *I shall descend with you to Egypt, and I shall surely bring you up*" (ibid. v. 4), Jacob knew with certainty that he had not fully comprehended the Divine plan. It then became clear to him why Egyptian exile had been decreed on his children.

אֶלָּא לָגוּר שָׁם — But only to sojourn there temporarily

◆§ The Struggle Against Settling in Egypt

At the time of his death, our forefather Jacob was engaged in a struggle against the Jewish people's wish to settle in

וַיֹּאמְרוּ אֶל פַּרְעֹה, לָגוּר בָּאָרֶץ בָּאנוּ, כִּי אֵין
מִרְעֶה לַצֹּאן אֲשֶׁר לַעֲבָדֶיךָ, כִּי כָבֵד הָרָעָב בְּאֶרֶץ
כְּנָעַן, וְעַתָּה יֵשְׁבוּ נָא עֲבָדֶיךָ בְּאֶרֶץ גֹּשֶׁן.[1]
בִּמְתֵי מְעָט – כְּמָה שֶׁנֶּאֱמַר, בְּשִׁבְעִים נֶפֶשׁ
יָרְדוּ אֲבֹתֶיךָ מִצְרָיְמָה, וְעַתָּה שָׂמְךָ יהוה אֱלֹהֶיךָ
כְּכוֹכְבֵי הַשָּׁמַיִם לָרֹב.[2]

Egypt and to establish it as their homeland. He was very
much afraid of being buried in Egypt, even temporarily.

Jacob, the original "pioneer" in Egypt, traveled there with the intention of
sojourning there only temporarily. He lived his last seventeen years in
Egypt, the most tranquil and peaceful years of his life. His yearning for his
beloved son Joseph, that yearning that had literally dragged Jacob to Egypt,
had been realized. However, Jacob's mind was not completely at ease. He
had been plagued all these years with the concern that perhaps his descendants would forget the land of Israel which had been designated for them and
would ultimately desire to settle permanently in Egypt. Therefore, when
Jacob was on his deathbed, he called to his son Joseph and made a request:
*"Please do not bury me in Egypt. And I will lie with my fathers and you shall
transport me out of Egypt and bury me in their grave"* (Bereishis 47:29-30).

Jacob, explains the commentators, was very specific in the wording of his
request. He wanted to be completely understood, and therefore left no room
for error. It was not sufficient for Jacob to request, "Please do not bury me in
Egypt." For then Joseph may have thought that Jacob simply wished not to be
permanently buried in the land of Egypt. But a temporary burial until the
eventual redemption from Egypt would suffice. In order that such an error
should not enter Joseph's mind, Jacob added, "And I will lie with my fathers
and you shall transport me out of Egypt" — immediately, without a moment's hesitation.

Joseph, having fully understood his father, replied, *"I will do in accordance
with your words"* (ibid. v. 30).

**Jacob feared being buried in Egypt. He knew that being buried there
could result in dangerous consequences.**

Amazingly, even Joseph's assurance did not assuage Jacob's concerns.
Even though he was well aware that Joseph would certainly do as he re-

"They (the sons of Jacob) said to Pharaoh: We have come to sojourn in the land, for there is no pasture for the flocks of your servants, because the famine is severe in the land of Canaan. And now, please let your servants dwell in the land of Goshen."[1]

With few people — as it says, "With seventy souls your fathers went down to Egypt, but now HASHEM, your God, has made you numerous as the stars of the heavens."[2]

---

(1) *Bereishis* 47:4. (2) *Devarim* 10:22.

---

quested, he wanted an additional assurance and asked Joseph to take an oath, swearing not to bury Jacob, even for a short period of time, in the land of Egypt. Only after Joseph's oath did Jacob offer thanks to Hashem that his final request would be fulfilled, as the verse states, *"And Israel prostrated himself toward the head of the bed"* (ibid. v. 31).

Jacob feared being buried in Egypt. He knew that being buried there could result in dangerous consequences. What was it that Jacob feared?

One of the answers given is as follows: *"In order that the Jewish nation should not wish to dwell there permanently. For they would say, 'If the land (of Egypt) was not holy, Jacob would not have been buried there'"* (*Sefer HaParshios*).

By requesting to be buried in the land of our forefathers, Jacob was in essence combating any whim or desire on the part of the Jewish people to live permanently in Egypt. This was a very real danger that was a tangible threat to the Jewish nation. The portion of the Torah dealing with this issue concludes with a verse that emphasizes just how real a threat this was: *"Thus Israel settled in the land of Goshen; they took holdings in it"* (Rashi explains that the "holdings" spoken of in the verse refer to "landholdings" which the Jews formed in Egypt — *Bereishis* 47:27).

Burying Jacob in Egypt, even temporarily, would be seen in the eyes of the Jewish people as giving them permission to settle there. For if the holy forefather Jacob could be buried in such a land then certainly it was sanctified enough for them to settle there.

This was the reason that Jacob requested — in a way that would be impossible to misconstrue — that his coffin should be sent immediately to the land of Israel, in order that the Jewish people should remember — in the midst of exile — where their true home really was.

וַיְהִי שָׁם לְגוֹי — מְלַמֵּד שֶׁהָיוּ יִשְׂרָאֵל מְצֻיָּנִים שָׁם.

גָּדוֹל עָצוּם — כְּמָה שֶׁנֶּאֱמַר, וּבְנֵי יִשְׂרָאֵל פָּרוּ וַיִּשְׁרְצוּ וַיִּרְבּוּ וַיַּעַצְמוּ בִּמְאֹד מְאֹד, וַתִּמָּלֵא הָאָרֶץ אֹתָם.[1]

וָרָב — כְּמָה שֶׁנֶּאֱמַר, רְבָבָה כְּצֶמַח הַשָּׂדֶה נְתַתִּיךְ, וַתִּרְבִּי וַתִּגְדְּלִי וַתָּבֹאִי בַּעֲדִי עֲדָיִים, שָׁדַיִם נָכֹנוּ וּשְׂעָרֵךְ צִמֵּחַ, וְאַתְּ עֵרֹם וְעֶרְיָה; וָאֶעֱבֹר עָלַיִךְ וָאֶרְאֵךְ מִתְבּוֹסֶסֶת בְּדָמָיִךְ, וָאֹמַר לָךְ, בְּדָמַיִךְ חֲיִי, וָאֹמַר לָךְ, בְּדָמַיִךְ חֲיִי.[2]

It is interesting to note a second reason why Jacob wished not to be buried in Egypt:

> For what reason did our forefather Jacob request not to be buried in Egypt? So that they should not turn him into a false god (Bereishis Rabbah 96).

Jacob was accorded great honor in Egypt. He was well respected even by the Egyptian population. If Jacob had been buried in Egypt, his grave would have been turned into a shrine and would have been worshiped. This would be a most tragic end for an individual whose entire life represented unwavering service of the One True God.

וָאֹמַר לָךְ, בְּדָמַיִךְ חֲיִי — And I said to you: "Through your blood you shall live!"

↝§ The Blood of Life

Behind circumcision lies the secret to the harmony which characterizes Judaism. It is the foremost sign of man's personal freedom from the chains of materialism. It has been triumphant where European culture has failed. In its merit we — and not the Arabs, who also practice circumcision — are worthy of receiving the land of Israel.

There he became a nation — This teaches us that the Jews were distinctive there.

Great, mighty — as it says, "And the Children of Israel were fruitful, increased greatly, multiplied, and became very very mighty; and the land was filled with them."[1]

Numerous — as it says, "I made you as numerous as the plants of the field; you grew and developed, and became charming, beautiful of figure, your hair grown long; but you were naked and bare. I passed over you and saw you downtrodden in your blood and I said to you: 'Through your blood you shall live!' And I said to you: 'Through your blood you shall live!' "[2]

---

(1) *Shemos* 1:7. (2) *Yechezkel* 16:7,6.

The blood referred to in the above verse is the type of blood from which life is drawn. It is blood that gives life to every individual Jew and to the Jewish nation as a whole. The blood that the verse is referring to is the blood of circumcision and the blood of the sacrificial lamb. It is this blood that gave the Jews in Egypt the ability to remove themselves from the sphere of Egyptian culture and from their idolatrous ways.

The spilling of both these bloods came about only through great peril. The blood of circumcision comes about through endangering the life of the infant, while the blood of the sacrificial lamb came about through endangering the lives of the entire Jewish nation. For it was safe to assume that the Egyptians would respond with a terrible pogrom in response to the slaughtering of their god. The ability of the Jewish people to overcome the natural fears they must have been feeling and to choose to obey the commandment of Hashem, was a clear indication that they had begun to achieve spiritual freedom from their previous status as slaves.

Let us take a few moments to discuss the commandment of circumcision. In relation to the fulfillment of this commandment, Hashem says to Abraham, *"Walk before Me and be perfect"* (Bereishis 17:1).

These words refer to the commandment of circumcision. Circumcision is the seal on the flesh of a man, a seal that teaches him about the wonderful harmony vested in the Jewish religion. It is the first sign of spiritual freedom, a freedom absolutely essential for a Jewish nation leaving Egypt.

What we must understand, however, is what exactly it is about this commandment that leads a Jew towards a state of perfection? Perhaps through understanding the meaning of the *orlah* (the word used to refer to the skin removed at the time of circumcision), we will be able to gain an insight into the profound depths of this commandment.

Let us examine the words of Rabbi Hirsch:

> Let us compare the following expressions: "blocked lips" ("aral sefasayim" — Shemos 6:12 — "aral" is the root of the word "orlah"), "their ear is blocked" ("areilah oznam" — Yirmiyah 6:10); in addition we have the laws of "orlah," the laws that pertain to a fruit in its first three years. From all of these expressions it is clear that the word "arel" (as it pertains to circumcision) connotes a predicament where one no longer has control. It connotes an individual's loss of control over a limb that by nature he has the ability to control. An individual who has "blocked ears" or "blocked lips" has attained such a state through his loss of control over both his ears and lips, and they no longer conform to his will. An individual is considered one who has a "barrier on his heart" ("aral lev"), if he is not in control of his heart's desires. The "arel" is in a total stupor, having lost complete control over himself. Who is considered the "arel of the flesh"? One who is not in control over his body and flesh. The body was not created to be a controller. The body was created to be no more than flesh and to serve the soul (Rabbi S. R. Hirsch, Commentary on the Torah).

The "arel" is in a total stupor, having lost complete control over himself. If this is the "orlah," than the purpose of circumcision is to remove it, as Rabbi Hirsch explains:

> The body of the "arel" has not been stamped with the sign of submission. When the "orlah" is removed the entire body is stamped with a sign indicating its submission to the soul — it being the soul which upholds the Divinely ethical statutes. For the covenant with Hashem is dependent first and foremost on not subordinating the soul, rather on submission of the flesh. Hashem's covenant with the Jewish people does not recognize a division of the body and soul, the soul sent soaring upwards through the upper worlds while the body is allowed to sink into the forty-nine levels of impurity. Rather, the first condition to upholding the covenant with Hashem is the ethical

submission of the body. Purity of the body is the foundation for the sanctification of a spiritual life.

Judaism is very much a battle against the division of the body, with all of its desires, and the soul, with all of its lofty virtues. As opposed to the cultures found in the Eastern part of world — cultures that are unknowledgeable of the techniques required to correctly control the desires of the body — which engage in crushing their bodies unnecessarily without properly utilizing their strengths, Western culture is altogether different. The materialistic culture of Western civilization is characterized by society's complet submission to any and every physical desire that makes itself available, without any intention to begin submitting the body to the soul and its higher purpose. Standing opposite them both is Judaism, which aims to *unite* the opposing forces of body and soul. As a means to achieving this purpose we have been granted the Divine commandments. Through utilizing our physical abilities to further a spiritual goal we grant our soul its proper position as controller of the body. Once in control, the soul is able to nurture and provide spiritual nourishment for the body, culminating in perfect balance and harmony.

It is most important to stress this concept which Judaism has bestowed on the world, namely, that there can exist a harmony between body and soul. One of the great Jewish philosophers of the previous generation wrote the following:

> Those who are wise in their own eyes have this to say: What is it that you want? Why do you confuse matters that are so simple? The main thing is for a person to be an upright individual, an individual who is benevolent, merciful, and one who favors justice and fair judgment. Then if all is in place there will be peace.
>
> It will never happen! The experiences that comprise the history of mankind are testimony to this fact! Simple logic demands that a person be upright. The heart of every normal individual is receptive to the voices of kindness and mercy. Yet despite it all, where is the peace? Why must we turn a blind eye to the reality that each and every individual recognizes to be true? There are tremendous, horrible, and savage forces that lie brewing within creation and within each individual. These forces are a part of creation, the "savage beast" inside each individual that desires existence. What becomes of these forces? They remain dozing inside the deepest depths of the individual, and the individual remains someone who is simply a being belonging to a "superior race." But woe is to the entire world if these forces are awoken from their slumber and they sever the chords of uprightness,

וַיָּרֵעוּ אתָנוּ הַמִּצְרִים, וַיְעַנּוּנוּ, וַיִּתְּנוּ עָלֵינוּ עֲבֹדָה קָשָׁה.[1]

of justice and fair judgment, of benevolence and mercy... Have we not seen the consequences of this in our days?

The Jewish culture is a "culture of the body," while the European culture is not.

What has been the greatest failure of the European culture? What is the difference between the European culture and the Jewish culture? Is there not wisdom in Edom (a title used to refer to the descendants of Esav)? Are benevolence and mercy not found among them, as are the traits of justice and fair judgment? The answer is as follows: The European culture is not a "culture of the body," while the Jewish culture is based on being a "culture of the body." The European culture views the body as no more than an object of sport, while the Jewish culture views the body as something holy. "My covenant is on your flesh"!

The European culture either renounces the uncontrollable forces vested within creation and within man, or it suffices to make of them an important "art form." There in its "art form" is revealed the tragedy that has become of man, man who has been born half angel and half man. There it is displayed to all onlookers the "very wicked individual" who, despite all his "refined culture," is oblivious to the concepts of good and evil, and the "very lustful individual," who is unable to bridle his lusts. The onlookers feel "mercy and fear" according to Aristotle, and it doesn't occur to them that this is more than simply an art form. Rather, at any given moment this art form has the potential to become a frightening reality, setting the entire world aflame. It is not within the power of art or any other visionary to bridle the "savage beast" within each individual, partly because it is an inherent part of his makeup, as it was not dealt with in a direct fashion from the time of his birth, nor from before his birth until the day of his death. The European culture is a blend of both the Greek culture and Christianity, of deifying the body and degrading the body, and from such a blend comes the concept of "sport." Dealing in such a fashion is not enough.

All true education aims to uncover and improve the mannerisms and attributes of the one being educated. However the European

The Egyptians did evil to us and afflicted us; and imposed hard labor upon us.[1]

---

(1) *Devarim* 26:6.

---

education is for the most part an intellectual education, barring the international educational system. However, history has shown that the mannerisms and attributes taught were based on a condition. That is, as long as the body continues to doze, the mannerisms and attributes stand firm. However, the mannerisms and attributes do not stand firm when the storm hits and the body is awakened from its slumber. Shortly after the storm has settled, the individual stands shocked and wonders: What have I done and how could I have done this? He asks himself these questions because he doesn't recognize his body. He never received an "education of the body" (Dr. Isaac Breuer, Nachliel, pp. 102-103).

This is the covenant represented by circumcision. It is a means with which to achieve harmony between body and soul.

However, this covenant is particularly amazing when viewed in comparison to the other commandments and covenants in the Torah. More than a thousand years ago our Sages established that this covenant would never be forgotten or nullified by the Jewish people. If the Jewish people would, God forbid, forget every other commandment in the Torah, the covenant of circumcision would still be kept. Our Sages have taught the following: "Any commandment [that the Jewish people] accepted upon themselves with joy, such as circumcision...they still perform with joy (*Shabbos* 130).

Our generation is the perfect example of our Sages' foretelling. Besides a few exceptions, the overwhelming majority of the Jewish nation still practices circumcision, even if they are negligent when it comes to the performance of the rest of Hashem's commandments.

In the merit of circumcision we are worthy of receiving the land of Israel.

From the words of the Ramban we learn that in the merit of performing the commandment of circumcision we will be worthy of returning to the land of Israel in the future:

With the permission of the nations of the world and with their assistance will they return to the land of Israel... It will be a generation which is entirely guilty and the Torah will be forgotten from Israel.

וַיָּרֵעוּ אֹתָנוּ הַמִּצְרִים — כְּמָה שֶׁנֶּאֱמַר, הָבָה נִתְחַכְּמָה לוֹ, פֶּן יִרְבֶּה, וְהָיָה כִּי תִקְרֶאנָה מִלְחָמָה, וְנוֹסַף גַּם הוּא עַל שֹׂנְאֵינוּ, וְנִלְחַם בָּנוּ, וְעָלָה מִן הָאָרֶץ.[1]

Nerve and insolence will abound... Nothing will remain in their hands except for the merit of circumcision (Ramban, Commentary to Shir HaShirim, Chapter 8).

However, the most startling piece of information of all, a portion of the Torah so strikingly applicable to our day and age that it seems as if it were pulled out of a present-day newspaper, is found in the *Zohar*:

Come and see: For four hundred years the ministering angel of Yishmael stood and beseeched the Master of the World. He said the following: "One who is circumcised has a portion in Your Name?" He (Hashem) said to him: "Yes." He (the ministering angel of Yishmael) said to Him: "But Yishmael is circumcised. Why does he not have a portion in Your Name like Isaac?" Hashem said to him: "Isaac was circumcised properly and according to that which was established and this one was not. Furthermore, these (the Jewish people) cling to me properly (circumcising their sons after) eight days, and these are distant from me for several more days (they are circumcised at the age of 13)."

He (the ministering angel of Yishmael) said to Him: "Even so, since he was circumcised, should he not receive a reward for this?"

Woe is to the time in which Yishmael was born and circumcised!

What did the Holy One, Blessed is He, do? He distanced Yishmael from deveikus (lit: "clinging") on high, and gave him a portion below, in the Holy Land, on account of the circumcision which he possesses.

And In the future the children of Yishmael will reign over the land of Israel for a long period of time when it is completely empty, like their circumcision, which is empty, lacking perfection. And they will prevent the Children of Israel from returning to their place. (This will last) until the merit of Yishmael has been exhausted (Zohar, Lech Lecha).

The Egyptians did evil to us — as it says, "Let us deal with them wisely lest they multiply and, if we happen to be at war, they may join our enemies and fight against us and then leave the country."[1]

---

(1) *Shemos* 1:10.

Amazing! The right of Yishmael (the father of the Arab nation) to the land of Israel, stems from the fact that he entered into the covenant with our forefather Abraham. This then is the background of the struggle over this small piece of Divine land. It is a struggle that we will eventually win although it will come at the cost of much suffering. Hashem should have mercy on us. We will be victorious because the blood of our circumcision is more perfect than the blood of the children of Yishmael. It is from the blood of our circumcision that we draw our life and our eternity in the land of Israel, because *"through your blood you shall live!"*

הָבָה נִתְחַכְּמָה לוֹ — Let us deal with them wisely

◄§ The Institution of "New" Policies

Pharaoh hated the Jewish people. However, in order to enslave them without revealing his hatred, he shrewdly instituted "new policies" that would eventually lead to the enslavement of the Jewish nation. This was a method used by the Nazis to carry out their plans of genocide.

Pharaoh had an intense hatred toward the Jewish people. However, the Egyptians remembered well the kindness of Joseph the Hebrew, who had saved Egypt and its entire population from starvation. Deep in their hearts lay a warm feeling of gratitude for all that he had done. But Pharaoh was well aware of the eternal "Jewish Problem" that now festered within his own country as well. He was faced with a separate nation — autonomous, and with its own identity — living among his own Egyptian nation. He lay awake at night, terrified of the political results that could arise from such a situation: *"Behold! the people, the Children of Israel are more numerous and stronger than we. Let us deal with them wisely, lest they multiply and, if we*

וַיְעַנּוּנוּ – כְּמָה שֶׁנֶּאֱמַר, וַיָּשִׂימוּ עָלָיו שָׂרֵי מִסִּים, לְמַעַן עַנֹּתוֹ בְּסִבְלֹתָם, וַיִּבֶן עָרֵי מִסְכְּנוֹת לְפַרְעֹה, אֶת פִּתֹם וְאֶת רַעַמְסֵס.[1]

---

happen to be at war, they may join our enemies and fight against us," Pharaoh told his nation (*Shemos* 1:9-10).

In the "Let us deal with them wisely" of Pharaoh, lies all of the shrewd "new" policies that Pharaoh wished to institute.

Pharaoh, a dictator from the old school, was wary of dealing in a direct manner with his enemies. Pharaoh ruled with an iron fist, permitting no one to voice feelings of dissent in relation to his manner of dictatorship. Even if he would choose to eliminate one of his many enemies from among his own people, he would do it with slyness, in his own "let us deal wisely with them" style.

Why was it necessary for Pharaoh to resort to such schemes? What exactly was he afraid of?

> *Pharaoh and his advisers did not see it wise to smite the Jewish nation with the sword. For it would surely be an act of terrible treason to smite without reason, the nation that came to the land in accordance with the command of the first king of Egypt. Even the inhabitants of the land would not allow Pharaoh to commit such an act of violence. Instead he proposed to do it (eliminate the Jewish people) in a shrewd way, so that the Jewish people would not realize that on account of hatred was this being done to them* (Ramban, Commentary to the Torah).

Interestingly enough, even in ancient Egypt, even in an absolute dictatorship, the opinion of the people was considered. Even the cruelest of all dictators took their view into account. Yet, since he in fact had absolute dominion over the entire land, instead of veering from his original course of action, he would simply attempt to change the views of the Egyptian people. He would modify their views slowly and carefully, without the people's suspecting that their opinions were in fact being changed. In addition, in order to succeed in his "brainwashing" of the Egyptian people, it would be absolutely essential that the Jews themselves would not realize that they were in fact being persecuted. For if they were to get wind of the fact that their lives were in danger, their screams of protest would certainly awaken their Egyptian neighbors, inciting them to demonstrate against

> **And afflicted us** — as it says, "And they appointed tax collectors over them in order to afflict them with their burdens. And they built store-cities for Pharaoh — Pithom and Raamses."[1]

---

(1) *Shemos* 1:11.

---

their dictator.

The Nazis understood this method quite well. This is in fact how they commenced with their plans of exterminating the Jewish people, very similar to Pharaoh in his day.

Pharaoh launched his plan: *"And they appointed tax collectors over them (the nation of Israel)"* (ibid. v. 11). Pharaoh taxed the Jewish nation. This didn't appear so terribly prejudiced to the Jews. After all, many governments lay taxes on foreign citizens who have chosen to reside in their countries. Such a step taken to discriminate against a minority is not likely to evoke the ire of a usually sympathetic majority. Ultimately, the taxing of a minority leads to greater prosperity for the majority.

Pharaoh's method of taxation was somewhat different from the method of taxing utilized in other countries, since it was a "labor tax" as opposed to a monetary tax. Foreigners were required to give of their manpower and time in order to build fortified cities for Pharaoh. Perhaps the Jews grumbled when they were informed of their new responsibilities, perhaps they felt feelings of anger as well. Yet they certainly did not feel that it was worthwhile to clash with their mighty dictator over such an issue.

Pharaoh was quite astute in instituting this "labor tax." From the moment the Jewish people were assigned this labor, the progression of discrimination and the erosion in their elevated social standing began to materialize in the eyes of the Egyptians. The Egyptian nation had begun to become acquainted with the fact that the Jews were second-class citizens, not deserving of equal treatment. The fact that the Egyptians saw the Jewish people going out to work for Pharaoh each morning belittled the Jew in the eyes of the Egyptians, and this gradually became their normal mode of perception.

The tax, however, simply concealed the much larger-scale plan of oppression, degradation, and eventual extermination of the entire Jewish race. The verse, therefore, adds to our understanding of what the aim of the tax truly was: *"In order to afflict them (the nation) with their burdens"* (ibid.).

The Jewish people were aware only of the immediate task which they had been given and therefore agreed to the tax. Their cruel taskmasters, how-

וַיִּתְּנוּ עָלֵינוּ עֲבֹדָה קָשָׁה – כְּמָה שֶׁנֶּאֱמַר,
וַיַּעֲבִדוּ מִצְרַיִם אֶת בְּנֵי יִשְׂרָאֵל בְּפָרֶךְ.[1]

---

ever, oppressed them and subjected them to crushing labor. Issuing a complaint over such harsh treatment is quite difficult, since it is hard to prove before a judicial court that the demand placed upon them exceeded the norm and that its purpose was debasement and eventual slavery.

It was not long before the atmosphere in Egypt changed entirely: *"The Egyptians enslaved the Children of Israel with crushing labor"* (ibid. v. 13).

It was no longer simply the taskmasters who oppressed the Jewish people. Rather, it was now "the Egyptians," the entire Egyptian nation that had begun to abuse them. It is worthwhile to note the change in the hearts of the Egyptians that had occurred from the time Pharaoh had instituted his plan of "Let us deal with them wisely" up until this very moment. Anti-Semitism had already taken hold of the entire nation. The atmosphere in Egypt was now ripe for the commencement of Pharaoh's murderous schemes: *"Pharaoh commanded all his people, saying, 'Every son that will be born — into the river you shall throw him!' "* (ibid. v. 22).

There was not a remnant of ethical behavior remaining in Egypt. A dictator was able to declare publicly his plan of genocide against a minority, and have his plan accepted by the people.

וַיַּעֲבִדוּ מִצְרַיִם אֶת בְּנֵי יִשְׂרָאֵל בְּפָרֶךְ — The Egyptians enslaved the Children of Israel with crushing labor

⊱ A Memory that Refines the Character

The suffering experienced in Egypt taught a newly redeemed Jewish nation a valuable lesson. It taught them how to deal with the weaker minority that would one day reside among them. The memories of the horrible oppression they endured would simply not allow them to mistreat a weaker population living in their midst. This is how the memories of Egyptian cruelty would refine the behavior of the Jewish people.

The Jewish exile in Egypt, the first exile the Jewish people would have to experience, was one that was characterized by much suffering and torment. This is depicted by the following verse: *"The Egyptians enslaved the*

They imposed hard labor upon us — as it says, "The Egyptians enslaved the Children of Israel with crushing labor."[1]

---

(1) *Shemos* 1:13.

Children of Israel with crushing labor. They embittered their lives with hard work" (*Shemos* 1:13-14).

The Midrash goes to great lengths to describe the atrocities experienced by the Jewish people in Egypt. The horrors of Egyptian slavery were such that we, along with the other commentators of the Torah, find ourselves groping for answers as to why such suffering was necessary. We find ourselves filled with harrowing questions such as: Why was such suffering required? Why were the Jewish people forced to endure such an exile? Why could we not have experienced an easier, less painful exile? After all the answers and explanations have been given, we certainly must admit, in retrospect, that the suffering we endured contributed greatly to the personality and character of a nation that was beginning to materialize. From an educational stand-point at least, we can clearly see a positive result to the many years of Egyptian torment. The years of Egyptian discrimination were responsible for teaching the Jewish nation the proper path in approaching their future relations with smaller, weaker minorities. Such groups are usually without much protection and are subject to the whims of the government in power, whose policies can often be implemented while turning a blind eye to the weaker minority. These groups can be viewed as lacking the basic human rights entitled to all individuals. This was society's predicament, not only in Egypt but even thousands of years after the Exodus as well. In Greece, while beauty was given much importance, the life of the common slave was most certainly not. Let us not even mention Rome, which despite boasting impressive laws and dictates did not necessarily boast impressive laws of equality. Once again standing opposite the accepted ways of the world is the Torah, which commands us to forever view the suffering that we endured in Egypt as a lesson to teach us the proper way to act with a slave and a foreigner. Says the Torah:

> *You shall not abuse a stranger and you shall not oppress him, for you were strangers in the land of Egypt* (ibid. 22:20).
>
> *You shall not oppress a stranger; you shall know the soul of a stranger, for you were strangers in the land of Egypt"* (ibid. 23:9).

We find a similar idea expressed in regard to the festivals:

> *You shall rejoice before Hashem, your God — you, your son, your*

וַנִּצְעַק אֶל יהוה אֱלֹהֵי אֲבֹתֵינוּ, וַיִּשְׁמַע יהוה אֶת קֹלֵנוּ, וַיַּרְא אֶת עָנְיֵנוּ, וְאֶת עֲמָלֵנוּ, וְאֶת לַחֲצֵנוּ.[1]

וַנִּצְעַק אֶל יהוה אֱלֹהֵי אֲבֹתֵינוּ — כְּמָה שֶׁנֶּאֱמַר, וַיְהִי בַיָּמִים הָרַבִּים הָהֵם, וַיָּמָת מֶלֶךְ מִצְרַיִם, וַיֵּאָנְחוּ בְנֵי יִשְׂרָאֵל מִן הָעֲבֹדָה, וַיִּזְעָקוּ, וַתַּעַל שַׁוְעָתָם אֶל הָאֱלֹהִים מִן הָעֲבֹדָה.[2]

וַיִּשְׁמַע יהוה אֶת קֹלֵנוּ — כְּמָה שֶׁנֶּאֱמַר, וַיִּשְׁמַע אֱלֹהִים אֶת נַאֲקָתָם, וַיִּזְכֹּר אֱלֹהִים אֶת בְּרִיתוֹ אֶת אַבְרָהָם, אֶת יִצְחָק, וְאֶת יַעֲקֹב.[3]

וַיַּרְא אֶת עָנְיֵנוּ — זוֹ פְּרִישׁוּת דֶּרֶךְ אֶרֶץ, כְּמָה שֶׁנֶּאֱמַר, וַיַּרְא אֱלֹהִים אֶת בְּנֵי יִשְׂרָאֵל, וַיֵּדַע אֱלֹהִים.[4]

וְאֶת עֲמָלֵנוּ — אֵלּוּ הַבָּנִים, כְּמָה שֶׁנֶּאֱמַר, כָּל הַבֵּן הַיִּלּוֹד הַיְאֹרָה תַּשְׁלִיכֻהוּ, וְכָל הַבַּת תְּחַיּוּן.[5]

---

daughter, your slave, your maidservant, the Levite who is in your cities, the convert, the orphan, and the widow who is among you . . . You shall remember that you were a slave in Egypt'' (Devarim 16:11-12).

It is also found regarding the requirement to abstain from activity on Shabbos:

In order that your slave and your maidservant may rest like you . . . And you shall remember that you were a slave in the land of Egypt (ibid. 5:14-15).

And, finally, in connection with the grants given to a freed slave:

Extend, you shall extend [a grant] to him . . . You shall remember that you were a slave in the land of Egypt, and Hashem, your God, redeemed you; therefore, I command you regarding this matter to-day (ibid. 15:14-15).

The Torah's demand for fair treatment of the weak doesn't stem from a

We cried out to HASHEM, the God of our fathers; and HASHEM heard our cry, and saw our affliction, our burden, and our oppression.[1]

We cried out to HASHEM the God of our fathers — as it says, "It happened in the course of those many days that the king of Egypt died, and the Children of Israel groaned because of the servitude and cried; their cry because of the servitude rose up to God."[2]

And HASHEM heard our cry — as it says, "God heard their groaning and God recalled His covenant with Abraham, with Isaac, and with Jacob."[3]

And saw our affliction — that is the disruption of family life, as it says, "God saw the Children of Israel, and God took note."[4]

Our burden — refers to the children, as it says, "Every son that will be born — into the river you shall throw him, but every daughter you shall let live."[5]

---

(1) *Devarim* 26:7. (2) *Shemos* 2:23. (3) 2:24. (4) 2:25. (5) 1:22.

"human rights" argument, such as "All men are created equal" and the like. Rather, because of the memories of our suffering and years of torment (*"You shall know the soul of a stranger, for you were slaves in the land of Egypt"*) we are able to feel, perhaps, sympathetic toward the weak and underprivileged.

כָּל הַבֵּן הַיִּלּוֹד הַיְאֹרָה תַּשְׁלִיכֻהוּ — **Every son that will be born — into the river you shall throw him**

◆§ *Women of Courage*

There were two courageous women who refused to heed Pharaoh's wicked decree. They did not fear the mighty dictatorship of Pharaoh, and couldn't be swayed to follow his commands. In direct opposition to Pharaoh's decree they saved Jewish babies from the clutches of death. The imminent danger that faced these midwives did not stop them. From where could they have drawn such courage?

וְאֶת לַחֲצֵנוּ – זוֹ הַדְּחַק, כְּמָה שֶׁנֶּאֱמַר, וְגַם רָאִיתִי
אֶת הַלַּחַץ אֲשֶׁר מִצְרַיִם לֹחֲצִים אֹתָם.[1]

_____

F rom within the darkness of a country that had lost all connection to a
code of ethics shone a beacon of light, generated by the bravery of two
women.

The story is as follows:

> The king of Egypt said to the Hebrew midwives, of whom the name
> of the first was Shifrah and the name of the second was Puah — and
> he said, "In your assisting the Hebrew women at childbirth and you
> see on the birthstool; if it is a son, you are to kill him" . . . But the
> midwives feared God and they did not do as the king of Egypt spoke
> to them, and they kept the boys alive (Shemos 1:15-17).

The great commentators differ on whether or not the midwives were in
fact Jewish or whether they were Egyptian. Regardless of whether they were
Jewish or not, there is little doubt that these midwives displayed extraordinary strength of character by refusing to conform to the vile atmosphere of
wickedness and cruelty that prevailed in Egypt at that time. Two women
who, for all intent and purposes, would never have been revealed as the
murderers of Jewish children — as they could have claimed that the infants
died during or shortly after childbirth — still refused to participate in such a
monstrous deed. However, not only did the midwives not murder the Jewish
children, "they kept the boys alive": "It was not enough for [the midwives]
that they did not kill [the baby boys], but they supplied water and food to
them as well" (Sotah 11b).

This wasn't, then, simply a refusal to perform a highly unethical and
immoral task, but rather an actual act of rebellion against a wicked king and
his corrupt nation. Perhaps one of the reasons that the Torah relates this
story is in order to teach future generations that under no condition should
one ever conform to the will of a tyrant. Even a lone individual must stand
up for justice in the face of corruption, for ethical behavior in the face of
wickedness, and for truth in the face of falsehood.

Perhaps the favorite excuse of a Nazi soldier, when forced to stand trial for
his crimes, was, "I was simply following orders," or maybe the alibi, "But
what could I have done? I was only one against many." The Torah does not
accept such excuses.

This is the message of the Torah's story of the courageous midwives. It is
a story that has served as a beacon of light for all those righteous individuals

Our oppression — refers to the pressure, as it says, "I have also seen how the Egyptians are oppressing them."[1]

---

(1) *Shemos* 3:9.

---

who, despite lacking moral support within a vast sea of immorality, have nonetheless stood alone and refused to compromise their principles. They have stood firm despite lack of approval, earning scorn from their respective societies, even placing their lives at risk.

From where did the midwives draw their courage, their strength to oppose an entire society?

The verse offers an answer: *"But the midwives feared God and they did not do as the king of Egypt spoke to them"* (*Shemos* 1:17).

The ability to withstand the forces of evil stems from fear of God. It is this fear that enables a person to choose to abide by his conscience and act with morality despite a society that has chosen otherwise.

⊷ The Royal Attitude

Pharaoh's attitude toward the Jewish people certainly expressed an overwhelming lack of appreciation for Joseph, the son of our forefather Jacob, and for all the kindness which he had bestowed upon the Egyptians. Many nations of the world have subsequently taken Pharaoh's lesson to heart and have abused the Jewish people, without showing even a minute amount of appreciation for all the profit and abundance which the Jewish people have brought to their lands. Yet even in the darkness of ancient Egypt there shone a light of mercy for the Jewish people.

---

*L*et us attempt to probe the mind of Pharaoh, king of Egypt. What could have been the thought process of the tyrant who, at any given moment, could decide to revoke the national rights that the Jewish people were entitled to as citizens? It is clear that Pharaoh's demographical concerns (*"Lest they multiply"* — *Shemos* 1:10) of which he feared the most disastrous repercussions (*"And if we happen to be at war, they may join our enemies and fight against us"* — ibid.) were farfetched and highly unlikely. Pharaoh was extremely concerned over even the most miniscule chance of danger.

וַיּוֹצִאֵנוּ יהוה מִמִּצְרַיִם בְּיָד חֲזָקָה, וּבִזְרֹעַ
נְטוּיָה, וּבְמֹרָא גָּדֹל, וּבְאֹתוֹת
וּבְמֹפְתִים.[1]

But how could Pharaoh have exhibited such ruthless cruelty against a nation that had never given even the slightest hint of rebellion? We are speaking of a nation that never once threw stones at the royal palace of Pharaoh, nor did they ever heave one Molotov cocktail. Why therefore did Pharaoh degrade them so, to the extent that his dictatorship had become one of absolute tyranny?

There are more issues that need to be addressed. For one, where was Pharaoh's appreciation and gratitude toward the Jewish people? After all, this is the nation that produced the great Joseph, the individual who only a generation ago had saved Egypt from utter destruction by transforming it into a literal "storage-house" of wheat, able to sustain all the nations of the world in a time of horrible famine. Joseph was responsible for bringing Egypt great prosperity and wealth. Was his visage not forever etched in the minds of the Egyptians, a face that would forever call to mind memories of his great salvation and call to heart feelings of immense gratitude?

Let us turn to a Midrash, a Midrash that mines the depths of the following verse: *"A new king arose over Egypt who did not know of Joseph"* (ibid. v. 8). Says the Midrash:

> *"A new king arose"* — but wasn't this Pharaoh? Rather (what happened was) that the Egyptians said to Pharaoh, *"Come and we shall deal (harmfully) with this nation."* He said to them: *"Fools! Until now we have been living from them (their sustenance), how can we go and deal (harmfully) with them? If not for Joseph, we would not have our lives!"* Since he did not listen to them, they dethroned him for three months, until he said to them: *"In all that you are doing, I am with you"* — and they returned him to his throne. Therefore the verse states: *"A new king arose"* (*Midrash Tanchuma, Shemos* 5).

The Midrash connects Egypt's drastic shift in their attitude toward the Jewish people to the same Pharaoh who placed Egypt's economic responsibilities in the hands of Joseph. In other words, it was this very king who understood so well the value of Joseph's contributions to Egypt — both on a national level and on an individual level — who had cast the lot of destruction on the Jewish people.

H ASHEM brought us out of Egypt with a mighty hand and with an outstretched arm, with great awe, with signs, and with wonders."[1]

_____
(1) *Devarim* 26:8.

Our Sages came to this conclusion through an in-depth analysis of the above verse. For if the verse were referring to an entirely new king, it should have stated as it has on numerous occasions, "And the king of Egypt died and another king was appointed in his place." Yet here, the verse mentions nothing of the death of a previous Pharaoh. Therefore our Sages inferred that the verse is speaking of a king who altered his views, in essence becoming a "new" king in his behavior and his approach.

In addition, the Midrash informs us that Pharaoh's feelings of gratitude toward Joseph did not simply evaporate overnight. Rather, they changed over an extended period of time, through the pressure applied by individuals in the upper echelon of Egyptian politics, as well as those who yielded political clout. While we are not certain just how long a period of time this actually was, it is clear that the topic of "Jewish extermination" was a highly debated one among the Egyptian hierarchy. Eventually the Egyptian hierarchy succeeded in having Pharaoh removed from his throne. For three months, Pharaoh refused to yield to their wicked plan, as the thoughts of Joseph's benevolence lingered on in his mind. However, in the end Pharaoh caved in to their pressure. The thought of losing his kingdom was more painful than the thought of betraying the kindness that Joseph had bestowed upon Egypt.

Yet it is in light of the above quoted Midrash that we find ourselves faced with some very serious questions: Perhaps we are able to understand Pharaoh's desire to return to the throne. Perhaps we could understand — but of course never agree — to Pharaoh's establishing decrees against the Jews, for he would have regained his throne in no other manner. But how can we ever reconcile such cruel and abominable decrees? From which dark recess in Pharaoh's mind could such waves of hatred stem? Waves of hatred that would eventually be focused on crushing the Jewish nation?

The answer is frighteningly simple — this is the nature of a human being!

From here we learn about the inner forces of a human being. In a short period of time they can descend at a frightening pace, from the correct path of life — the lofty level of a scholar — to the pit below, the lowest level possible. From "And he said to his servants: Could we find one like this — a man in whom is the spirit of God," to "He said to his people . . . Let us deal with them wisely," we behold a man who was able to erase from his heart the entire trait of gratitude he once had possessed. (For three months he refused to surrender to the desires of those who surrounded him, even though he had been dethroned.) In the end he became a different person, a new king "who did not know of Joseph." It was as if Joseph had never existed (Ohr Yahel).

Why did Pharaoh forget Joseph?

Indeed, it is most frightening how the unchecked inner forces of a human being can cause immeasurable harm to both him and his surroundings. Lack of gratitude, as repulsive as it may be, is still a trait that can be refined and improved if sufficient effort is invested. As far as our relations with the other nations of the world are concerned, Pharaoh was simply the first in a long line of political leaders to conveniently erase any memory of the good that the Jewish people had bestowed upon their nations. Spain, as well, forgot the greatness it had achieved because of the Jewish nation, and cruelly expelled them from their land. In truth, which European country has not treated the Jewish nation in the same fashion? It was specifically a German sociologist, who had no great love for the Jewish people, who compared the Jews to the sun, which brings life and warmth to all areas on which it shines. Has there been an economy that has not received a boost from the Jewish people? Has there been a country that hasn't seen the Jews make a profitable economic contribution to their land? It isn't only in the financial spectrum that the Jews have made their mark. Be it politics, philosophy, or science — the Jews have been at the forefront of it all. Yet the repayment for our contributions has inevitably been a lack of appreciation. Not only a lack of appreciation, however, but harsh decrees of every possible horror have been our reward. The root of all the ingratitude is the original "who did not know of Joseph," that base hatred nestled inside the human being, that simply hates all those who give to him.

Pharaoh's hatred drove him to attempt to destroy the Jewish nation: "Pharaoh commanded to all his people, saying, "Every son that will be born — into the river you shall throw him, but every daughter you shall let live" (Shemos 1:22).

Pharaoh's concern over the Jewish people had finally driven him completely mad. A psychologist, no doubt, would identify Pharaoh's growing wickedness as a subconscious attempt to quiet an inner voice of guilt, haunting Pharaoh for not showing gratitude for Joseph's kindness. Pharaoh's astrologers had recently informed him that they had been able to discern that Israel's savior had been born. Pharaoh, in a panic, extended his decree of annihilation even to the Egyptian sons:

> *"To all his people" — he decreed upon the [the Egyptian people] too. For on the day that Moses was born, [Pharaoh's] astrologers told him, "Today Israel's savior has been born, but we do not know if he was born of the Egyptians or of the Israelites" (Rashi, quoting the Midrash).*

The slaughtering of innocent children was a plan of action that had been accepted by the Egyptians. Such a heinous plan could have been accepted by an entire nation only if the very last spark of mercy that had remained until this point had finally been snuffed out. Apparently, Pharaoh and his cohorts had succeeded in doing just that. They succeeded in uniting Egypt under their cruel reign, allowing such a travesty to come to fruition. The years of terror perpetrated by the Nazi regime are clear proof to the fact that inhumane cruelty can also become the lot of the masses.

Yet even in the ocean of cruelty there remained a drop of mercy.

> *Pharaoh's daughter went down to bathe by the river . . . She saw the basket among the reeds and she sent her maidservant and she took it. She opened it and saw him, the boy, and behold! A youth was crying. She took pity on him and said, "This is one of the Hebrew boys" (ibid. 2:5-6).*

"She took pity on him." From this pity sprang the redemption of the Jewish people. The daughter of Pharaoh rebelled against her father and his cruel decrees. The trait of mercy flickered in her heart as she gazed upon a crying infant who had been sentenced to death. The threat of punishment did not prevent her from following her feelings of mercy, even though her handmaidens attempted to persuade her otherwise:

> *They said to her, "Our lady, the following is the norm in the world: When a flesh and blood king issues a decree, if the entire world doesn't observe it at least his children and the members of his household could be counted on to observe it; yet you are violating the decree of your father!" (Sotah 12b).*

Interesting indeed. It is the alibi of all the Nazis who have stood trial on account of their "involvement" with the extermination of European Jewry; at some point they inevitably answer that they were "just following orders."

However, the daughter of Pharaoh was from the righteous few who had the courage to stand firm in their values and principles. She did not demonstrate publicly, announcing her views to the world. Nor did she gather groups of people together or arrange a protest march. She simply *acted.*

וַיּוֹצִאֵנוּ יהוה מִמִּצְרַיִם — לֹא עַל יְדֵי מַלְאָךְ, וְלֹא עַל יְדֵי שָׂרָף, וְלֹא עַל יְדֵי שָׁלִיחַ, אֶלָּא הַקָּדוֹשׁ בָּרוּךְ הוּא בִּכְבוֹדוֹ וּבְעַצְמוֹ. שֶׁנֶּאֱמַר, וְעָבַרְתִּי בְאֶרֶץ מִצְרַיִם בַּלַּיְלָה הַזֶּה, וְהִכֵּיתִי כָל בְּכוֹר בְּאֶרֶץ מִצְרַיִם מֵאָדָם וְעַד בְּהֵמָה, וּבְכָל אֱלֹהֵי מִצְרַיִם אֶעֱשֶׂה שְׁפָטִים, אֲנִי יהוה.[1]

וְעָבַרְתִּי בְאֶרֶץ מִצְרַיִם בַּלַּיְלָה הַזֶּה — אֲנִי וְלֹא מַלְאָךְ. וְהִכֵּיתִי כָל בְּכוֹר בְּאֶרֶץ מִצְרַיִם — אֲנִי וְלֹא שָׂרָף. וּבְכָל אֱלֹהֵי מִצְרַיִם אֶעֱשֶׂה שְׁפָטִים — אֲנִי וְלֹא הַשָּׁלִיחַ. אֲנִי יהוה — אֲנִי הוּא, וְלֹא אַחֵר.

When she saw this infant in the river, even though she knew that he was one if the "Hebrew boys," she decided to raise him, amazingly, in Pharaoh's very own palace!

Yet one question continues to persist. Why did Pharaoh — so obsessed with the destruction of Israel's future savior — not immediately kill this infant who had been brought into his palace? Why did he exonerate his daughter?

Our great teachers of ethics — who had profound insight into the human character — offer the following explanation: This is a case study in the contradictions that can exist within the human personality. Pharaoh the murderer, the slaughterer of the innocent, would not hesitate to kill a Jewish child, yet if his beloved daughter brought this child home he would shower it with mercy. His feelings of sensitivity were able to be brought out by his daughter, yet were unable to be evoked by a defenseless child. Quite similar in fact to the Nazis, who on one hand were able to butcher Jews yet were able to act in a completely refined manner when enjoying a symphony, cultivating a garden, or raising their own families.

This is — for better and for worse — the human being. It allows for the opportunity of Pharaoh's merciful daughter raising the future savior of the Jewish people in front of Pharaoh himself, the merciless king "who did not know of Joseph."

HASHEM **brought us out of Egypt** — not through an angel, not through a *saraph*, not through a messenger, but the Holy One, Blessed is He, in His glory, Himself, as it says, "I will pass through the land of Egypt on that night; I will slay all the firstborn in the land of Egypt from man to beast; and upon all the gods of Egypt will I execute judgments. I am HASHEM."[1]

"I will pass through the land of Egypt on that night" — I and no angel. "I will slay all the firstborn in the land of Egypt" — I and no *saraph*. "And upon all the gods of Egypt will I execute judgments" — I and no messenger. "I, HASHEM" — it is I and no other.

_____
(1) *Shemos* 12:2.

‏אֲנִי וְלֹא מַלְאָךְ . . . אֲנִי וְלֹא הַשָּׁלִיחַ —‏
I and no angel . . . I and no messenger

✑ Why Is Moses not Mentioned in the Haggadah?

Why is the name of our great teacher Moses not mentioned in the Haggadah? How is it that Hashem's faithful messenger, the man who stood fearlessly before Pharaoh and was the medium through which the redemption was wrought, was not privileged to have been associated with the Seder night?

Moses our teacher, the great savior and redeemer of Israel, the man whose name is mentioned most frequently in the *parshiyos* (Torah portions) which deal with the redemption — does not receive mention in our Haggadah. He is completely forgotten, as if he were not even an active participant in the great victory achieved in Egypt.

It seems as if our forgetfulness does not correspond to the attitude of the nations of the world. It is absolutely amazing to observe the honor and respect they afford to a "savior" and "redeemer." Even those nations that

בְּיָד חֲזָקָה — זוֹ הַדֶּבֶר, כְּמָה שֶׁנֶּאֱמַר, הִנֵּה יַד יהוה הוֹיָה בְּמִקְנְךָ אֲשֶׁר בַּשָּׂדֶה, בַּסּוּסִים בַּחֲמֹרִים בַּגְּמַלִּים בַּבָּקָר וּבַצֹּאן, דֶּבֶר כָּבֵד מְאֹד.[1]

וּבִזְרֹעַ נְטוּיָה — זוֹ הַחֶרֶב, כְּמָה שֶׁנֶּאֱמַר, וְחַרְבּוֹ שְׁלוּפָה בְּיָדוֹ, נְטוּיָה עַל יְרוּשָׁלָיִם.[2]

_____

believe in Divine Providence spare no words of praise and adulation when referring to such individuals. One simply has to open up a history book and he will quickly become aware of this fact. Especially on the days celebrating the independence of those nations, we find the memories of these individuals recalled most frequently.

Yet by the Jewish people, this clearly seems not to be the case!

How can we explain such a thing? Could it be that the author of the Haggadah intentionally chose not to mention Moses? Could it possibly be, God forbid, that He would want to lessen the stature of Moses, the most faithful servant of Hashem, the "man of God," as stated by the verse?

Of course not. After all, the entire account of Moses' meeting with Pharaoh is clearly stated and accounted for by the Torah. The Jewish people read it over the course of the year, as well as on the festival of Pesach.

Why, then, is it specifically on this night that he is forgotten?

After pondering this most troubling question, the following answer begins to surface. The mentioning of Moses' name on the Seder night is potentially quite dangerous. It is quite possible that recalling Moses on this night would jeopardize our ability to absorb the Seder's eternal message, thereby placing ourselves, as well as the future generations of the Jewish nation, at great risk.

We have mentioned several times that the Exodus was not simply a chance event, occurring naturally on its own. It was Hashem Who redeemed the Jewish nation from Egypt. The concept of the existence of a Creator was forever established through the Exodus, as this was its main purpose. Only once such a concept was firmly established could there begin to be understood the ethical responsibilities of man and his ability to achieve true freedom through his actions.

This fundamental truth stands at risk of being left unrecognized if Moses would be mentioned in the Haggadah. For the tendency to "deify," so to speak, an outstanding personality, an individual who represents qualities of excellence, seems to be almost ingrained within human nature. The greater the individual, and the more years that have elapsed since his period of activity — the greater an icon he becomes. Has history not seen scores of

With a mighty hand — refers to the pestilence, as it says, "Behold, the hand of HASHEM shall strike your cattle which are in the field, the horses, the donkeys, the camels, the herds, and the flocks — a very servere pestilence."[1]

With an outstretched arm — refers to the sword, as it says, "His drawn sword in his hand, outstretched over Jerusalem."[2]

---

(1) *Shemos* 9:3. (2) *I Divrei HaYamim* 21:16.

---

remarkable individuals who have essentially been turned into "deities" by their respective societies?

This danger, explain the commentators, is one that is very much a threat to the Jewish people as well. Should Moses, the man of God, be portrayed as the hero of the Haggadah, or at least be given a central role in the night's events, there is a distinct possibility that a portion of the Jewish nation would come to view Moses as, God forbid, almost godly. The Exodus, the prime antithesis of idolatry, would be turned into an idolatrous affair. Therefore, Moses' name is stricken from the Haggadah and not mentioned on the Seder night, in order that we should be able to sing songs of praise only to Hashem. For it is wrong to "deify" even an individual as great as Moses, as the Psalmist writes, *" Yet, you have made him but slightly less than the angels"* (*Tehillim* 8:6). For by adulating a human being to such a degree, it is possible to create, God forbid, a new form of idolatry.

The Torah was obviously well aware of such a potential danger. It therefore depicts the death of Moses in great detail: *"He (Moses) said to them: 'I am a hundred and twenty years old today; I can no longer go out and come in, and Hashem has said to me: You shall not cross this Jordan'"* (*Devarim* 31:2).

This was a very sad moment for the Jewish nation, for they knew that all too soon, their great leader would leave them forever. Their hearts were pained at the thought of Moses being unable to witness the materialization of his dream of entering the land of Israel.

Rashi, the great Torah commentator, explains that when Moses told the Jewish people, *"I am a hundred and twenty years old today,"* he was telling them *" . . . that the knowledge handed down and the wellsprings of wisdom had become closed to him."* In other words, Moses informed them that they would no longer be able to make use of his leadership and advice, for his vast knowledge of Torah and his wisdom were taken from him and given

וּבְמוֹרָא גָדֹל — זוֹ גִּלּוּי שְׁכִינָה, כְּמָה שֶׁנֶּאֱמַר, אוֹ הֲנִסָּה אֱלֹהִים לָבוֹא לָקַחַת לוֹ גוֹי מִקֶּרֶב גּוֹי, בְּמַסֹּת, בְּאֹתֹת, וּבְמוֹפְתִים, וּבְמִלְחָמָה, וּבְיָד חֲזָקָה, וּבִזְרוֹעַ נְטוּיָה, וּבְמוֹרָאִים גְּדֹלִים, כְּכֹל אֲשֶׁר עָשָׂה לָכֶם יהוה אֱלֹהֵיכֶם בְּמִצְרַיִם לְעֵינֶיךָ.[1]

וּבְאֹתוֹת — זֶה הַמַּטֶּה, כְּמָה שֶׁנֶּאֱמַר, וְאֶת הַמַּטֶּה הַזֶּה תִּקַּח בְּיָדֶךָ, אֲשֶׁר תַּעֲשֶׂה בּוֹ אֶת הָאֹתֹת.[2]

וּבְמוֹפְתִים — זֶה הַדָּם, כְּמָה שֶׁנֶּאֱמַר, וְנָתַתִּי מוֹפְתִים בַּשָּׁמַיִם וּבָאָרֶץ —

to the future leader of the Jewish people. Another interpretation of this verse is that Moses was telling the Jewish people that he was no longer capable of waging the wars that were to be fought by a nation on the brink of conquering a new land.

Moses' words seem a bit puzzling, however. For did Moses wish to add to the sorrow presently being felt by a people about to lose their leader? What could have been the purpose of relating such depressing information?

The Ramban explains that Moses' intentions were exactly the opposite. Moses was in fact trying to console the Jewish people. He was displaying to them his undying love and concern for them even at the time of his death. He did not wish that they be saddened over his physical demise, for that was simply the result of the aging process, a process experienced by everyone. He wanted to assure them that, subsequent to his passing, they would inherit a new leader who was assured Divine assistance. As Moses related to the Jewish nation: *"Hashem, your God — He will cross before you; He will destroy these nations from before you and you shall possess them; Joshua — he shall cross over before you, as Hashem has spoken"* (ibid. v. 3).

Moses visited the encampments of each tribe, *". . . to console Israel on his (approaching) death"* (*Sforno*). The Jewish people were deeply moved by their awareness of how the great love for them burning within his heart was now complemented by his deep concern over their future.

With great awe — alludes to the revelation of the *Shechinah,* as it says, "Has God ever attempted to take unto Himself a nation from the midst of another nation, by trials, miraculous signs, and wonders, by war and with a mighty hand and out-stretched arm and by awesome revelations, as all that HASHEM your God did for you in Egypt, before your eyes?"[1]

With signs — refers to the miracles performed with the staff, as it says, "Take this staff in your hand, that you may perform the miraculous signs with it."[2]

With wonders — alludes to the blood, as it says, "And I will show wonders in the heavens and on the earth:

_____

(1) *Devarim* 4:34. (2) *Shemos* 4:17.

This was a particularly sad moment for Moses, who had just recently felt for the first time that he was no longer able to "go out and come in," as the Midrash (brought by Rashi) explains: *"To go out and come in, in words of Torah. This teaches (us) that the knowledge handed down and the wellsprings of wisdom had become closed to him."* It was then that Moses knew that his time on this earth had drawn to a close, and that he would no longer be the leader of the Jewish nation.

The certainty of Moses' eventual passing became even more concrete in the eyes of the nation when Moses received the following commandment from Hashem: *"Behold, your days are drawing near to die; summon Joshua, and both of you shall stand in the Tent of Meeting, and I shall command him"* (ibid. v. 14).

This is similar to the events that took place in *Bamidbar,* when Moses became aware of the fact that it was Joshua who was to follow him as leader of the Jewish people — similar but with one exception. The verse states:

> *Hashem said to Moses, "Take to yourself Joshua son of Nun . . . You shall stand him . . . before the entire assembly, and command him before their eyes"* (ibid. 27:18-19).

In *Bamidbar* it was Moses who was to command Joshua, yet in *Devarim,* at the very end of Moses' life, it was Hashem who commanded him. The

As each of the words דָּם, "blood," אֵשׁ, "fire," and עָשָׁן, "smoke," is said,
a bit of wine is removed from the cup, with the finger or by pouring.

דָּם וָאֵשׁ וְתִמְרוֹת עָשָׁן.[1]

דָּבָר אַחֵר — בְּיָד חֲזָקָה, שְׁתַּיִם. וּבִזְרֹעַ
נְטוּיָה, שְׁתַּיִם. וּבְמֹרָא גָדֹל, שְׁתַּיִם.
וּבְאֹתוֹת, שְׁתַּיִם. וּבְמֹפְתִים, שְׁתַּיִם.

אֵלּוּ עֶשֶׂר מַכּוֹת שֶׁהֵבִיא הַקָּדוֹשׁ בָּרוּךְ הוּא עַל
הַמִּצְרִים בְּמִצְרַיִם, וְאֵלּוּ הֵן:

---

authority of Moses, which had been granted to him by Hashem all those
years in the wilderness, had now been taken away. It had been taken away
in front of the entire nation; now Hashem would command Joshua and
Moses would simply observe.

The Midrash vividly describes these monumental last moments of Moses'
life:

> Moses arose and made his way to the opening (of the tent) of Joshua,
> while it was still early. Joshua was sitting and expounding . . . and
> Joshua's eyes were closed and he did not see Moses. The people of
> Israel went to (the tent of) Moses to learn Torah, and they asked:
> "Where is Moses our teacher?" They were told: "He arose early and
> went to the opening of Joshua's (tent)." They went and found him
> (Moses) at the opening of Joshua's tent . . . They said to him (to
> Joshua): "Joshua . . . Moses our teacher stands, while you sit?" Once
> Joshua saw him, he immediately tore his clothes, screamed, cried,
> and said: "My teacher! My teacher, my father and my master!"
>
> Said the people of Israel to Moses: "Moses, teach us Torah!" He
> said to them: "I am not permitted!" They said to him: "We will not
> relent."
>
> A heavenly voice rang out and exclaimed, "Learn from Joshua."
>
> . . . And so Joshua sat and expounded in front of Moses . . . The
> knowledge that had been handed down to Moses was taken from
> him and given over to Joshua, and he did not know that which Joshua
> was expounding.
>
> After the people of Israel arose (from before Joshua), they said to
> Moses: "We do not understand the words of Joshua." He (Moses)

As each of the words דָּם, "blood," אֵשׁ, "fire," and עָשָׁן, "smoke," is said,
a bit of wine is removed from the cup, with the finger or by pouring.

Blood, fire, and columns of smoke."[1]

Another explanation of the preceding verse: [Each phrase represents two plagues,] hence: **mighty hand** — two; **outstretched arm** — two; **great awe** — two; **signs** — two; **wonders** — two.

These are the ten plagues which the Holy One, Blessed is He, brought upon the Egyptians in Egypt, namely:

----

(1) *Yoel* 3:3.

----

said to them: "I don't know what to answer you." And Moses was downcast (Midrash Tanchuma, Va'eschanan 6).

This is only one of several gloomy portrayals the Midrash offers us in describing the final hours of Moses, our teacher. What must be understood is, why would Hashem desire, as it were, for the Jewish nation to remember Moses in his last moments on earth bereft of the mantle of leadership he had held for so long? Why is it that the entire nation had to be aware of the physical and intellectual demise of Moses?

The answer is that this was done in order to prevent the outgrowth of false legends and myths. It was entirely necessary so that future generations should not come to view Moses as godlike, something that has happened to individuals who have established their own religions, basing them on the principles they have garnished from the same Torah that Moses transmitted to the Jewish people. We are all aware of the man who was turned into "the Son of God," and his Eastern counterpart who was said to have ascended to the heavenly firmament on his donkey.

Opposite them stands Moses, the master of all prophets, the greatest of all men — but still a man. A man who, over the course of an incredible life, reached the highest levels of spirituality that a human being has ever reached, without denying the boundaries that separate man and the Eternal God. This is implicit in the final words of Moses: *He washed his two hands, placed them on his chest, and said to the people of Israel, "See the end of flesh and blood"* (ibid.).

This is the fundamental message learned on Seder night, by not mentioning the man so directly involved in the redemption, the "man of God," Moses our teacher.

As each of the plagues is mentioned, a bit of wine is removed from the cup. The same is done at each word of Rabbi Yehudah's mnemonic.

דָּם. צְפַרְדֵּעַ. כִּנִּים. עָרוֹב. דֶּבֶר. שְׁחִין. בָּרָד. אַרְבֶּה. חֹשֶׁךְ. מַכַּת בְּכוֹרוֹת.

דָּם צְפַרְדֵּעַ כִּנִּים — Blood, frogs, lice

⊷§ Plagues That Were Able to Topple an Entire Culture

There was a major philosophical debate taking place between Pharaoh and Moses. In essence, it was a war, in every sense of the word, between two diametrically opposed cultures. The terrible plagues, which mercilessly devastated Egypt, were the undeniable proof to the legitimacy of the outlook of Moses.

Why did Hashem afflict the Egyptians with ten terrible plagues that entirely decimated the land of Egypt? It certainly wasn't in order to enable the redemption to occur. For the Exodus to take place it would have been sufficient to simply strike Egypt with the final plague, the Plague of the Firstborn. As the Midrash states:

Originally, when The Holy One, Blessed is He, sought to bring the plagues upon Egypt, he wanted to bring the Plague of the Firstborn first . . . Said The Holy One, Blessed is He: "If I first bring (upon Egypt) the Plague of the Firstborn — they will send them away (in other words, the horror of the Plague of the Firstborn will force Pharaoh to succumb to releasing the Jewish people). Rather, I will bring upon them the other plagues first" (Midrash Rabbah, Shemos 18:5).

It is obvious then, that Hashem did not wish for Pharaoh to free the Jewish people immediately. The Egyptians would have to suffer before Pharaoh would relent to release the Jews from bondage.

Why did Hashem do this? Why was it necessary for the Egyptians to endure ten brutal plagues, each one further crippling the land of Egypt?

The answer provided by the verses, at first glance, appears quite odd. It is an answer that is stated not once, but ten times over the course of the Torah portions which deal with the Ten Plagues:

As each of the plagues is mentioned, a bit of wine is removed from the cup.
The same is done at each word of Rabbi Yehudah's mnemonic.

1. Blood 2. Frogs 3. Lice 4. Wild Beasts 5. Pestilence 6. Boils 7. Hail 8. Locusts 9. Darkness 10. Plague of the Firstborn.

"And Egypt shall know that I am Hashem" (*Shemos* 7:5).

"Through this shall you know that I am Hashem" (ibid. v. 17).

"So that you will know that there is none like Hashem, your God" (ibid. 8:6).

"So that you will know that I am Hashem in the midst of the land" (ibid. v. 18).

"So that you should know that there is none like Me in all the world" (ibid. 9:14).

"So that you should know that the earth is Hashem's" (ibid. v. 29).

"That you may know that I am Hashem" (ibid. 10:2).

"So that you shall know that Hashem will distinguish between Egypt and Israel" (ibid. 11:7).

"And Egypt will know that I am Hashem" (ibid. 14:4).

"And Egypt will know that I am Hashem" (ibid. v. 18).

If we are understanding these verses correctly, then they are suggesting an idea that is quite difficult to swallow. They are suggesting that Egypt was not decimated in order that the Jewish people should be redeemed. Nor was its destruction a result of the harsh cruelty the Egyptians had inflicted upon their Jewish slaves. Rather, Egypt was destroyed and much of its population annihilated in order for Hashem to teach a lesson, namely — Who He was! Egypt was stricken with ten plagues so that Pharaoh should never again say, *"Who is Hashem . . . I do not know Hashem!"* (ibid. 5:2).

Hashem is obviously not in any way stricken with a desire for honor and recognition. We must therefore attempt to comprehend why it was so important to Him to be "recognized," so to speak.

The classical as well as the modern commentators have delved into the Torah's verses and have discovered a profound struggle between two opposing cultures taking place in the portion of the Torah dealing with Moses' monumental first meeting with Pharaoh. Theirs was not simply a technical discussion revolving around the improvement of social conditions, or the freeing of the Jewish slaves. It was a deep philosophical discussion about issues which stand at the center of the universe. They discussed the standing of man and his capacity to subsist in the world as a model of ethical behavior. The redemption or non-redemption of the Jewish people hung on the outcome of this spiritual clash.

These are the words of the commentator Rabbi Don Isaac Abarbanel:

> Pharaoh disagreed with Moses over three fundamentals: Moses held that existence itself is the first and foremost reason to validate Hashem's existence. And Pharaoh denied His existence with his statement: "I do not know Hashem."
>
> The second fundamental: Moses held that the Lord oversees all of man's ways, allowing him to do that which he chooses. And Pharaoh denied this with his statement, "Who is God?"
>
> And the third fundamental: Moses held that the Lord, the Overseer, the Lord of Israel is the master of all forces (that exist in the universe), and is able to do anything (He wishes). He is able to change the nature of elements and reinvent them in any way He desires. And Pharaoh denied this with his statement, "Who is Hashem that I should heed His voice?" He intended to say as follows: What ability does He have, that I should humble myself before Him and heed His voice?"

Pharaoh was a God in his own eyes. Moses shattered Pharaoh's illusion.

In order to get a clearer impression of who it was that Moses was confronting, we will attempt to delineate the powers and strengths attributed to Pharaoh by the Egyptians. Let us try to understand Pharaoh's standing in the eyes of the Egyptian people:

> Pharaoh was not a mere mortal, but a god. This was the basic perception of the Egyptian kingship. In other words, Pharaoh had a godly essence, a godliness that was clothed in a body. It is incorrect to speak about the deification of Pharaoh. The kingship was not simply a "ceremony" of deification, rather one of "divine" service . . .
>
> The king in Mesopotamia was considered a great man, endowed with supernatural abilities, however he remained one of the nation . . . The prophets of Israel rejected these two approaches . . . They attributed all lofty and sanctified values to the Lord (Professor Henry Frankfurt, *God and Kingship*).

It becomes clear that there is wide gap separating these approaches from one another, with each one fashioning a different philosophy and society. On one hand we have Egypt, a land in which idolatry prevails. It is a society which places its faith in the unseeing and savage forces upon which the universe operates. They beget a society, which conducts itself solely according to the laws of determinism, with man possessing no free will whatsoever. It is a land bound to the predictions of astrologers and stargazers, as astrology provided much assistance to those involved in predicting the future, witchcraft, and the like. It is a land subservient to the forces of nature alone, with Pharaoh's reign among the "primary" forces of nature. In Egyptian society, man was simply a link — but by no means the most significant link — in the long chain of "cause and effect" that had served to define the Egyptian perspective on life. Terms such as "good and evil," "personal responsibility," or "responsibility to one's nation" simply had no place within such a society. For of what value is man in this Egyptian culture, a culture that celebrates little more than the natural forces to which the world seemingly "abides"?

It was in this very Egypt that Moses stood before Pharaoh in the name of Hashem and demanded the freedom of the oppressed Jewish slaves. Diametrically opposed to "Pharaoh the god" stood Moses, the representative of the One True God, the Creator of the entire universe Who created the world with a specific goal and purpose. In direct opposition to the Egyptian astrology and idol worship, Moses announced that a man was brought into this world with the explicit purpose of becoming a "free man." For in man is vested a soul, a spark from the Creator Himself, and he is therefore to be "free," much like his Creator. Man has the lofty ability to choose to lead a life bound to ethics and morality, thereby uplifting himself and freeing himself from the chains of instinct and base animalistic drives. He has the ability to choose between good and evil and then bear responsibility for his actions.

Man is not a puppet, to be controlled by an overseer pulling the strings. Nor is he a robot, programmed to do actions without giving them any thought. On these grounds, Moses demanded that the Jewish people be set free. For all men are inherently equal, and no one is given the right to impose his will upon another.

This was Moses' challenge to Egyptian culture and society. It was not simply a philosophical lecture geared around proving the existence of God, but rather a confrontation between two diametrically opposed approaches to life. How did Pharaoh respond? In a way befitting a man of his low stature. Pharaoh retorted, "Who is Hashem?" In other words, "How can you prove to me that this God of which you speak is truly the controller of the entire universe? Through what means will you be able to make me surrender to the fact that this world is not simply a collection of chance events, and that the elements of nature have not always existed?"

This was the challenge that Pharaoh — led to err by haughtiness, which clouded his judgment — placed before Moses and his God. The answer given to such a person must be perfectly clear, without any room for even

רַבִּי יְהוּדָה הָיָה נוֹתֵן בָּהֶם סִמָּנִים:
דְּצַ"ךְ • עֲדַ"שׁ • בְּאַחַ"ב.

the slightest denial, as the fate of mankind quite literally depended on it. Whether the world would continue to consist of corrupt societies such as the one in Egypt, or whether there would rise up a different society — a society that placed ethics and proper values on the top rung of their ladder of priorities — entirely depended on the answer delivered to Pharaoh.

It was therefore necessary to momentarily alter the normal course of nature, in order to demonstrate to Egypt — which would serve as an example for the rest of the world — that there exists a Supreme Being with the power to adjust the laws of nature in conformance with His will. This is a concept that would have an immeasurably profound significance for Egypt and the entire world for many generations to come.

The Ten Plagues that Moses brought upon the Egyptians certainly demonstrated, beyond a shadow of a doubt, that there exists such a Supreme Being, all-powerful without any limitation. The Plagues were responsible for far-reaching and devastating damage. From the "holy" Nile River until Pharaoh's firstborn son, nothing in Egypt remained unaffected and unharmed by the Ten Plagues. The Egyptian culture was forever toppled by the Ten Plagues, toppled, but enlightened — together with their freed Jewish slaves — as to what it means to be a human being.

דְּצַ"ךְ עֲדַ"שׁ בְּאַחַ"ב — D'TZACH, ADASH, B'ACHAV

⋅§ The Code

The Ten Plagues that descended upon Egypt were vested with much educational quality. They solved many deep-rooted dilemmas and philosophical difficulties. *D'TZACH, ADASH, B'ACHAV* is the code that enables us to begin to comprehend the many philosophical implications upon which the Ten Plagues are based.

D'TZACH, ADASH, B'ACHAV — this is the "code" that is an acronym for the following words: *Dam* (Blood), *Tzefarde'a* (Frogs), *Kinim* (Lice), *Arov* (Wild Beasts), *Dever* (Pestilence), *Shechin* (Boils), *Barad* (Hail), *Arbeh* (Locusts), *Choshech* (Darkness), *Bechoros* (Plague of the Firstborn). This is

Rabbi Yehudah abbreviated them thus:
D'tzach, Adash, B'achav.

---

a "code" that was contrived by the great *Tanna,* Rabbi Yehudah. The Ten Plagues were codified, not only as a means for remembering them, but also in order to get us to focus on their very essence, on their deeper meaning. We are meant to realize that the Ten Plagues were not simply a Divine punishment meant to afflict the cruel Egyptians. Through deepening our understanding of the Ten Plagues it will become clear that when we speak about the Plagues we are not speaking of a mere punishment alone. Rather, we are speaking of a form of harsh education. The Plagues, as previously stated, made it possible to re-educate both Egyptian and Jew alike. They taught the world about the significance of man and of his importance, which entitles him to a certain standard of treatment. Let us attempt to understand those "problems" which the Plagues were sent to correct.

We previously explained the mode of thinking that was prevalent in Egypt before the Plagues, and we described the philosophical awakening that was experienced after they occurred.

We will now take this a step further. We will focus on the contribution of the Ten Plagues toward the rectification of the disturbed psyche of the slave driver, who sees his "dominance" over another segment of society as inherent in nature.

The Egyptians erred in three ways: 1) by improperly treating foreigners in their midst; 2) by enslaving the Jewish people; and 3) by subjecting them to cruel tortures. The low level which the foreigner and stranger occupied in Egyptian society is basically the "mother" of the aforementioned errors, each one automatically resulting from this major flaw. The haughtiness of the Egyptians prevented the foreigner from having even the basic privileges entitled to any individual. It is not long before such an attitude breeds the enslavement and brutal treatment that became the lot of the Jewish people, depending only on whether or not the "master" feels he has something to gain from subjecting the minority to slavery. Words, whether in the form of lectures or simple persuasion, are unable to rectify a deep-rooted character flaw such as this one. For the belief that the "elite" has the right to subordinate the "lower class" is an idea that was adhered to and followed for many generations. Physical strength and economic superiority defined the "upper class," whose behavior was severely lacking in ethical quality. Did philosophers such as Aristotle and Appleton ever condemn such an idea? Did they not in fact justify it? When an idea or belief — as mistaken as it may be — becomes rooted in the psyche of an individual, it is extremely difficult,

The cups are refilled. The wine that was removed is not used.

רַבִּי יוֹסֵי הַגְּלִילִי אוֹמֵר: מִנַּיִן אַתָּה אוֹמֵר שֶׁלָּקוּ
הַמִּצְרִים בְּמִצְרַיִם עֶשֶׂר מַכּוֹת, וְעַל
הַיָּם לָקוּ חֲמִשִּׁים מַכּוֹת? בְּמִצְרַיִם מָה הוּא אוֹמֵר,
וַיֹּאמְרוּ הַחַרְטֻמִּם אֶל פַּרְעֹה, אֶצְבַּע אֱלֹהִים הוּא.[1]
וְעַל הַיָּם מָה הוּא אוֹמֵר, וַיַּרְא יִשְׂרָאֵל אֶת הַיָּד
הַגְּדֹלָה אֲשֶׁר עָשָׂה יהוה בְּמִצְרַיִם, וַיִּירְאוּ הָעָם
אֶת יהוה, וַיַּאֲמִינוּ בַּיהוה וּבְמֹשֶׁה עַבְדּוֹ.[2] כַּמָּה לָקוּ
בְּאֶצְבַּע? עֶשֶׂר מַכּוֹת. אֱמוֹר מֵעַתָּה, בְּמִצְרַיִם לָקוּ
עֶשֶׂר מַכּוֹת, וְעַל הַיָּם לָקוּ חֲמִשִּׁים מַכּוֹת.

barring certain exceptions, to rid oneself of it.

The Ten Plagues made for such an exception.

We have explained above how the sin of the Egyptian people was basically comprised of three different misdeeds. If one were to examine the structure and order of the Ten Plagues according to the acronym of Rabbi Yehudah, one would notice that they are in fact split up into three distinct groups, with each group corresponding to a different aspect of the Egyptian exile.

Rabbi Yehudah's acronym allows us to divide the Plagues into categories, unrelated to their chronological order. Let us take the first plague of each category (Blood, from *D'TZACH*; Wild Beasts, from *ADASH*; Hail, from *B'ACHAV*) and group them together. Let us do the same for the second plague and for the third plague in each group. Our groups would be divided as follows: **Group 1:** Blood, Wild Beasts, and Hail. **Group 2:** Frogs, Pestilence, and Locusts. **Group 3:** Lice, Boils, and Darkness. The Plague of the Firstborn stands alone as the plague which sealed the redemption for the Jewish people.

❏ The first group of plagues (Blood, Wild Beasts, and Hail) served the purpose of freeing the Egyptian from his foolish and warped method in dealing with foreigners who had come to settle in the land of Egypt. The Egyptian's attitude stemmed, for the most part, from a feeling that *he* was the master of the land in which he dwelled. The land of Egypt was entirely his and his ownership knew of no boundaries or limitations. Since it was *he* who "reigned" in his homeland, he certainly felt entitled to having an opinion of how his land should appear demographically, and to whom would be

The cups are refilled. The wine that was removed is not used.

Rabbi Yosi the Galilean said: "How does one derive that the Egyptians were struck with ten plagues in Egypt, but with fifty plagues at the sea? Concerning the plagues in Egypt the Torah states: 'The magicians said to Pharaoh: It is the finger of God.'[1] However, of those at the Sea, the Torah relates:'Israel saw the great "hand" which HASHEM laid upon the Egyptians, the people feared HASHEM and they believed in HASHEM and in His servant Moses.'[2] How many plagues did they receive with the finger? Ten! Then conclude that if they suffered ten plagues in Egypt [where they were struck with a finger], they must have been made to suffer fifty plagues at the Sea [where they were struck with a whole hand]."

---

(1) *Shemos* 8:15. (2) 14:31.

---

granted civil rights and liberties. It was this insane way of thinking that was pervasive throughout Egypt and appeared to be far from extinction. For the most part, much of the Egyptian's arrogance in relation to his land stemmed from the fact that he was convinced that his land would always receive a healthy supply of sustenance from the Nile. He believed that he had an endless supply of irrigation and could afford to take pride in a land that saw little sign of facing agricultural threat. This resulted in the Egyptian putting his faith in the Nile and not in God, believing he could suffice without Divine mercy. He would not need to beseech the Lord for rain and irrigation, for the Nile would provide him with all that he needed. His arrogance was expressed by the words of Yechezkel the prophet, who portrayed the Egyptian as proclaiming the following statement: *"My river is my own, and I have made it for myself"* (29:3).

Through afflicting them with the Plague of Blood, it was as if Hashem were informing the Egyptians, "This Nile of which you are so proud, and in whose free-flowing waters you place so much faith, can be turned into a foul, undrinkable river of blood, if I so desire. Instead of blessing and prosperity, it will be a river of contamination, until all the fish in it die. As for you, you proud Egyptian, if this situation persists, you will be forced to abandon your land. This will serve to teach you that even you are in fact a stranger in your

רַבִּי אֱלִיעֶזֶר אוֹמֵר. מִנַּיִן שֶׁכָּל מַכָּה וּמַכָּה שֶׁהֵבִיא הַקָּדוֹשׁ בָּרוּךְ הוּא עַל הַמִּצְרִים בְּמִצְרַיִם הָיְתָה שֶׁל אַרְבַּע מַכּוֹת? שֶׁנֶּאֱמַר, יְשַׁלַּח בָּם חֲרוֹן אַפּוֹ – עֶבְרָה, וָזַעַם, וְצָרָה, מִשְׁלַחַת מַלְאֲכֵי רָעִים.[1] עֶבְרָה, אַחַת. וָזַעַם, שְׁתַּיִם. וְצָרָה, שָׁלשׁ. מִשְׁלַחַת מַלְאֲכֵי רָעִים, אַרְבַּע. אֱמוֹר מֵעַתָּה, בְּמִצְרַיִם לָקוּ אַרְבָּעִים מַכּוֹת, וְעַל הַיָּם לָקוּ מָאתַיִם מַכּוֹת.

רַבִּי עֲקִיבָא אוֹמֵר. מִנַּיִן שֶׁכָּל מַכָּה וּמַכָּה שֶׁהֵבִיא הַקָּדוֹשׁ בָּרוּךְ הוּא עַל הַמִּצְרִים בְּמִצְרַיִם הָיְתָה שֶׁל חָמֵשׁ מַכּוֹת? שֶׁנֶּאֱמַר, יְשַׁלַּח בָּם חֲרוֹן אַפּוֹ, עֶבְרָה, וָזַעַם, וְצָרָה, מִשְׁלַחַת מַלְאֲכֵי רָעִים.[1] חֲרוֹן אַפּוֹ, אַחַת. עֶבְרָה, שְׁתַּיִם. וָזַעַם, שָׁלשׁ. וְצָרָה, אַרְבַּע. מִשְׁלַחַת מַלְאֲכֵי רָעִים, חָמֵשׁ. אֱמוֹר מֵעַתָּה, בְּמִצְרַיִם לָקוּ חֲמִשִׁים מַכּוֹת, וְעַל הַיָּם לָקוּ חֲמִשִּׁים וּמָאתַיִם מַכּוֹת.

---

land, and a stranger you shall remain, as long as I, the Master of the World, allow you to remain living there."

The Wild Beasts — the plague that saw all the wild animals in the jungle stampede throughout the land of Egypt — sent this message as well. There is a boundary that separates the wilderness — a haven for the wild and savage beasts of creation — from the land in which mankind dwells. This is a boundary that has existed from the day that Hashem formed the heaven and earth, and it allows man to continue to settle and expand his habitat in this world. Yet it is vital that man remember that this separation between man and beast is ultimately dependent on the desire of the One Above to sustain it. One should not feel secure in the confines of his home if he is guilty of robbing strangers and foreigners of the security that they seek to find inside their own places of dwelling.

Rabbi Eliezer said: "How does one derive that every plague that the Holy One, Blessed is He, inflicted upon the Egyptians in Egypt was equal to four plagues? As it says, 'He sent upon them His fierce anger: wrath, fury, and trouble, a band of emissaries of evil.'[1] [Since each plague in Egypt consisted of] 1) wrath, 2) fury, 3) trouble, and 4) a band of emissaries of evil, therefore conclude that in Egypt they were struck by forty plagues and at the Sea by two hundred!"

Rabbi Akiva said: "How does one derive that each plague that the Holy One, Blessed is He, inflicted upon the Egyptians in Egypt was equal to five plagues? As it says, 'He sent upon them His fierce anger: wrath, fury, trouble, and a band of emissaries of evil.'[1] [Since each plague in Egypt consisted of] 1) fierce anger, 2) wrath, 3) fury, 4) trouble, and 5) a band of emissaries of evil, therefore conclude that in Egypt they were struck by fifty plagues and at the Sea by two hundred and fifty!"

(1) *Tehillim* 78:49.

Finally — the Plague of Hail. This plague also served to shatter the feelings of security felt by the Egyptians. In front of their eyes they witnessed a total reversal of the laws of nature, a complete change in their usual day-to-day climate. Egypt had never seen such hail in its entire history. The fact that the land in which they had placed so much of their faith had become a land they could no longer recognize, frightened the Egyptians terribly. They feared the future, which up until recently had appeared to be so bright and secure. The personal pride and confidence of the Egyptians had taken a major blow that would impart to them a most valuable lesson.

The Egyptian was arriving at the realization that his faith in his land and in the Nile was being taken from him. His land, its waters turned to blood; its outer boundaries no longer secure due to the wild beasts that invaded them from all directions; and its climate, having undergone a supernatural up-heaval — all indicated that his trust in the land of Egypt was unwarranted.

כַּמָּה מַעֲלוֹת טוֹבוֹת לַמָּקוֹם עָלֵינוּ.

אִלּוּ הוֹצִיאָנוּ מִמִּצְרַיִם

וְלֹא עָשָׂה בָהֶם שְׁפָטִים   דַּיֵּנוּ.

אִלּוּ עָשָׂה בָהֶם שְׁפָטִים

וְלֹא עָשָׂה בֵאלֹהֵיהֶם   דַּיֵּנוּ.

אִלּוּ עָשָׂה בֵאלֹהֵיהֶם

וְלֹא הָרַג אֶת בְּכוֹרֵיהֶם   דַּיֵּנוּ.

אִלּוּ הָרַג אֶת בְּכוֹרֵיהֶם

וְלֹא נָתַן לָנוּ אֶת מָמוֹנָם   דַּיֵּנוּ.

❑ Egypt's sin of enslaving the Jewish people also enjoyed a most exquisite rectification.

The tiny frog was responsible for teaching the Egyptian oppressor an important chapter in the laws which delineate the proper ways to treat one's slave. It taught him the extent to which even he is a "free man" and a "superior being." In the words of Rabbi S. R. Hirsch: "The frog, the scared beast that slips away from man to his egg and reed, forsakes his place of hiding and appears with brazenness in all of man's dwelling places . . . And it taught them that even the most petty and lowliest vermin no longer feared them, in order that their crazed conceit and hubris be weakened."

The Frogs, though small in size, were able to teach Pharaoh a gigantic, valuable lesson in the evil of haughtiness and the greatness of humility.

The master, the one who delights in exalting himself above his lowly slaves, does not seem to feel any remorse when faced with the sad sight of one of his slaves crumbling beneath the sharp lashes of his whip. The feeling of "owning" a lowly slave, and the recognition of the authority placed in his hands, serve to drown him in a sea of arrogance, and direct him to engage in a life of self-indulgence. He is convinced that he has the inherent right to control others. This concept of the "elite" and the "superior man" is not a concept that has been lost to our generation either, unfortunately.

An individual who is unable to defend himself against a tiny frog is forced to think twice about his standing as a "superior man," the standing that entitles him to greater rights and liberties. And if the Plague of Frogs was not enough to jog the minds of the Egyptians, than along came the Plague of Pestilence to decimate a major part of the Egyptian economy, and much of

The Omnipresent has bestowed so many favors upon us!

Had He brought us out of Egypt,
    but not executed judgments against the Egyptians,
        it would have sufficed us.
Had He executed judgments against them,
    but not upon their gods,
        it would have sufficed us.
Had He executed judgments against their gods,
    but not slain their firstborn,
        it would have sufficed us.
Had He slain their firstborn,
    but not given us their wealth,
        it would have sufficed us.

---

the Egyptian superiority along with it. The Pestilence killed the horses, the animals that symbolized the strength of the Egyptian economy; it wiped out the sheep and cattle, Egypt's main source of capital. (Amazingly enough, the pestilence did not harm the Egyptians' Jewish slaves. Could there be any clearer indication to the Egyptians that a slave is neither "property" nor the capital of any man?) The Plague of Locusts concluded the overall decimation of the once thriving Egyptian economy, destroying the Egyptian grain that had remained after the Plague of Hail.

❑ The third sin of the Egyptians was their cruel torture of the Jewish people.

The Plague of Lice was sent in order to awaken the "mighty" Egyptians and make them aware of the pain and suffering they were so mercilessly inflicting upon a weaker people. Perhaps the physical discomfort and anguish experienced by a nation suffering with horrible lice would be sufficient to arouse feelings of sympathy from the Egyptian slave drivers, who were causing the Jewish people similar levels of anguish. The Plague of Boils served to further engrave the aforementioned message in the minds of the Egyptians. The Plague of Darkness entailed the Egyptians being smitten with a darkness that had actual density, a thickness of such proportion that they were actually unable to move for three days! The Egyptians were in fact "prisoners," lacking the ability to move, restricted in every way, shape, and form. Perhaps they would now get a most miniscule taste of their own medicine, experiencing life as "prisoners," a life of restriction — the life which they had been responsible for creating for the Jewish nation.

אִלּוּ נָתַן לָנוּ אֶת מָמוֹנָם

וְלֹא קָרַע לָנוּ אֶת הַיָּם דַּיֵּנוּ.

אִלּוּ קָרַע לָנוּ אֶת הַיָּם

וְלֹא הֶעֱבִירָנוּ בְּתוֹכוֹ בֶּחָרָבָה דַּיֵּנוּ.

אִלּוּ הֶעֱבִירָנוּ בְּתוֹכוֹ בֶּחָרָבָה

וְלֹא שִׁקַּע צָרֵינוּ בְּתוֹכוֹ דַּיֵּנוּ.

קָרַע לָנוּ אֶת הַיָּם — Split the Sea for us

⋖§ A Restrained Rejoicing

On the bank of the Red Sea stood the nation of Israel singing songs of praise and adulation to Hashem. They saw the bodies of their Egyptian enemies sinking beneath the stormy water. Their joy was a spontaneous one, yet incomplete.

O n the seventh day since the Jewish people had left Egypt, they found themselves standing on the bank of the Red Sea, having just experienced a miraculous salvation. They saw that their Egyptian oppressors had been defeated and they now watched them for the very last time, sinking to the depths of the Sea along with their chariots and horsemen.

While standing by the Sea, after days of fearing the Egyptian pursuers who were quite literally seething on account of the Plagues they had just endured, the Jewish people suddenly realized that they were finally free. They were finally free men after years of crushing slavery.

It was then that song erupted from their very essence, as the verse states: *"Then Moses and the Children of Israel chose to sing this song to Hashem"* (*Shemos* 15:1).

It was "then" that the amazement at all that had transpired was realized, and the Jews were led to joyful song. It was a glorious symphony of gratitude, a song of pure faith in the One Above, a song which contained the hopes of a brilliant future.

It was "then" — at the greatest, most exciting moment in the history of the Jewish nation — that the Jewish people learned a most valuable lesson. They learned the proper way to rejoice at the downfall of an enemy.

Had He given us their wealth,
but not split the Sea for us,
it would have sufficed us.
Had He split the Sea for us,
but not let us through it on dry land,
it would have sufficed us.
Had He let us through it on dry land,
but not drowned our oppresors in it,
it would have sufficed us.

Chazal teach us that at this very moment the ministering angels of Hashem desired to sing songs of praise to Hashem. They were well aware that this moment was unlike any other in the history of mankind. They, too, wanted to participate in the Jewish nation's rise to greatness, and celebrate the miracle of their salvation by singing songs of praise to Hashem.

However, *Chazal* continue and reveal to us that Hashem prevented them from doing so. As it is stated in the Midrash: *"My handiwork drowns in the Sea and you sing songs (of praise)?"* (*Midrash*).

The Jewish people were certainly required to sing songs of praise to Hashem. After all, they were just saved — in most miraculous fashion — from the sword of the enemy. But it was *they,* and they alone, who were the recipients of Hashem's redemption. The world at large, however, had not yet experienced redemption, nor had creation arrived at its ultimate rectification. The handiwork of Hashem was drowning in the Sea, and even though they were wicked in every way, even though they were cruel and involved in the abomination of idolatry — they were nonetheless the "handiwork" of Hashem.

Therefore, despite it all, the Divine Presence was saddened, as it were, saddened that the redemption could not have occurred without the destruction of the enemy.

We learn from this episode that true happiness will prevail in the world only at a time when there will be complete redemption. It will be a redemption without the slightest trace of death or injury, when even those who vehemently oppose it will walk away unharmed. Only the collective happiness of all the world's inhabitants can truly be viewed as a complete redemption.

It has therefore been permanently slated in Jewish law that on the seventh day of Pesach — the day on which the Splitting of the Red Sea occurred — a complete *Hallel* is not recited. On this day the Jew skips several chapters

אִלּוּ שִׁקַּע צָרֵינוּ בְּתוֹכוֹ וְלֹא סִפֵּק צָרְכֵּנוּ
בַּמִּדְבָּר אַרְבָּעִים שָׁנָה דַּיֵּנוּ.
אִלּוּ סִפֵּק צָרְכֵּנוּ בַּמִּדְבָּר אַרְבָּעִים שָׁנָה
וְלֹא הֶאֱכִילָנוּ אֶת הַמָּן דַּיֵּנוּ.
אִלּוּ הֶאֱכִילָנוּ אֶת הַמָּן
וְלֹא נָתַן לָנוּ אֶת הַשַּׁבָּת דַּיֵּנוּ.

---

in *Hallel* in order to remember and remind others that we are partners in the sadness experienced by the Divine Presence on this day. For while there is certainly tremendous joy to be felt, it is a joy that is incomplete. For the true redemption, which will be consummated in true happiness, can be experienced only when no individual has to be sacrificed in order for it to occur.

הֶאֱכִילָנוּ אֶת הַמָּן ... דַּיֵּנוּ — Had He fed us the manna ... it would have sufficed us

◄§ The Sustenance That Defies Every Theory

For what purpose did Hashem choose to sustain the Jewish people in the desert by supplying them with the supernatural manna? Why was it specifically this form of daily nourishment that Divine Providence sent the way of the Jewish nation and why did Hashem wait for their complaints before He supplied them with it?

L et us take a quick glance at the events which took place shortly after the Jewish people's redemption from Egypt.

Exactly a month has passed since the historical Exodus from Egypt. Three weeks have passed since the Jews became completely aware of the power of the Almighty God, as He split the Sea for them, miraculously delivering them from the hands of the pursuing enemy. They knew that Hashem was all-powerful, not simply in a theoretical, philosophical sense, but rather they knew it as fact and were able to feel its truth surging through their bones. We

Had He drowned our oppressors in it,
>   but not provided for our needs in the wilderness
>   for forty years,   it would have sufficed us.
Had He provided for our needs in the wilderness
>   for forty years,
>   but not fed us the manna,
>
>   it would have sufficed us.
Had He fed us the manna,
>   but not given us the Sabbath,
>
>   it would have sufficed us.

---

must therefore try to understand: How was it possible for a nation that had so recently experienced such miracles to begin complaining the moment the first pang of hunger struck?

> *The entire assembly of the Children of Israel complained against Moses and Aaron in the wilderness. The Children of Israel said to them, "If only we would have died by the hand of Hashem in the land of Egypt, as we sat by the pot of meat, when we ate bread to satiety, for you took us out to this wilderness to kill this entire congregation by famine" (Shemos 16:2-3).*

Such words! Had the Jewish people forgotten all that had transpired not more than a month ago? Had the memories of Hashem's salvation been cast away, now beyond recollection? If the Jewish people were undergoing a period of hardship, why did they not simply turn their hearts in prayer to the One Above, the One True God, Who had been responsible for their sustenance and survival up until now? Why did they immediately make such extreme statements and draw such drastic conclusions ("In Egypt we enjoyed unlimited delicacies, and now we have only death to look forward to")? Furthermore, why did Hashem not provide His nation with the bread and water they and their families desperately needed, *before* they began complaining?

Indeed, it was in those hours of starvation that a most frightening concern began creeping into the minds of the Jewish people. They sensed for the first time since leaving Egypt that perhaps they had not achieved a complete redemption. While they had been freed from the chains of cruel oppression, they were still subject to the laws that dictate man's existence in this world. They feared the future, unsure of what lay in store for them. Would they be able to survive in the dangerous wilderness? Would they be able to provide

אִלּוּ נָתַן לָנוּ אֶת הַשַּׁבָּת

וְלֹא קֵרְבָנוּ לִפְנֵי הַר סִינַי דַּיֵּנוּ.

אִלּוּ קֵרְבָנוּ לִפְנֵי הַר סִינַי

וְלֹא נָתַן לָנוּ אֶת הַתּוֹרָה דַּיֵּנוּ.

אִלּוּ נָתַן לָנוּ אֶת הַתּוֹרָה

וְלֹא הִכְנִיסָנוּ לְאֶרֶץ יִשְׂרָאֵל דַּיֵּנוּ.

אִלּוּ הִכְנִיסָנוּ לְאֶרֶץ יִשְׂרָאֵל

וְלֹא בָנָה לָנוּ אֶת בֵּית הַבְּחִירָה דַּיֵּנוּ.

---

for their families? They were now acutely aware of their hunger, growing stronger and more bothersome by the moment. The fear of starvation was now first and foremost in their minds, conquering all the memories of Hashem's benevolence. For they were still "enslaved," so to speak, to the demands of the physical world, not yet having been granted the true, eternal freedom that will one day be the lot of the virtuous. It was therefore deemed necessary by them to find a means with which to sustain themselves and their families in the wilderness.

This is, indeed, the message that Hashem wished to impart to the Jewish nation, a nation on the verge of redefining world history. He therefore did not immediately provide them with the manna, despite the fact that it would have made the transition from Egypt to the wilderness substantially easier. Rather, only after they felt as if they were on the brink of starvation, only after they had gotten to the point where they would complain bitterly to Moses, did Hashem provide them with the "heavenly bread." But they first had to arrive at the realization that they were still subordinate to the realities of day-to-day life (such as concern over one's sustenance, a concern that has the ability to clutter one's spiritual perspective and hinder an individual's efforts to inculcate within himself proper values and priorities).

Let us examine the verses that deal with Hashem's bestowal of the manna to the Jewish people:

> Hashem said to Moses, "Behold! — I shall rain down for you food from heaven; let the people go out and pick each day's portion on its day, so that I may test him, whether he will follow My Torah or not. And it shall be that on the sixth day when they prepare what they will bring, and it will be double what they pick every day" (ibid. vs. 4-5).

Had He given us the Sabbath,
  but not brought us before Mount Sinai,
                it would have sufficed us.
Had He brought us before Mount Sinai,
  but not given us the Torah,
                it would have sufficed us.
Had He given us the Torah,
  but not brought us into the land of Israel,
                it would have sufficed us.
Had he brought us into the land of Israel,
  but not built the Temple for us,
                it would have sufficed us.

In these verses lie the keys to understanding the heavenly sustenance provided to the Jewish people. This was a form of sustenance that ran contrary to every accepted form of philosophy that has been recognized by the world at one time or another, be it communism or capitalism. It was an unprecedented form of sustenance, able to mold the character of the Jewish nation, instilling within the people proper values while imbedding within them the foundations of faith that would be the hallmark of the Jewish people. These would be foundations that would carry on long after the Jewish people would leave the confines of the wilderness and would be forced to engage in what seemed to be a more "worldly" existence, having to exert considerable effort in securing a livelihood.

Why was it so important that the Children of Israel learn these principles and absorb the lofty message of the manna?

> *Danger of starvation, whether real or imagined, undermines every principle and nullifies each and every good decision. And as long as an individual is not redeemed — not necessarily from his worry over his sustenance — but from the weight of his worry over his sustenance, there is no room for Hashem's Torah to materialize (in his life) . . . As long as an individual is harnessed to the yolk of earning a livelihood alone — he alone with his own limited abilities — there is no end to such worry. This worry is liable to turn his world into a wilderness . . . Even within an inhabited world, (having) much property — yet many rivals — a person is likely to think that his concern must encompass not only tomorrow, but also his entire future as well as the future of his children, grandchildren, and great-grandchildren.*

עַל אַחַת כַּמָּה, וְכַמָּה טוֹבָה כְפוּלָה וּמְכֻפֶּלֶת לַמָּקוֹם עָלֵינוּ. שֶׁהוֹצִיאָנוּ מִמִּצְרַיִם, וְעָשָׂה בָהֶם שְׁפָטִים, וְעָשָׂה בֵאלֹהֵיהֶם, וְהָרַג אֶת בְּכוֹרֵיהֶם, וְנָתַן לָנוּ אֶת מָמוֹנָם, וְקָרַע לָנוּ אֶת הַיָּם, וְהֶעֱבִירָנוּ בְתוֹכוֹ בֶּחָרָבָה, וְשִׁקַּע צָרֵינוּ בְּתוֹכוֹ, וְסִפֵּק צָרְכֵּנוּ בַּמִּדְבָּר אַרְבָּעִים שָׁנָה, וְהֶאֱכִילָנוּ אֶת הַמָּן, וְנָתַן לָנוּ אֶת הַשַּׁבָּת, וְקֵרְבָנוּ לִפְנֵי הַר סִינַי, וְנָתַן לָנוּ אֶת הַתּוֹרָה, וְהִכְנִיסָנוּ לְאֶרֶץ יִשְׂרָאֵל, וּבָנָה לָנוּ אֶת בֵּית הַבְּחִירָה, לְכַפֵּר עַל כָּל עֲוֹנוֹתֵינוּ.

It is this thought that drives him to pile achievement on top of achievement, without rest and without introspection, until he is left with no space in his heart for any other purpose (Rabbi S. R. Hirsch, Commentary on the Torah).

In this concise statement lies the principal battle that mankind has faced since Hashem uttered the words, *"By the sweat of your brow shall you eat bread"* (*Genesis* 3:19). It is this age-old concern of earning a livelihood that has been greatly responsible for shaping the world in which we live. It has corrupted man's character, created an upper class and a lower class, and established the goal of high profit as man's number one priority, both on a personal and a national level. The worry and concern over lack of sustenance has enslaved man's spirit and "entitled" him to step on anything and anyone who gets in the way of his making a living. It makes little difference whether it be a neighbor, a "rival" at work, an opposing party, or another country. None will come in the way of his sustenance. The main thoughts and deeds of a society that makes such ideals its first order revolve entirely around the struggle to earn a living, leaving very little room for any spiritual aspirations whatsoever. It will even begin to oppose spiritual ideals, combating their very essence.

The sustenance provided by the manna did not yield such a materialistic ideology. Its very purpose was to free the Jewish people from this natural inclination that resides within the heart of every human being. Their complaints revealed to them that they, too, were vulnerable to this fear and concern over the unknown future. They, too, were liable to succumb to the

Thus, how much more so should we be grateful to the Omnipresent for all the numerous favors He showered upon us: He brought us out of Egypt; executed judgments upon them and against their gods; slew their firstborn; gave us their wealth; split the Sea for us; led us through it on dry land; drowned our oppressors in it; provided for our needs in the wilderness for forty years; fed us the manna; gave us the Sabbath; brought us before Mount Sinai; gave us the Torah; brought us to the land of Israel; and built for us the Temple to atone for all our sins.

---

degeneration of ethical behavior and proper judgment due to the stresses that earning a living might appear to present. Therefore the manna was presented to the Jewish people as a test, a "spiritual practice session," so to speak, that would prepare them for the future and strengthen them, in order to prevent any such spiritual decline in the future.

How was the manna able to accomplish this?

The first stage was as follows, explain Rabbi Hirsch:

> The profound recognition within the heart, that also the worry over one's livelihood — the foremost of all of man's worries — is not dependent first and foremost upon man alone. A man is permitted and required to do that which Hashem has required of him, yet the success of (his actions) is in the hands of Hashem . . . .
>
> Therefore: " . . . Let the people go out and pick each day's matter on its day, so that I may test him, whether he will follow My Torah or not" (Shemos 16:4).
>
> "Follow My Torah" is predicated upon My finding individuals who are satisfied with their sustenance, and the sustenance of their wives and children "with each day's portion on its day." Those who make what they require each day, eating each day with gladness and goodness of heart, they cast upon Hashem their worries over tomorrow, (knowing that He) Who created today and its sustenance will create tomorrow and its sustenance. Only the one who trusts in Hashem without any reservation is assured that he will not violate His Torah due to worries over his livelihood, whether they be real or imagined. One who has not learned to cast (his worry over) tomorrow's sustenance upon Hashem will ultimately stray from Hashem and from His

רַבָּן גַּמְלִיאֵל הָיָה אוֹמֵר. כָּל שֶׁלֹּא אָמַר שְׁלֹשָׁה דְבָרִים אֵלּוּ בַּפֶּסַח, לֹא יָצָא יְדֵי חוֹבָתוֹ, וְאֵלּוּ הֵן,

פֶּסַח. מַצָּה. וּמָרוֹר.

פֶּסַח שֶׁהָיוּ אֲבוֹתֵינוּ אוֹכְלִים בִּזְמַן שֶׁבֵּית הַמִּקְדָּשׁ הָיָה קַיָּם, עַל שׁוּם מָה? עַל שׁוּם שֶׁפָּסַח הַקָּדוֹשׁ בָּרוּךְ הוּא עַל בָּתֵּי אֲבוֹתֵינוּ בְּמִצְרָיִם. שֶׁנֶּאֱמַר, וַאֲמַרְתֶּם, זֶבַח פֶּסַח הוּא לַיהוה,

---

Torah, due to many years of worries. Here it is fitting to mention the great saying of Rabbi Eliezer of Modi'in: "(He) Who has created the day has created its sustenance . . . Anyone who has what to eat today, but says: 'What will I have to eat tomorrow?' is lacking in faith."

Over the course of forty years of wandering in the wilderness, the Jewish nation became conditioned not to worry about what tomorrow may bring. Hashem provided their sustenance each and every day. However, it was the Jewish people themselves who were required to go out each and every day and collect the manna that had fallen from the heavens. If someone would choose not to go out and collect his portion of manna, he and his family would go hungry that day. This teaches us that we are required to invest a certain amount of effort in our attempts to earn a livelihood. Heaven forbid that our faith in Hashem should lead us to become parasitic, or the opposite, that our lack of faith should lead us to endlessly pursue financial gain. For as the Torah relates, one who gathered more manna than was to be his portion was greeted with a most surprising realization upon returning home: " . . . *He who took much and he who took little. They measured in an omer and whoever took more had nothing extra and whoever took less was not lacking; everyone according to what he eats . . . Moses said to them, 'No man may leave over from it until morning.' But they did not obey Moses and people left over from it until morning and it became infested with worms and it stank"* (Shemos 16:17-20).

The nation's experience of collecting the manna for six days and the approach of Judaism toward earning one's sustenance as established by these experiences, bequeathed to them and to all future genera-tions a most important inheritance, as regards this approach. Most

Rabban Gamliel used to say: Whoever has not
explained the following three things on Passover
has not fulfilled his duty, namely:

Pesach — the Passover offering; Matzah —
the Unleavened Bread; Maror — the Bitter Herbs.

Pesach — Why did our fathers eat a Pesach
offering during the period when the Temple still
stood? Because the Holy One, Blessed is He, passed
over the houses of our fathers in Egypt, as it says,
"You shall say: It is a Pesach offering for HASHEM,

---

*repugnant is the trait of laziness, as is chasing profit, stinginess, and
pettiness. Praiseworthy are the traits of diligence, and contentment
with little, happiness with one's lot, and deriving pleasure from that
which he has. (He) places his trust in Hashem and casts his burden
upon Him (Rabbi S.R. Hirsch, ibid.).*

This is the lesson that the manna has taught us. It is the only guide we shall
ever need in order to show us that the road to sustenance in this world can
be one of happiness and faith in Hashem.

עַל שׁוּם מָה . . . פֶּסַח שֶׁהָיוּ אֲבוֹתֵינוּ אוֹכְלִים — Pesach —
Why did our fathers eat a Pesach offering?

⇜ Slaughtering False Gods

On the night that the Jewish people were to leave Egypt,
they were commanded to slaughter a lamb and eat it. The
redemption of the Jewish people depended greatly on the
performance of this action. It was this action that enabled
them to truly absorb the eternal message of the Exodus.

The "Pesach" — this is the title given to the sacrificial offering, offered
by the Jewish nation on the night they left Egypt. It is called "The
Pesach" or "Passover," in memory of Hashem's decision to pass over the
Jewish homes, leaving them unmarred by the Plague of the Firstborn that
was soon to be unleashed upon the Egyptians.

אֲשֶׁר פָּסַח עַל בָּתֵּי בְנֵי יִשְׂרָאֵל בְּמִצְרַיִם בְּנָגְפּוֹ אֶת
מִצְרַיִם, וְאֶת בָּתֵּינוּ הִצִּיל, וַיִּקֹּד הָעָם וַיִּשְׁתַּחֲווּ.

The broken matzah is lifted and displayed
while the following paragraph is recited.

מַצָּה זוּ שֶׁאָנוּ אוֹכְלִים, עַל שׁוּם מָה? עַל שׁוּם
שֶׁלֹּא הִסְפִּיק בְּצֵקָם שֶׁל אֲבוֹתֵינוּ
לְהַחֲמִיץ, עַד שֶׁנִּגְלָה עֲלֵיהֶם מֶלֶךְ מַלְכֵי הַמְּלָכִים
הַקָּדוֹשׁ בָּרוּךְ הוּא וּגְאָלָם. שֶׁנֶּאֱמַר, וַיֹּאפוּ אֶת

What was the purpose of this commandment? Why was it so vital that the Jews sacrifice a lamb, offering it to Hashem?

In order to answer this question, it is of utmost importance that we be aware of the following: Before the Jewish people would be able to be redeemed by Hashem, they were first required to enact their own redemption. Before Hashem would do His part and free the Jews from their bondage, the Jews were first obligated to free themselves. The slaughtering of the Pesach Lamb was the first step toward this freedom.

As the Plague of Darkness — the ninth in the series of tragedies that had befallen Egypt — came to a close (*Shemos* 10:21-23), the Jewish people received a Divine commandment: *"On the tenth of this month they shall take for themselves — each man — a lamb/kid for each household . . . It will be unto you for safekeeping until the fourteenth day of this month; the entire congregation of the assembly of Israel shall slaughter it . . . They shall take some of its blood and place it on the two doorposts and on the lintel of the houses in which they will eat it"* (ibid. 12:3-7).

This commandment — a commandment that the Jewish nation would continue to fervently adhere to for ensuing generations — up until the destruction of the Temple — was bequeathed to them on foreign soil, in the land of Egypt, specifically before the redemption was to take place. This itself points to a strong bond between this commandment and the eventual Exodus.

Upon investigation, it becomes quite clear that this commandment was a perfect fit for the Jewish people, considering their spiritual predicament at that time. The Midrash states:

> You find that the Jewish people, when they were in Egypt, worshiped false gods and refused to part with them. The Holy One, Blessed is He, said to Moses, "As long as the Jewish people worship the gods of Egypt, they will not be redeemed. Go and tell them that they

Who passed over the houses of the Children of Israel in Egypt when He struck the Egyptians, and spared our houses. And [upon hearing this] the people bowed down and prostrated themselves."[1]

The broken matzah is lifted and displayed while the following paragraph is recited.

Matzah — Why do we eat this unleavened bread? Because the dough of our fathers did not have time to become leavened before the King of kings, the Holy One, Blessed is He, revealed Himself to them and redeemed them, as it says, "They baked

_____
(1) *Shemos* 12:27.

---

should leave their ways of wickedness and renounce idolatry." As the verse states, "Draw forth and take for yourselves . . . " — In other words, "Draw your hands from the worship of false gods and take for yourselves sheep. Slaughter the gods of the Egyptians and perform the Pesach offering" (Shemos Rabbah 16:2).

The Torah commentators, both classic as well as contemporary, ask a rather striking question, which results in a most amazing insight. They ask the following:

Was not the entire purpose of the Ten Plagues to shatter the great illusion of mankind, namely that there exists more than one Supreme Being to whom control of the universe belongs? Yet we find that the Jewish people themselves were in fact steeped in idolatrous practices up until the moment of redemption! The years of exile and hardship had taken their toll on the Children of Israel. The influence of the idolatrous and immoral Egyptian environment had worked its way into the Jewish community as well. As long as the imprint from that influence remained, the Jewish People would not be worthy of redemption. For it was of vital importance that they arrive at the realization that a physical redemption alone, with the soul left writhing in captivity, is of no value. **There is simply no purpose to freedom if it is only materialistic and mundane, lacking any spiritual advancement.** Yet while the physical aspect of redemption is completely in the all-powerful hands of Hashem, redemption of one's soul has been placed squarely on the shoulders of man himself. It is his responsibility to free himself from spiritual bondage, and only then can a physical redemption be forthcoming.

Hashem provided the Jew in Egypt with more than adequate means with which to escape from spiritual slavery. He guided him, showing him the road

הַבָּצֵק אֲשֶׁר הוֹצִיאוּ מִמִּצְרַיִם עֻגֹת מַצּוֹת כִּי לֹא
חָמֵץ, כִּי גֹרְשׁוּ מִמִּצְרַיִם, וְלֹא יָכְלוּ לְהִתְמַהְמֵהַּ,
וְגַם צֵדָה לֹא עָשׂוּ לָהֶם.[1]

The *maror* is lifted and displayed while the following paragraph is recited.

מָרוֹר זֶה שֶׁאָנוּ אוֹכְלִים, עַל שׁוּם מָה? עַל שׁוּם
שֶׁמֵּרְרוּ הַמִּצְרִים אֶת חַיֵּי אֲבוֹתֵינוּ
בְּמִצְרָיִם. שֶׁנֶּאֱמַר, וַיְמָרְרוּ אֶת חַיֵּיהֶם, בַּעֲבֹדָה
קָשָׁה, בְּחֹמֶר וּבִלְבֵנִים, וּבְכָל עֲבֹדָה בַּשָּׂדֶה, אֵת
כָּל עֲבֹדָתָם אֲשֶׁר עָבְדוּ בָהֶם בְּפָרֶךְ.[2]

---

that would lead to such freedom. It was through slaughtering the lamb that this freedom would be achieved.

Let us understand how.

What, in fact, was the great significance of the lamb? Why was it so important that the Jewish people take specifically *that* animal, and slaughter it? The answer is that the lamb was one of the gods of the Egyptian people. "The Egyptians worshiped the constellation of *T'leh* ("Lamb")," says the Rambam in his classic work, *Moreh Nevuchim*. It was the lamb to which the Egyptians afforded honor, the lamb in which the Egyptians placed their faith. It was given the status of a god and was certainly never harmed or mistreated in any way.

Now the Jewish people were to take that Egyptian god and slaughter it. They were to slaughter it on a most auspicious day as well — the fourteenth of Nissan:

> On the tenth of this month (Nissan) its reign begins — yet it is still young, and (its power) only a third developed. It (was) slaughtered and subsequently eaten on the fourteenth day, when its strength is fully realized through the great light that stands together with it in its vicinity (Akeidas Isaac).

In other words, the Egyptians believed that the sheep, due to its corresponding constellation, reached its maximum strength in the month of Nissan.

The strength of this constellation began to flourish and reveal itself on the tenth of the month, and from the twentieth onwards it began to wane. Therefore, according to Egyptian belief, the constellation of *T'leh* reached its peak on the fifteenth day of Nissan. It was on this day that the control it

the dough which they had brought out of Egypt into unleavened bread, for it had not fermented, because they were driven out of Egypt and could not delay; nor had they prepared any provisions for themselves."[1]

The *maror* is lifted and displayed while the following paragraph is recited.

Maror — Why do we eat this bitter herb? Because the Egyptians embittered the lives of our fathers in Egypt, as it says, "They embittered their lives with hard labor, with mortar and bricks, and with all manner of labor in the field. All of the work which they made them do was with hard labor."[2]

---

(1) *Shemos* 12:39. (2) 1:14.

---

influenced on the universe and on mankind as a whole was fully realized.

It was therefore specifically on this day that Hashem commanded the Jewish people to slaughter the lamb. This would be clear, undeniable proof of the lamb's absolute lack of power and inability to assert any form of control on the forces of this world. Slaughtering the lamb, eating it, and subsequently smearing its blood on the lintel of the doorposts, was an open defiance against those who believed in its Divine abilities. For the Jews did not attempt to conceal their "sacrilege" by stealing a lamb in the darkness of night, and then slaughtering it in utmost secrecy. Quite the contrary, they carried out that which they had been commanded to do, in public view and with great self-sacrifice.

It goes without saying that to perform such a feat, one must possess incredible mental strength and a tremendous degree of courage. We find, in fact, that the Jews were required to rid themselves of various fears in order that they be assured success in carrying out Hashem's commandment:

> The reason that we were commanded to slaughter a lamb on Pesach and sprinkle its blood on the outside of the doorways when we were in Egypt, was in order to cleanse ourselves of the prevailing ideologies and to publicly oppose them. We were to have faith that the action, which we reasoned would bring about our deaths, would actually be the cause of our salvation (Rambam, Moreh Nevuchim 3:46).

Fear of death was one fear that Hashem wished the Jewish people to be rid of. But there was yet another fear that Hashem wished to be regarded:

בְּכָל דּוֹר וָדוֹר חַיָּב אָדָם לִרְאוֹת אֶת עַצְמוֹ
כְּאִלּוּ הוּא יָצָא מִמִּצְרָיִם. שֶׁנֶּאֱמַר, וְהִגַּדְתָּ לְבִנְךָ בַּיּוֹם הַהוּא לֵאמֹר, בַּעֲבוּר
זֶה עָשָׂה יהוה לִי, בְּצֵאתִי מִמִּצְרָיִם.¹ לֹא אֶת
אֲבוֹתֵינוּ בִּלְבָד גָּאַל הַקָּדוֹשׁ בָּרוּךְ הוּא, אֶלָּא אַף
אֹתָנוּ גָּאַל עִמָּהֶם. שֶׁנֶּאֱמַר, וְאוֹתָנוּ הוֹצִיא מִשָּׁם,
לְמַעַן הָבִיא אֹתָנוּ לָתֶת לָנוּ אֶת הָאָרֶץ אֲשֶׁר
נִשְׁבַּע לַאֲבוֹתֵינוּ.²

Therefore Hashem commanded the Jewish people to perform three
acts upon publicly slaughtering their (the Egyptians') god. They were
not to fear the enormity of danger involved, that the Egyptians would
become enraged and attempt to annihilate them. Rather they were
to do as Moses instructed (Shemos 8:22). They were not to be dis-
suaded from fulfilling this commandment, from venturing out into
the streets and marketplaces (and purchasing sheep) to bring back to
their homes. Despite the attention this would draw to themselves,
they were not to fear the Egyptians. Furthermore, they were to
slaughter the Pesach Lamb in groups and with much fanfare, families
upon families, for all to see, and they were not to fear their enemies
(HaKesav V'HaKabbalah).

If we would be able to understand just how greatly the Jewish People had
been influenced by the ideologies and culture of Egypt and the extent to
which they themselves actually believed in the "Divine powers" of the lamb,
we would begin to comprehend the spiritual upheaval that the slaughtering
of the lamb provoked within their hearts and minds. In one fell swoop it was
able to uproot and entirely eradicate any attribution of power to anything
other than the One True God. It also put an end to the fear which the Jew
had felt for the Egyptian oppressor, a fear that had been so prevalent over the
course of the Jewish people's stay in Egypt.

Perhaps the most important outcome of all, more important than everything
that had been achieved up until that point, was the Jewish people's newfound
understanding of what it meant to be truly free. They now understood that
freedom meant so much more than mere physical freedom, freedom to establish a sovereign state, design a flag, and build an army. They learned that it was
possible to be free, even when one's hands are bound and he is physically

In every generation one is obligated to see himself as though he personally had gone out of Egypt, as it says, "And you shall tell your son on that day, saying, 'It is because of this that HASHEM did so for me when I went out of Egypt.'"[1] Not only did the Holy One, Blessed is He, redeem our ancestors, but He redeemed us, too, with them, as it is said, "He took us out of there to bring us, to give us the land which He had sworn to our fathers."[2]

(1) *Shemos* 13:8. (2) *Devarim* 6:23.

---

restricted. **For an individual's freedom is measured by his freedom of the spirit, and this is a freedom that only he himself is able to take away.**

It was only when the Jewish people tasted the sweet taste of spiritual freedom that they became worthy of receiving physical freedom as well. It was only then that the Egyptians were stricken with the Plague of the First-born, opening the gates of total freedom and redemption.

חַיָּב אָדָם לִרְאוֹת אֶת עַצְמוֹ כְּאִלּוּ הוּא יָצָא מִמִּצְרַיִם —
One is obligated to see himself as though he personally had gone out of Egypt

✥ To Erect a Monument in the Heart

Why did the Jewish people not erect monuments of stone and metal, in commemoration of the Exodus? How is it possible for an individual, thousands of years after the redemption from Egypt, to view himself as if he personally left Egypt? The secret lies in the mind's power of imagery.

Why, you may ask, did the Jewish nation not build statues and monuments in memory of the miracle that took place in Egypt? Why did the earlier generations not eternalize the greatest of all events, by carving out in stone and metal the images that comprised the Exodus? Is it possible to ascribe to the notion that they did not give thought to the impact that a visual effect, such as a craftily designed statue, would achieve for the remembrance of this event? Would the placement of such an image on the peak of Mount Carmel or atop one of the hills of Jerusalem not have far-reaching effects for

The matzos are covered and the cup is lifted and held until it is to be drunk. According to some customs, however, the cup is put down after the following paragraph, in which case the matzos should once more be uncovered.

לְפִיכָךְ אֲנַחְנוּ חַיָּבִים לְהוֹדוֹת, לְהַלֵּל, לְשַׁבֵּחַ, לְפָאֵר, לְרוֹמֵם, לְהַדֵּר, לְבָרֵךְ, לְעַלֵּה, וּלְקַלֵּס, לְמִי שֶׁעָשָׂה לַאֲבוֹתֵינוּ וְלָנוּ אֶת כָּל הַנִּסִּים הָאֵלּוּ, הוֹצִיאָנוּ מֵעַבְדוּת לְחֵרוּת, מִיָּגוֹן לְשִׂמְחָה, וּמֵאֵבֶל לְיוֹם טוֹב, וּמֵאֲפֵלָה לְאוֹר גָּדוֹל, וּמִשִּׁעְבּוּד לִגְאֻלָּה, וְנֹאמַר לְפָנָיו שִׁירָה חֲדָשָׁה, הַלְלוּיָהּ.

all future generations? The Egyptians, for example, thoroughly understood this concept. They left a countless number of statues and carvings that would preserve the memory of past events that took place in their history. Whether it is the pyramids, sphinxes, or ancient temples, each one lends credence and testifies to the fact that at one time there existed a mighty Egyptian empire. They tell the story of ancient Egypt, painting vivid pictures of an empire at its peak. Each one conveys to the world a most remarkable tale, yet it is a tale without words. For all it takes is a simple gaze, and one is immediately detached from the present and instantly connected to the past. It enables one to develop sensitivities to the endless flow of memories associated with the nation's history.

Why does the Exodus not have anything of the sort?

But surely such a thing is forbidden, you will say. Anyone with even an elementary knowledge of Judaism knows that it is strictly forbidden to carve or construct forms and images! Yet you would be sorely mistaken. To fashion an image of this sort is most certainly permissible. For did not the great Joshua himself act similarly, after the Jewish people passed through the Jordan River prior to conquering the land of Israel? He himself inscribed the entire Torah — in seventy different languages — on tremendous stones, on the heights of Mount Eival. Joshua was, of course, not acting on his own volition; rather he was fulfilling the commandment of Hashem, Who desired, as it were, that all should be familiar with the eternal Torah and that it should be etched in the minds of all nations of the world. Why was a similar action not performed in order to preserve the memory of the monumental Exodus? Doesn't the Torah require that we forever remember this great event? As the verse states: "Remember this day on which you departed from Egypt" (Shemos 13:3).

The matzos are covered and the cup is lifted and held until it is to be drunk. According to some customs, however, the cup is put down after the following paragraph, in which case the matzos should once more be uncovered.

Therefore it is our duty to thank, praise, laud, glorify, aggrandize, extol, bless, exalt and acclaim the One Who performed all these miracles for our ancestors and for us. He has brought us from slavery to freedom, from anguish to joy, from mourning to festivity, from darkness to great light, and from servitude to redemption. And we will say before Him, Halleluyah!

If we ponder our question for a moment it will dawn on us that from our very question emerges the answer which we so desperately seek. Let us think for a moment: Can anyone in our present day pinpoint the exact location of those stones which Joshua inscribed? Where are they precisely? Does there remain from them even the slightest remnant? The answer is a most resounding, no. We are clueless as to what has become of these stones, and there is no one who can testify to having seen them. Even the pyramids, sphinxes, and ancient temples of Egypt — their testimony is but a silent one. They cannot truly tell us, nor paint vibrant pictures that will profoundly influence the life of another human being. Perhaps they do let us in on some historical data, but do they serve to send us any redeeming messages? They may certainly produce enough of a flicker of awe in the heart of the tourist — who will not miss the opportunity to have himself photographed, posing next to the site — to make a place for the subsequent photograph in a photo album, but it will accomplish little more than that.

If our goal was to inspire feelings of nostalgia, then we could not argue that monuments and statues are of inestimable value. But the Exodus and its memories serve a much loftier purpose than the simple inspiration of nostalgia. The Exodus has a message that is crystal clear and of utmost importance. It is a message that is meant to mold and transform the life of the Jewish nation, inspiring it, not just for a trip or tour, but for all eternity. It would therefore be absolutely impossible to preserve such an event and its eternal message by inscribing it upon mere stones. After all, the monument or statue would be in direct contradiction to the desired goal. Gone would be the eternal remembrance of the Exodus — for why expend effort in remembering it when all one needs to do is glance at the monument from time to time?

Fine, you say. It is a valid point and let us assume that it is correct. But what

הַלְלוּיָהּ הַלְלוּ עַבְדֵי יהוה, הַלְלוּ אֶת שֵׁם יהוה. יְהִי שֵׁם יהוה מְבֹרָךְ, מֵעַתָּה וְעַד עוֹלָם. מִמִּזְרַח שֶׁמֶשׁ עַד מְבוֹאוֹ, מְהֻלָּל שֵׁם יהוה. רָם עַל כָּל גּוֹיִם יהוה, עַל הַשָּׁמַיִם כְּבוֹדוֹ. מִי כַּיהוה אֱלֹהֵינוּ, הַמַּגְבִּיהִי לָשָׁבֶת. הַמַּשְׁפִּילִי לִרְאוֹת, בַּשָּׁמַיִם וּבָאָרֶץ. מְקִימִי מֵעָפָר דָּל, מֵאַשְׁפֹּת יָרִים אֶבְיוֹן. לְהוֹשִׁיבִי עִם נְדִיבִים, עִם נְדִיבֵי עַמּוֹ. מוֹשִׁיבִי עֲקֶרֶת הַבַּיִת, אֵם הַבָּנִים שְׂמֵחָה, הַלְלוּיָהּ.[1]

other alternative is there? How else can the Torah instruct us, in hopes of achieving the desired result of establishing the redemption from Egypt as an eternal memory, alive and vibrant in the hearts and minds of the Jewish nation?

The Torah has instructed us to achieve its goal by our creating mental images and subsequently performing physical actions that will enable the message of the Exodus to be permanently absorbed in our hearts and minds.

There is a verse in the Torah that contains within it the key to preserving essential memories on a nationalistic level. It is a verse that appears in the Torah reading that we read on the festival of Pesach.

Let us examine the following verse carefully and attempt to understand it thoroughly: *"And you shall tell your son on that day, saying, 'It is because of this that Hashem did so for me when I went out of Egypt' "* (ibid. v. 8).

Did you pay careful attention? There are indeed two distinct parts to this verse: 1) the requirement to relate the story of the Exodus to one's children; 2) the requirement to tell over the story of the redemption from Egypt as if he were relating a personal experience (*"Hashem did so for me when I went out of Egypt"*).

When we are reminded of the fact that this commandment was issued not only to the generation that actually left Egypt but to all subsequent generations as well, there arises a most perplexing question in regard to that which we have just stated:

What can it possibly mean that I — a Jew who is 2,000, or even 1,000, or even 100 years removed from the Exodus — am intended to, or better yet, *commanded* to tell over the story of the Jewish nation's redemption from

Halleluyah! Praise, servants of HASHEM. Praise the Name of HASHEM! Blessed be the Name of HASHEM from now and forever. From the dawning place of the sun to its setting place, praised is the Name of HASHEM. Exalted above all nations is HASHEM. Above the heavens is His glory. Who is like HASHEM, our God, Who dwells on high, yet deigns to look upon heaven and earth? He raises the impoverished from the dust. From the trash heaps He lifts the indigent. To seat them with nobles, with the nobles of His people. He transforms a barren woman into a happy mother of children. Halleluyah![1]

---

(1) *Tehillim* 113.

Egypt as if I were relating a personal experience? After all, I personally did not experience the redemption from Egypt! Was I among the multitude of Jews who witnessed and had their perceptions and lives forever changed by the splitting of the Red Sea? I am but a recipient of those memories transmitted from generation to generation! Therefore, how is it conceivable that I should be commanded to pronounce, "Hashem did so for me when I went out of Egypt"?

It is worthwhile to note that this verse has not been understood by the commentators of the Torah as simply a figure of speech, but rather as an absolute requirement:

The Talmud (Pesachim 116a) expresses the requirement in the following manner: *"In every generation one is obligated to see himself as though he personally had gone out of Egypt, as it is written* (ibid. v. 8): *"It is because of this that Hashem did so for me when I went out of Egypt."*

The question, however, remains: How is it possible to demand from us such a seemingly unusual requirement?

The explanation is hidden in two words that were cited in the above quotation: "to see"! We must "see," through the eyes of our minds, in other words — by utilizing our imagination. We have to conjure up in our minds images of our glorious past. Our consciousness must stream with lucid and vivid images, images that sparkle and shimmer with an endless rainbow of colors. We must then attempt to fulfill . . . "to see himself." We must inject ourselves into the mental images we have created in our minds, and try to see ourselves as Jewish slaves in Egypt, tasting for the very first time the

בְּצֵאת יִשְׂרָאֵל מִמִּצְרָיִם, בֵּית יַעֲקֹב מֵעַם לֹעֵז. הָיְתָה יְהוּדָה לְקָדְשׁוֹ, יִשְׂרָאֵל מַמְשְׁלוֹתָיו. הַיָּם רָאָה וַיָּנֹס, הַיַּרְדֵּן יִסֹּב לְאָחוֹר. הֶהָרִים רָקְדוּ כְאֵילִים, גְּבָעוֹת כִּבְנֵי צֹאן. מַה לְּךָ הַיָּם כִּי תָנוּס, הַיַּרְדֵּן תִּסֹּב לְאָחוֹר. הֶהָרִים תִּרְקְדוּ כְאֵילִים, גְּבָעוֹת כִּבְנֵי צֹאן. מִלִּפְנֵי אָדוֹן חוּלִי אָרֶץ, מִלִּפְנֵי אֱלוֹהַּ יַעֲקֹב. הַהֹפְכִי הַצּוּר אֲגַם מָיִם, חַלָּמִישׁ לְמַעְיְנוֹ מָיִם.[1]

sweet taste of freedom, having just witnessed the miracles that Hashem wrought for us in the Red Sea. We must try to imagine — with the utmost clarity and down to the minutest details — how we would have trembled in absolute horror upon seeing the Egyptian army closing in behind us, knowing all too well that the wilderness was but a closed door on each side of us, faced with nothing other than a raging sea directly in front of us. How we would have experienced an almost nauseating dread knowing that we were trapped, with simply nowhere to turn. The feeling of jubilation that accompanied our salvation is a feeling that must be felt in a very deep and profound way. Yet it will only be experienced after putting forth an earnest effort at producing those images, which portray our miraculous salvation, and through constantly reviewing those images drawn on that easel, which is our mind. We must attempt to relive the songs of thanks that emanated from our throats, throats that were choked up from the overwhelming overflow of emotion that must have been felt by the Jewish people at that glorious moment.

Why must we go to such seemingly drastic lengths? As the Haggadah so clearly states: "One is obligated to see himself as though he personally had gone out of Egypt."

Yet you might pose the following question: A very fine exercise indeed, but what comes next? Where has this most unusual drill led us?

First of all, you must realize that this is anything but an "unusual drill." It is a concept that lies at the source, and is the foundation, of any and every action or deed that we perform in this world. Our brain is constantly flashing images in front of our mind's eye, and this is precisely how we think — in pictures. Our minds are comprised of a countless array of pictures, each one exerting its influence on our overall behavior. This is

When Israel went out of Egypt, the house of Jacob from a slanderous nation, Judah became His holy one; Israel, His dominion. The Sea saw and fled. The Jordan stayed to the rear. The mountains skipped like rams; the hills — like lambs. What is it, Sea, that makes you flee? Jordan, what makes you stay back? Mountains, why do you prance like rams? Hills, why do you skip like lambs? Before the presence of the Master Who created the earth. Before the presence of the God of Jacob, Who turns the rock into a pond of water, the flint into a fountain of water.[1]

---

(1) *Tehillim* 114.

---

what psychologists term the "self-image":

> *Conjure up a certain picture of yourself in your mind's eye for an extended period of time, and you will come to be drawn after it. If you have painted a lifelike picture of yourself, depicting yourself as someone who is beaten and is a loser — this picture itself will make success impossible. Paint a lifelike picture of yourself (realistically acknowledging your strengths and weaknesses), as someone who is successful, and this picture itself will project you toward success in a way that you simply would not believe. Those who have lived great lives have always possessed great self-images (Dr. Harry Emerson Fustic, cited by Dr. Maxwell Milts, Psycho Cybernetics).*

Today we are well aware that the key to understanding the human personality and the life experiences that comprise man's existence, lies in understanding the image that he possesses of himself, and his ability to alter that self-image. We understand that there is very little discrepancy between the image that one possesses of himself and his true self. It is quite clear therefore, that knowledge of one's self-image is a most valuable tool that can be put to use by each and every individual to improve his or her mental predicament. In recent years, studies have proven that improvement of one's self-image can be instrumental in the recovery from physical illnesses as well. The technique known as "biofeedback" — a method that attempts to cure the ill by improving their own mental images of themselves — has been recognized as an effective measure in combating certain illnesses. Perhaps it is for this reason that the Torah, in the aforementioned verse, establishes the

The cup is lifted and the matzos covered while reciting the following blessing.
[On Saturday night substitute the bracketed phrase for the preceding phrase.]

בָּרוּךְ אַתָּה יהוה אֱלֹהֵינוּ מֶלֶךְ הָעוֹלָם, אֲשֶׁר
גְּאָלָנוּ וְגָאַל אֶת אֲבוֹתֵינוּ מִמִּצְרַיִם,
וְהִגִּיעָנוּ הַלַּיְלָה הַזֶּה לֶאֱכָל בּוֹ מַצָּה וּמָרוֹר. כֵּן
יהוה אֱלֹהֵינוּ וֵאלֹהֵי אֲבוֹתֵינוּ, יַגִּיעֵנוּ לְמוֹעֲדִים
וְלִרְגָלִים אֲחֵרִים הַבָּאִים לִקְרָאתֵנוּ לְשָׁלוֹם,
שְׂמֵחִים בְּבִנְיַן עִירֶךָ וְשָׂשִׂים בַּעֲבוֹדָתֶךָ, וְנֹאכַל שָׁם
מִן הַזְּבָחִים וּמִן הַפְּסָחִים [מִן הַפְּסָחִים וּמִן הַזְּבָחִים]
אֲשֶׁר יַגִּיעַ דָּמָם עַל קִיר מִזְבַּחֲךָ לְרָצוֹן. וְנוֹדֶה לְךָ
שִׁיר חָדָשׁ עַל גְּאֻלָתֵנוּ וְעַל פְּדוּת נַפְשֵׁנוּ. בָּרוּךְ
אַתָּה יהוה, גָּאַל יִשְׂרָאֵל.

---

use of mental imagery as an absolute commandment!

> *And it is self-understood that it is simply impossible for the amazement generated by an event that occurred several years ago to leave an imprint that will, in the future, generate that amazement once again. Therefore Chazal have instructed us in a similar fashion to that which was mentioned above . . . to draw it closer to our senses by forming a realistic image in our minds (time and time again until the image penetrates our self-conscious, nestling itself among the multitude of personal experiences that comprise our lives) . . . And through this above-mentioned image the memory of the Exodus will become firmly imprinted upon him (Rabbi Simcha Zissel Ziv of Kelm, Chochmah U'Mussar 1:27).*

Instead of chiseling out lifeless stones we turn the chisel toward our hearts of flesh and blood. It is there, in the depths of our hearts, that we erect the historical monument that will enable us to develop a healthy sense of identity. It is an identity that will permeate our entire being and, in turn, shape our present-day values and future existence.

This time we have not discussed the eternal message of the Exodus, but rather the means with which to transmit that message, that continually burning torch of the Jewish people, from generation to generation and from heart to heart.

The cup is lifted and the matzos covered while reciting the following blessing. [On Saturday night substitute the bracketed phrase for the preceding phrase.]

Blessed are You, HASHEM, our God, King of the Universe, Who has redeemed us and redeemed our ancestors from Egypt, and enabled us to live to this night, to eat on it matzah and *maror*. So, HASHEM, our God and the God of our fathers, bring us to future festivals and holidays in peace, happy in the reconstruction of Your city and joyful in Your worship. May we eat there of the offerings and Passover sacrifices [the Passover sacrifices and the offerings] whose blood will reach the wall of Your altar for acceptance. And may we thank You with a new song for our redemption and the liberation of our soul. Blessed are You, HASHEM, Who redeemed Israel.

וְנֹאכַל שָׁם מִן הַזְּבָחִים וּמִן הַפְּסָחִים — May we eat there of the offerings and Passover sacrifices

⊷§ A Trip to the Innermost Depths of a Human Being

Contemporary man is confounded by the concept of the sacrificial offerings that were brought in the *Beis HaMikdash*. It is a subject that he considers to be disconsonant with the messages of the prophets and human sensibility. However, it is specifically the sacrificial offerings that served as the prophets' medium to deliver their lofty lessons and messages to the Jewish people.

In this blessing/prayer, we express our hopes of one day witnessing the renewal of the sacrificial animal offerings in the *Beis HaMikdash*. It seems that few other issues so effectively evoke the disdain of modern-day man. It stands in opposition to many of the values he holds dear and true, and he therefore rejects the concept of animal sacrifice in its entirety.

These arbiters of propriety flinch in disgust and cringe in abject horror when forced to contemplate the thought of spilling the blood of an animal.

Some recite the following before the second cup:

הֲרֵינִי מוּכָן וּמְזוּמָן לְקַיֵּם מִצְוַת כּוֹס שֵׁנִי מֵאַרְבַּע כּוֹסוֹת. לְשֵׁם יִחוּד קֻדְשָׁא בְּרִיךְ הוּא וּשְׁכִינְתֵּיהּ, עַל יְדֵי הַהוּא טָמִיר וְנֶעְלָם, בְּשֵׁם כָּל יִשְׂרָאֵל. וִיהִי נֹעַם אֲדֹנָי אֱלֹהֵינוּ עָלֵינוּ, וּמַעֲשֵׂה יָדֵינוּ כּוֹנְנָה עָלֵינוּ, וּמַעֲשֵׂה יָדֵינוּ כּוֹנְנֵהוּ:

בָּרוּךְ אַתָּה יהוה אֱלֹהֵינוּ מֶלֶךְ הָעוֹלָם, בּוֹרֵא פְּרִי הַגָּפֶן.

The second cup is drunk while leaning on the left side —
preferably the entire cup, but at least most of it.

They ascribe these practices to a primitive time in Jewish history; and find our prayer here offensive.

Though these individuals may admit that they find much in the Torah that guides them to live morally and ethically, they distinguish between the lessons they choose to take from the Torah and a practice the Torah specifically commands. In fact, according to these erroneous critics, the great prophets — who exhorted the populace to conduct themselves with justice, peace, truth and honesty — disparaged animal sacrifice.

To support their contention, they cite the prophet Samuel's admonition of king Saul: *"Does Hashem delight in elevation-offerings and feast-offerings as in obedience to the voice of Hashem? Behold! — to obey is better than a choice offering, to be attentive than the fat of rams"* (I Shmuel 15:22). They also proffer the words of Jeremiah: *"For I did not speak with your forefathers, nor did I command them, on the day I took them out of the land of Egypt, concerning burnt- or peace-offerings"* (Yirmiyah 7:22), as well as citations from the prophets Isaiah and Hosea, and others.

The Sages of the Talmud and Midrash were well aware of these verses — and they regarded them with far greater reverence than we do. Yet they understood that the offering of animals as sacrifices to Hashem is a central and vital concept of Torah and Judaism. They saw these offerings as components of Jewish belief and practice fully consonant with the words of the prophets mentioned.

What was the Sages' view of sacrificial offerings? Let us take two examples:

> *"Hashem took the man and placed him in the Garden of Eden, to work it and to guard it"* (Bereishis 2:15) — *These refer to the sacrificial offerings* (Bereshis Rabbah 16:8).

Some recite the following before the second cup:

Behold, I am prepared and ready to fulfill the mitzvah of the second of
the Four Cups. For the sake of the unification of the Holy One,
Blessed is He, and His Presence, through Him Who is hidden and
inscrutable — [I pray] in the name of all Israel. May the pleasantness of
my Lord, our God, be upon us — may He establish our handiwork for
us; our handiwork may He establish.

Blessed are You, HASHEM, our God, King of the
Universe, Who creates the fruit of the vine.

The second cup is drunk while leaning on the left side —
preferably the entire cup, but at least most of it.

"He (Abraham) said . . . Whereby shall I know that I am to inherit
it?" (Bereishis 15:8). Rabbi Chiya, son of Rabbi Chanina said: He said
to Him (Abraham to Hashem): "In what merit (will I merit to inherit
the land)?" He responded: "In the merit of the sacrificial offerings"
(Bereishis Rabbah 44:17).

The words of our Sages certainly indicate that the sacrificial offerings play
a central role in sustaining humanity and the Jewish people.

However, let us approach this issue from a different perspective.

Even modern-day, anti-religious philosophers are hesitant to artificially
and conveniently differentiate between the ritual aspects of the Torah and
the ethical messages of the prophets. Take this short excerpt by Professor
Yechezkel Koifman:

The demand of Jeremiah is consistent with the entire theme of
his prophecy: Do not simply offer sacrifices, rather fulfill the
entire covenant. He was opposed to the following: performing rituals
in a superficial manner, all the while lacking true faith and the
proper devotion in regard to the fulfillment of the Torah's commandments . . . That Jeremiah was not condemning the sacrificial
offering itself can be easily discerned from verses 7:11 and 7:12 . . .
And if he (Jeremiah) exclaims that the sacrifices of the Jewish
people were not finding favor in the eyes of Hashem due to the
fact that they were not obeying His words (verses 7:20-21), it can
be inferred (see the final verses of Hosea 9) that should they in
fact heed His words, their sacrificial offerings would be readily accepted.
. . . To oppose the ritual of sacrificial offerings would be in
line with the theology of Christian liberalism which customarily

רחצה

The hands are washed for matzah and the following blessing is recited. It is preferable to bring water and a basin to the head of the household at the Seder table.

בָּרוּךְ אַתָּה יהוה אֱלֹהֵינוּ מֶלֶךְ הָעוֹלָם, אֲשֶׁר קִדְּשָׁנוּ בְּמִצְוֹתָיו, וְצִוָּנוּ עַל נְטִילַת יָדָיִם.

מוֹצִיא / מצה

The following two blessings are recited over matzah; the first is recited over matzah as food, and the second for the special mitzvah of eating matzah on the night of Pesach. [The latter blessing is to be made with the intention that it also apply to the *korach*, "sandwich," and the *afikoman*.] The head of the household raises all the matzos on the Seder plate and recites the following blessings:

Some recite the following before the blessing *hamotzi*:

הִנְנִי מוּכָן וּמְזוּמָן לְקַיֵּם מִצְוַת אֲכִילַת מַצָּה. לְשֵׁם יְחוּד קֻדְשָׁא בְּרִיךְ הוּא וּשְׁכִינְתֵּיה, עַל יְדֵי הַהוּא טָמִיר וְנֶעְלָם, בְּשֵׁם כָּל יִשְׂרָאֵל. וִיהִי נֹעַם אֲדֹנָי אֱלֹהֵינוּ עָלֵינוּ, וּמַעֲשֵׂה יָדֵינוּ כּוֹנְנָה עָלֵינוּ, וּמַעֲשֵׂה יָדֵינוּ כּוֹנְנֵהוּ:

בָּרוּךְ אַתָּה יהוה אֱלֹהֵינוּ מֶלֶךְ הָעוֹלָם, הַמּוֹצִיא לֶחֶם מִן הָאָרֶץ.

Those who use three matzos put down the bottom matzah at this point.

בָּרוּךְ אַתָּה יהוה אֱלֹהֵינוּ מֶלֶךְ הָעוֹלָם, אֲשֶׁר קִדְּשָׁנוּ בְּמִצְוֹתָיו, וְצִוָּנוּ עַל אֲכִילַת מַצָּה.

---

erases and amends" (*Toldos HaEmunah HaYisraelis, Vol. 3, pp. 443-444*).

We are left with a question that requires some clarification. How do these rituals coincide with all the ethical and moral teachings of the prophets? How could the prophets preach such lofty values, yet at the very same moment be involved in the slaughter and subsequent offering of countless animals? How can we resolve this apparent contradiction?

The answer begins with understanding the fundamental concepts that underlie the sacrifices. The root of the word "*korban*" ("sacrificial offering")

RACHTZAH

The hands are washed for matzah and the following blessing is recited. It is preferable to bring water and a basin to the head of the household at the Seder table.

Blessed are You, HASHEM, our God, King of the Universe, Who has sanctified us with His commandments and commanded us with regard to washing the hands.

MOTZI / MATZAH

The following two blessings are recited over matzah; the first is recited over matzah as food, and the second for the special mitzvah of eating matzah on the night of Pesach. [The latter blessing is to be made with the intention that it also apply to the *korach*, "sandwich," and the *afikoman*.] The head of the household raises all the matzos on the Seder plate and recites the following blessings.

Some recite the following before the blessing *hamotzi:*
Behold, I am prepared and ready to fulfill the mitzvah of eating matzah. For the sake of the unification of the Holy One, Blessed is He, and His Presence, through Him who is hidden and inscrutable — [I pray] in the name of all Israel. May the pleasantness of my Lord, our God, be upon us — may He establish our handiwork for us; our handiwork may He establish.

Blessed are You, HASHEM, our God, King of the Universe, Who brings forth bread from the earth.

Those who use three matzos put down the bottom matzah at this point.

Blessed are You, HASHEM, our God, King of the Universe, Who has sanctified us with His commandments and commanded us with regard to eating matzah.

---

is *"krav,"* which means "to draw close," as the Ramban states: "Whenever the word *"korban"* appears, it connotes closeness and unity" (*Ramban, Vayikra* 1:9). In many other religions, a sacrifice is an "offering" — a gift to the deity, for the benefit of the deity. In Judaism, however, a sacrifice is a vehicle to bring oneself closer to God; it transforms man's relationship to his Creator, but the Creator Himself remains unaffected.

Judaism rejected the view that the ritual possesses any sort of Divine quality — a view embraced by idol worshipers. The performance of

The matzos are to be eaten while reclining on the left side and without delay; they need not be dipped in salt. Each participant is required to eat an amount of matzah equal in volume to an egg. Since it is usually impossible to provide a sufficient amount of matzah from the two matzos for all members of the household, other matzos should be available at the head of the table from which to complete the required amounts. However, each participant should receive a piece from each of the top two matzos.

מרור

The head of the household takes a half-egg volume of the *maror*, dips it into *charoses*, and gives each participant a like amount. The following blessing is recited with the intention that it also apply to the *maror* of the "sandwich." The *maror* is eaten without reclining, and without delay.

Some recite the following before *maror*:

הִנְנִי מוּכָן וּמְזוּמָּן לְקַיֵּם מִצְוַת אֲכִילַת מָרוֹר. לְשֵׁם יִחוּד קֻדְשָׁא בְּרִיךְ הוּא וּשְׁכִינְתֵּיהּ, עַל יְדֵי הַהוּא טָמִיר וְנֶעְלָם, בְּשֵׁם כָּל יִשְׂרָאֵל. וִיהִי נֹעַם אֲדֹנָי אֱלֹהֵינוּ עָלֵינוּ, וּמַעֲשֵׂה יָדֵינוּ כּוֹנְנָה עָלֵינוּ, וּמַעֲשֵׂה יָדֵינוּ כּוֹנְנֵהוּ:

בָּרוּךְ אַתָּה יהוה אֱלֹהֵינוּ מֶלֶךְ הָעוֹלָם, אֲשֶׁר קִדְּשָׁנוּ בְּמִצְוֹתָיו, וְצִוָּנוּ עַל אֲכִילַת מָרוֹר.

---

rituals in the world of idolatry carried with it the fate of their god . . . However, according to the Jewish faith, the ritual itself contains absolutely no godly quality whatsoever, and the "fate" of Hashem is not dependent on the ritual in even the most minute form . . . The ritual is a commandment. It is a revelation of Hashem's kindness, and He does not "need" it in any way (Toldos HaEmunah HaYisraelis, Vol. 3, p. 80).

Thus, we view animal sacrifices as a means for us to draw closer to Hashem. Sacrifice without commitment is meaningless. It was — as mentioned — this sort of hollow sacrifice that was denounced by the prophets.

"But," the modern-day thinker may wonder, "is this truly the optimum way for man to draw closer to Hashem? Can we expect to strengthen the bond that binds us to our Creator, by slaughtering a sheep?"

For this, we must look at the dynamic of a person's relationship to God. An individual comes close to Hashem by constantly struggling to achieve mastery over the instinctive urges that rage within him. If left uncontrolled, these desires could draw man very far away from Hashem. To the degree that a person masters his animalistic instincts — choosing instead to act with

The matzos are to be eaten while reclining on the left side and without delay; they need not be dipped in salt. Each participant is required to eat an amount of matzah equal in volume to an egg. Since it is usually impossible to provide a sufficient amount of matzah from the two matzos for all members of the household, other matzos should be available at the head of the table from which to complete the required amounts. However, each participant should receive a piece from each of the top two matzos.

MAROR

The head of the household takes a half-egg volume of the *maror,* dips it into *charoses,* and gives each participant a like amount. The following blessing is recited with the intention that it also apply to the *maror* of the "sandwich." The *maror* is eaten without reclining, and without delay.

Some recite the following before *maror:*

Behold, I am prepared and ready to fulfill the mitzvah of eating maror. For the sake of unification of the Holy One, Blessed is He, and His Presence, through Him Who is hidden and inscrutable — [I pray] in the name of all Israel. May the pleasantness of my Lord, our God, be upon us — may He establish our handiwork for us; our handiwork may He establish.

Blessed are You, HASHEM, our God, King of the Universe, Who has sanctified us with His commandments and commanded us with regard to eating *maror.*

---

dignity, fairness, and with full adherence to the commandments of Hashem — it is to that degree that he perfects his personality and earns closeness to Hashem.

When a man sins, he severs, to a certain degree, his ties with Hashem. He distances himself from his Creator. The pursuit of base desires creates a barrier, so to speak, between man and God. In order to lessen the gap between man and his God, man was granted the sacrificial offering.

How does this sacrificial offering influence a person to realign his values, prioritize his goals and set himself to the task of serving the One Above?

For we have said that the main ways of the heart are dependent upon the actions (of a person). Therefore, when a man sins he will not be able to properly purify his heart with the words of his lips alone, that he should say between himself and a wall, "I have sinned. I will not continue to do so." But by performing an important action on account of his sin, "taking goats from your pen" (see Tehillim 50:9),

כּוֹרֵךְ

The bottom matzah is now taken. From it, with the addition of other matzos if needed, each participant receives a half-egg's volume of matzah with an equal volume of *maror* (dipped into *charoses* which is shaken off). The following paragraph is recited and the "sandwich" is eaten while reclining.

זֵ֫כֶר לְמִקְדָּשׁ כְּהִלֵּל. כֵּן עָשָׂה הִלֵּל בִּזְמַן שֶׁבֵּית הַמִּקְדָּשׁ הָיָה קַיָּם. הָיָה כּוֹרֵךְ (פֶּסַח) מַצָּה וּמָרוֹר וְאוֹכֵל בְּיַחַד. לְקַיֵּם מַה שֶׁנֶּאֱמַר, עַל מַצּוֹת וּמְרֹרִים יֹאכְלֻהוּ.[1]

שלחן עורך

The meal should be eaten in a combination of joy and solemnity, for the meal, too, is a part of the Seder service.

It is customary to eat an egg, in remembrance of the *chagigah* offering, and meat (but not roasted), in remembrance of the Pesach offering.

While it is desirable that *zemiros* and discussion of the laws and events of Pesach be part of the meal, extraneous conversation should be avoided.

It should be remembered that the *afikoman* must be eaten while there is still some appetite for it. In fact, if one is so sated that he must literally force himself to eat it, he is not credited with the performance of the mitzvah of *afikoman*. Therefore, it is unwise to eat more than a moderate amount during the meal.

---

and expending the effort to bring them to the Kohen . . . As a result of performing this important act, the evil of the sin he had performed will be fully realized by him, and he will refrain from performing it another time (Sefer HaChinuch, commandment 95).

In essence it is one deed coming to counteract another. Counterbalancing the sin — an action that involved the entire personality of the sinner in a pursuit which distanced him from Hashem — is the sacrificial offering, which responds to the sin by demanding the full involvement of the offerer in a Divine pursuit. Through the offering, the sinner's entire personality is refocused on the service of Hashem; he is redirected to strive upward, closing the gap between man and his Creator.

There is an additional way that the heart can be inspired by the offering of an animal: through similarity. The physical bodies of man

KORECH

The bottom matzah is now taken. From it, with the addition of other matzos if needed, each participant receives a half-egg's volume of matzah with an equal volume of *maror* (dipped into *charoses* which is shaken off). The following paragraph is recited and the "sandwich" is eaten while reclining.

In remembrance of the Temple we do as Hillel did in Temple times: He would combine the Passover offering, matzah and *maror* in a sandwich and eat them together, to fulfill that which is written, "With matzos and *maror* they should eat it."[1]

SHULCHAN ORECH

The meal should be eaten in a combination of joy and solemnity, for the meal, too, is a part of the Seder service.

It is customary to eat an egg, in remembrance of the *chagigah* offering, and meat (but not roasted), in remembrance of the Pesach offering.

While it is desirable that *zemiros* and discussion of the laws and events of Pesach be part of the meal, extraneous conversation should be avoided.

It should be remembered that the *afikoman* must be eaten while there is still some appetite for it. In fact, if one is so sated that he must literally force himself to eat it, he is not credited with the performance of the mitzvah of *afikoman*. Therefore, it is unwise to eat more than a moderate amount during the meal.

(1) *Bamidbar* 9:11.

and animal bear many resemblances. They differ from one another only by virtue of the fact that one was given intelligence while the other was not. Being that the body of man parts with his intellect at the time of sin, he should realize that he has entered into the realm of the animals, as this is all that differentiates between them. He has therefore been commanded to take a physical body . . . to burn it . . . (and thereby) strengthen in his mind the thought that the entire matter — (the pursuit of the) physical without intellect — must perish and become completely nullified (ibid.).

In other words, the shocking sight of the burning animal stirs the mind of the sinner, and enables him to recognize the bestial quality of his actions. This is the optimum way to begin purifying one's sullied personality and redirect it down a path of spiritual achievement.

צָפוּן

From the *afikoman* matzah (and from additional matzos to make up the required amount), a half-egg's volume portion — according to some, a full egg's volume portion — is given to each participant. It should be eaten before midnight, while reclining, without delay, and uninterruptedly. Nothing may be eaten or drunk after the *afikoman* (with the exception of water and the like) except for the last two Seder cups of wine.

Some recite the following before eating the *afikoman*:

הִנְנִי מוּכָן וּמְזוּמָן לְקַיֵּם מִצְוַת אֲכִילַת אֲפִיקוֹמָן. לְשֵׁם יִחוּד קֻדְשָׁא בְּרִיךְ הוּא וּשְׁכִינְתֵּיהּ, עַל יְדֵי הַהוּא טָמִיר וְנֶעֱלָם, בְּשֵׁם כָּל יִשְׂרָאֵל. וִיהִי נְעַם אֲדֹנָי אֱלֹהֵינוּ עָלֵינוּ, וּמַעֲשֵׂה יָדֵינוּ כּוֹנְנָה עָלֵינוּ, וּמַעֲשֵׂה יָדֵינוּ כּוֹנְנֵהוּ:

בָּרֵךְ

The third cup is poured and *Bircas HaMazon* (Grace After Meals) is recited. According to some customs, the Cup of Elijah is poured at this point.

שִׁיר הַמַּעֲלוֹת, בְּשׁוּב יהוה אֶת שִׁיבַת צִיּוֹן, הָיִינוּ כְּחֹלְמִים. אָז יִמָּלֵא שְׂחוֹק פִּינוּ וּלְשׁוֹנֵנוּ רִנָּה, אָז יֹאמְרוּ בַגּוֹיִם, הִגְדִּיל יהוה לַעֲשׂוֹת עִם אֵלֶּה. הִגְדִּיל יהוה לַעֲשׂוֹת עִמָּנוּ, הָיִינוּ שְׂמֵחִים. שׁוּבָה יהוה אֶת שְׁבִיתֵנוּ, כַּאֲפִיקִים בַּנֶּגֶב. הַזֹּרְעִים בְּדִמְעָה בְּרִנָּה יִקְצֹרוּ. הָלוֹךְ יֵלֵךְ וּבָכֹה נֹשֵׂא מֶשֶׁךְ הַזָּרַע, בֹּא יָבֹא בְרִנָּה, נֹשֵׂא אֲלֻמֹּתָיו.

תְּהִלַּת יהוה יְדַבֶּר פִּי, וִיבָרֵךְ כָּל בָּשָׂר שֵׁם קָדְשׁוֹ לְעוֹלָם וָעֶד.[1] וַאֲנַחְנוּ נְבָרֵךְ יָהּ, מֵעַתָּה וְעַד עוֹלָם, הַלְלוּיָהּ.[2] הוֹדוּ לַיהוה כִּי טוֹב, כִּי לְעוֹלָם חַסְדּוֹ.[3] מִי יְמַלֵּל גְּבוּרוֹת יהוה, יַשְׁמִיעַ כָּל תְּהִלָּתוֹ.[4]

TZAFUN

From the *afikoman* matzah (and from additional matzos to make up the required amount), a half-egg's volume portion — according to some, a full egg's volume portion — is given to each participant. It should be eaten before midnight, while reclining, without delay, and uninterruptedly. Nothing may be eaten or drunk after the *afikoman* (with the exception of water and the like) except for the last two Seder cups of wine.

Some recite the following before eating the *afikoman*:

Behold, I am prepared and ready to fulfill the mitzvah of eating the *afikoman*. For the sake of the unification of the Holy One, Blessed is He, and his Presence, through Him who is hidden and inscrutable — [I pray] in the name of all Israel. May the pleasantness of my Lord, our God, be upon us — may He establish our handiwork for us; our handiwork may He establish.

BARECH

The third cup is poured and *Bircas HaMazon* (Grace After Meals) is recited. According to some customs, the Cup of Elijah is poured at this point.

A song of the steps. When HASHEM will bring the exiles back to Zion, it will be as if we were dreaming. Then our mouth will be filled with laughter and our tongue with joy. Then they will say among the nations, "HASHEM is the One Who has done great things with these." HASHEM has indeed done great things with us. We have been made happy. HASHEM, return our captives like dry streams that run again in the south. Those who sow in tears will reap in song. He who goes crying, carrying his load of seed, will return singing, carrying his sheaves of grain.

May my mouth declare the praise of HASHEM and may all flesh bless His Holy Name forever.[1] We will bless HASHEM from this time and forever. Halleluyah![2] Give thanks to HASHEM for He is good, for His kindness is eternal.[3] Who can express the mighty acts of HASHEM? Who can declare all His praise?[4]

---

(1) *Tehillim* 145:21. (2) 115:18. (3) 118:1. (4) 106:2.

Some recite the following before *Bircas HaMazon:*

הִנְנִי מוּכָן וּמְזוּמָּן לְקַיֵּם מִצְוַת עֲשֵׂה שֶׁל בִּרְכַּת הַמָּזוֹן, כַּכָּתוּב,
וְאָכַלְתָּ וְשָׂבָעְתָּ וּבֵרַכְתָּ אֶת יהוה אֱלֹהֶיךָ עַל הָאָרֶץ הַטֹּבָה
אֲשֶׁר נָתַן לָךְ.[1]

If three or more males, aged thirteen or older, participate in the meal, the leader
is required to formally invite the others to join him in the recitation of *Bircas
HaMazon.* Following is the *zimun,* or formal invitation.

The leader begins:

רַבּוֹתַי נְבָרֵךְ.

The group responds:

יְהִי שֵׁם יהוה מְבֹרָךְ מֵעַתָּה וְעַד עוֹלָם.[2]

The leader continues [if ten men join the *zimun,*
the words in parentheses are included]:

יְהִי שֵׁם יהוה מְבֹרָךְ מֵעַתָּה וְעַד עוֹלָם.[2] בִּרְשׁוּת מָרָנָן
וְרַבָּנָן וְרַבּוֹתַי, נְבָרֵךְ (אֱלֹהֵינוּ) שֶׁאָכַלְנוּ מִשֶּׁלּוֹ.

The group responds:

בָּרוּךְ (אֱלֹהֵינוּ) שֶׁאָכַלְנוּ מִשֶּׁלּוֹ וּבְטוּבוֹ חָיִינוּ.

The leader continues:

בָּרוּךְ (אֱלֹהֵינוּ) שֶׁאָכַלְנוּ מִשֶּׁלּוֹ וּבְטוּבוֹ חָיִינוּ.

The following line is recited if ten men join the *zimun.*

בָּרוּךְ הוּא וּבָרוּךְ שְׁמוֹ.

וְאָכַלְתָּ וְשָׂבָעְתָּ, וּבֵרַכְתָּ אֶת ה' — **And you shall eat
and you shall be satisfied and you shall bless Hashem**

⇜ The Golden Key

Grace After Meals is a tool that, if put to proper use, can
lead an individual to a life of happiness and contentment.
Within the blessing lies a most thrilling and revolutionary
approach toward sustenance. It is an approach that has
the potential to solve much of the hardship and stress that
face present-day society. Its central theme is: Hashem
created the world in order to bestow kindness upon man.

Grace After Meals, *Bircas HaMazon* — as hard as this may be for many
of us to believe — is the golden key that can enable us to rectify the

Some recite the following before *Bircas HaMazon:*

Behold, I am prepared and ready to fulfill the mitzvah of Grace After Meals, as it is written; "And you shall eat and you shall be satisfied and you shall bless HASHEM, your God, for the good land which He gave you."[1]

If three or more males, aged thirteen or older, participate in the meal, the leader is required to formally invite the others to join him in the recitation of *Bircas HaMazon.* Following is the *zimun,* or formal invitation.

The leader begins:

Gentlemen, let us make the blessing.

The group responds:

May the Name of HASHEM be blessed from this moment and forever![2]

The leader continues [if ten men join the *zimun,* the words in parentheses are included]:

May the Name of HASHEM be blessed from this moment and forever![2]

With the permission of the distinguished people present,

let us bless [our God], for we have eaten from what is His.

The group responds:

Blessed is [our God] He of Whose we have eaten

and through Whose goodness we live.

The leader continues:

Blessed is [our God] He of Whose we have eaten

and through Whose goodness we live.

The following line is recited if ten men join the *zimun.*

Blessed is He and Blessed is His Name.

_____

(1) *Devarim* 8:10. (2) *Tehillim* 113:2.

---

problems of society, both on a general and an individual level. The philosophy that lies behind this oft-recited blessing (and in truth behind all blessings that we recite) is capable of navigating the ships of society — strewn to and fro on the stormy seas of dissatisfaction — toward the shores of contentment.

What is the psychological process that takes place in the heart of the believing Jew at the time when he recites the *Bircas HaMazon?*

In order to answer this question, let us gain some insight from the book entitled "East and West." After the author, Dr. Raphael Eisenberg, dissects and analyzes all the relevant theories dealing with man's sustenance that have been eschewed over the course of several generations, and pinpoints each one's mistakes and failures, he presents Judaism's approach, showering it with praise and adulation. It is an approach, he explains, that centers on Hashem's affection for the world He created and His concern for each and every one of his creations: *The human being, with all his physical needs*

בָּרוּךְ אַתָּה יהוה אֱלֹהֵינוּ מֶלֶךְ הָעוֹלָם, הַזָּן אֶת
הָעוֹלָם כֻּלּוֹ, בְּטוּבוֹ, בְּחֵן בְּחֶסֶד וּבְרַחֲמִים,
הוּא נֹתֵן לֶחֶם לְכָל בָּשָׂר, כִּי לְעוֹלָם חַסְדּוֹ.[1]
וּבְטוּבוֹ הַגָּדוֹל, תָּמִיד לֹא חָסַר לָנוּ, וְאַל יֶחְסַר לָנוּ
מָזוֹן לְעוֹלָם וָעֶד. בַּעֲבוּר שְׁמוֹ הַגָּדוֹל, כִּי הוּא אֵל
זָן וּמְפַרְנֵס לַכֹּל, וּמֵטִיב לַכֹּל, וּמֵכִין מָזוֹן לְכָל
בְּרִיּוֹתָיו אֲשֶׁר בָּרָא. בָּרוּךְ אַתָּה יהוה, הַזָּן אֶת
הַכֹּל. (אָמֵן. —Others)

---

and basic necessities, is capable of sensing the flow of blessing that emanates from Hashem.

He commences his commentary on the Jewish approach toward sustenance by stating as follows:

> *Man, however, is not lost. For there exists a philosophy that is capable of relieving his stress, even in our turbulent times, a time that lives with the fear of nuclear warfare that is capable of putting an end to human existence. We live in a generation in which the natural drives and tendencies that are present within each individual, those which motivate him toward the pursuit of wealth and physical satisfaction, remain unbridled and unchecked. Mankind's drive to improve its material standing has resulted in a world outlook that affords no mercy to one who is guilty of standing in the way of another man's pursuit of big profit.*
>
> *Our aim is not to prove the validity of the following doctrine. Our aim is simply to point out that it works in accordance with the psychological process of the human mind. Vested in it is the potential to bestow lifelong satisfaction of one's desires and drives without rejecting them.*
>
> *At the very core of this philosophy lies the approach that defines the Jewish perspective toward sustenance. It accepts as a basic principle and foundation of Judaism, that Hashem created the world in order to bestow good upon man. Since this is the first and foremost desire, as it were, of Hashem, it is most logical to conclude that Hashem is concerned with the materialistic aspect of man's existence. If man is able to recognize that the fulfillment of his wants and needs are a direct result of the bounty which Hashem bestows upon*

Blessed are You, Hashem, our God, King of the Universe, Who nourishes the entire world with His goodness, with grace, kindness, and mercy. He gives nourishment to all flesh, for His kindness is eternal.[1] And in His great goodness, nourishment has never been lacking for us, nor may it ever be, for the sake of His great Name. For He feeds and supports all and does good to all and readies food for all His creatures that He created. Blessed are You, Hashem, Who feeds all.

---

(1) *Tehillim* 136:25.

---

him, then the gratification of these wants can awaken within him feelings of extreme love and closeness to his God. It does not inspire fear of God; it will result only in a deep appreciation and feelings of warmth towards the One Who has bestowed upon him all that he has.

The awareness of the personal concern that Hashem feels for each and every human being can potentially uplift and sanctify man's materialistic urges themselves, as he is able to see within them a prerequisite toward achieving the spiritual bliss that is the result of feeling intense love for Hashem. It is only because man has wants and desires that he is able to grasp the infinite kindness that Hashem has bestowed upon him, and experience the love that He feels for man. A man is able to come to this recognition only upon experiencing a sense of gratification upon having his needs met. This approach is in direct contrast to the views of other religions and societies who consider material desires as something evil and ultimately destructive to society at large.

The recognition of Hashem's infinite love for man is a recognition that has the power to eradicate the prevailing view that the pursuit of sustenance is not simply a means to an end, but an end in itself. A world that espouses the Jewish approach toward sustenance is a world that abides by the notion that materialistic pursuits are by no means an end in themselves, but rather a vehicle with which to experience spiritual pleasure. It doesn't reject the desires a human being may have for materialistic items, but rather transforms them into something noble and sacred. The following analogy illustrates the point we are trying to get across: To derive pleasure from a bouquet of flowers, by enjoying

נוֹדֶה לְךָ יהוה אֱלֹהֵינוּ, עַל שֶׁהִנְחַלְתָּ לַאֲבוֹתֵינוּ אֶרֶץ חֶמְדָּה טוֹבָה וּרְחָבָה. וְעַל שֶׁהוֹצֵאתָנוּ יהוה אֱלֹהֵינוּ מֵאֶרֶץ מִצְרַיִם, וּפְדִיתָנוּ

its appearance and by inhaling its pleasant fragrance, is an activity that can be viewed as an end in itself, or as a means toward an end. For example, if the present holder of the bouquet is a girl who recently received the bouquet as a token of affection from her chasan, she is certain to derive far more pleasure from the appearance and fragrance of the bouquet than would the person who just happened to find it lying on a street corner. This person's feelings of satisfaction upon gazing at the lovely bouquet pale in comparison to the feelings of delight felt by the kallah, who is well aware that the bouquet is a token of true affection from her chasan.

This is the gift that the Grace After Meals has given to mankind. It enables modern-day man to overcome the problems that face him. But since man does not recognize his Divine sustainer, he views material pursuit as an end in itself. It is this desire that drives him to amass wealth and aggressively pursue a life of inordinate luxury. It is only after he experiences many years of disappointment that he begins to search for ways to control his destructive urges.

However, if among man's many wants would be a sincere yearning for closeness with the One Above, many of the daily pressures that stem from those very wants would gradually dissipate. They would evolve from a source of anxiety and stress into a medium for achieving Divine closeness. The happiness he would feel upon having his desires fulfilled would be far greater than that of one whose wants were met but who lacked this mode of thought, as in the case of the kallah and the stranger.

This is the lofty transformation that can sanctify the otherwise mundane physical desires of man. It is capable of doing away with the following social flaws:

1) One's interest in bettering his material predicament would no longer be deemed an ethical flaw, but a means with which to get closer to Hashem.

2) Awareness of Hashem's concern over one's well-being would result in a much-needed sense of security in his relationship with Hashem, a feeling rarely felt by one who would not necessarily be termed scholarly as far as his spiritual erudition is concerned.

We thank You, HASHEM, our God, for giving to our ancestors as a heritage a desirable, good, and spacious land, and for taking us out, HASHEM, our God, from the land of Egypt, and redeeming us

3) *This act of sanctification is far different from the theories that have been experimented with by the other "major" religions and social orders of our time, such as communism, capitalism, and liberalism. It is a theory that does not place its sole focus on man, nor does it diminish the lofty purpose of man. For the man that arrives at the understanding that Hashem is truly concerned over his state of affairs, will undoubtedly come to trust in Hashem wholeheartedly. He will no longer expend an endless amount of energy trying to amass — be it for himself, his friend, or his nation — hordes of wealth and material goods, all of which enable him to exert more control and influence in society. Control is not without its price. It usually comes at the expense of another, leaving a trail of broken relationships, jealousy, and mistrust. Judaism provides an alternative that will lay the foundation for peaceful interaction with others.*

4) *It goes without saying that in such a society there exists no need for the theories — such as communism and individualism — which state that physical strength is the only means through which one is able to better his materialistic standing. The hardships facing much of today's world have their roots in these theories.*

These are the wise words of Dr. Eisenberg. Within them lies the secret of living a blissful existence and a life of enduring contentment.

אֶרֶץ חֶמְדָּה טוֹבָה וּרְחָבָה — A desirable, good, and spacious land

◆§ In Praise of the Good Land

How did Moses describe the land that was destined for the people of Israel? Which praises did he laud upon it when telling the Jewish people of its outstanding qualities, and which did Moses choose not to relate? Why does the land of Israel not contain rivers or carvings of gold? Why is everyone living upon it content?

מִבֵּית עֲבָדִים, וְעַל בְּרִיתְךָ שֶׁחָתַמְתָּ בִּבְשָׂרֵנוּ, וְעַל
תּוֹרָתְךָ שֶׁלִּמַּדְתָּנוּ, וְעַל חֻקֶּיךָ שֶׁהוֹדַעְתָּנוּ, וְעַל
חַיִּים חֵן וָחֶסֶד שֶׁחוֹנַנְתָּנוּ, וְעַל אֲכִילַת מָזוֹן
שָׁאַתָּה זָן וּמְפַרְנֵס אוֹתָנוּ תָּמִיד, בְּכָל יוֹם וּבְכָל עֵת
וּבְכָל שָׁעָה.

"**A** desirable, good, and spacious land" — these were the words used by Moses to describe the land of Israel. In the Book of *Devarim*, when Moses speaks longingly about the land of Israel, he chooses a description that speaks volumes about the love he feels for the land. Moses describes the land as "good." Time and time again, throughout his lengthy diatribe to the Jewish people, Moses mentions "the good land." Even we, so many years and miles away from those Valleys of Moav, from which Moses addressed the Jewish people shortly before his passing, are able to sense the deep love Moses felt for the land of Israel at the moment he expressed the words, "the good land."

Here is a verse that illustrates Moses' deep longing for the land of Israel, and the pain he experienced upon being denied entry:

> "Let me now cross and see the good land that is on the other side of the Jordan, this good mountain and the Lebanon" (Devarim 3:25).

In *Parashas Eikev* there is a lengthy description detailing the outstanding qualities of the land of Israel:

> "For Hashem, your God, is bringing you to a good land: a land with streams of water, of springs and underground water coming forth in valley and mountain; a land of wheat, barely, grape, fig, and pomegranate; a land of oil-olives and date-honey; a land where you will eat bread without poverty — you will lack nothing there; a land whose stones are iron and from whose mountains you will mine copper" (ibid. 8:7-9).

We can almost hear a delicate splashing sound arising from the streams of water. In our mind's eye we are able to visualize a field full of wheat, swaying to and fro, as a warm breeze gently passes through it. We can easily picture the green vines dangling from the hilltops, the glistening honey and pure olive-oil that flows so plentifully through the valleys of Israel. In short, we can

from the house of bondage, and for the covenant which You sealed into our flesh, and for Your Torah which You taught us, and for Your laws which You made known to us, and for life, grace, and kindness which You have bestowed upon us, and for the food with which You feed and sustain us every day, at every time, at every moment.

---

experience the many delights of the Holy Land, the land in which *"you will lack nothing there"* (ibid. v. 9).

If one reads carefully, he will note that Moses was very particular and exact in describing the land of Israel. He did not choose his adjectives indiscriminately, nor by random. Each and every description contained great significance, and was delivered to the ears of the Jewish people for a specific purpose, namely, the laying of the foundation for a new sovereignty that was to be established in the land of Israel. It was to be a sovereignty unlike any other that had come before it. It would be based upon spiritual values, and would be capable of imparting true happiness to its citizens. It would be a society that would spawn a people who would be honored and respected worldwide, a people who contained the potential to illuminate even the farthest and most distant corners of the universe. This was the pretense upon which this society was created, and these are the challenges that lay before it.

It is for this reason that Moses was rather concise, and offered but a brief description of the land. He described the streams, underground waters and springs of the Holy Land, yet made no mention of its rivers. Moses described hills that harbored copper and iron, yet "forgot" to mention all the silver and gold that hides within them. He told the Jewish people of the seven species of fruit through which the land of Israel is praised (wheat, barley, grape, fig, pomegranates, oil-olives and date-honey), but left out the remaining fruits of the land, of which there are an abundance.

Rabbi Don Isaac Abarbanel explains:

> It is well known that there are additional fruits in the land of Israel, apples, for example, as well as other fruits. Moses, of blessed memory, mentioned only those items whose benefits and uses are essential for the sustenance of man, such as bread, wine, grapes, and dates, of which Galinus, the head of the doctors, said that the necessary quantity should be consumed, as they are instrumental in guarding one's health. This applies to olive oil and honey as well, as they

וְעַל הַכֹּל יהוה אֱלֹהֵינוּ אֲנַחְנוּ מוֹדִים לָךְ, וּמְבָרְכִים אוֹתָךְ, יִתְבָּרַךְ שִׁמְךָ בְּפִי כָּל חַי תָּמִיד לְעוֹלָם וָעֶד. כַּכָּתוּב, וְאָכַלְתָּ וְשָׂבָעְתָּ, וּבֵרַכְתָּ אֶת יהוה אֱלֹהֶיךָ, עַל הָאָרֶץ הַטֹּבָה אֲשֶׁר נָתַן לָךְ.[1] בָּרוּךְ אַתָּה יהוה, עַל הָאָרֶץ וְעַל הַמָּזוֹן. (אָמֵן. — Others)

רַחֵם יהוה אֱלֹהֵינוּ עַל יִשְׂרָאֵל עַמֶּךָ, וְעַל יְרוּשָׁלַיִם עִירֶךָ, וְעַל צִיּוֹן מִשְׁכַּן כְּבוֹדֶךָ, וְעַל מַלְכוּת בֵּית דָּוִד מְשִׁיחֶךָ, וְעַל הַבַּיִת הַגָּדוֹל וְהַקָּדוֹשׁ שֶׁנִּקְרָא שִׁמְךָ עָלָיו. אֱלֹהֵינוּ אָבִינוּ רְעֵנוּ זוֹנֵנוּ פַּרְנְסֵנוּ וְכַלְכְּלֵנוּ וְהַרְוִיחֵנוּ, וְהַרְוַח לָנוּ יהוה אֱלֹהֵינוּ מְהֵרָה מִכָּל צָרוֹתֵינוּ. וְנָא אַל תַּצְרִיכֵנוּ יהוה אֱלֹהֵינוּ, לֹא לִידֵי מַתְּנַת בָּשָׂר וָדָם, וְלֹא לִידֵי הַלְוָאָתָם, כִּי אִם לְיָדְךָ הַמְּלֵאָה הַפְּתוּחָה הַקְּדוֹשָׁה וְהָרְחָבָה, שֶׁלֹּא נֵבוֹשׁ וְלֹא נִכָּלֵם לְעוֹלָם וָעֶד.

---

are needed in order to maintain one's health. Moses, however, did not make mention of the remaining fruits as they are prone to erosion (*Commentary on the Torah*).

Moses spoke of only those fruits that are vital and basic elements of sustenance. By intentionally overlooking the other fruits of the land, Moses taught the Jewish nation about the intended purpose of food: to sustain the body and to strengthen it, in order that an individual should be able to maximize his spiritual potential and carry out his mission in this world. Should one derive pleasure from the act of food consumption? Certainly. Yet it is of utmost importance to realize that one should not be eating simply for the sake of eating alone, for this leads to gluttony. Gluttony is a symptom of an empty and morally disintegrated society.

This is the first step toward a life full of happiness that Moses imparted to the Jewish nation.

As far as the actual land was concerned, upon describing it Moses men-

Ｆor it all, Hashem, our God, we thank You and bless
You. May Your Name be blessed by the mouths of
all who live constantly, forever, as it is written, "You
will eat and you will be satisfied, and bless Hashem,
your God, for the good land which He has given
you."[1] Blessed are You, Hashem, for the land and the
food.

Ｈave mercy, Hashem, our God, on Israel, Your
people, and on Jerusalem, Your city, and on Zion,
the abode of Your glory, and on the monarchy of the
House of David, Your anointed, and on the great and
holy House upon which Your name is called. Our
God, our Father, tend us, nourish us, support us,
sustain us, and rescue us. And rescue us, Hashem, our
God, speedily from all of our troubles. Please,
Hashem, our God, do not put us in need of gifts or
loans from men. May we need only Your full, open,
holy, and ample hand, so that we may never be
ashamed or embarrassed.

---

(1) *Devarim* 8:10.

---

tioned its streams and underground waters, yet noticeably excluded any
mention of its rivers. The commentators explain that Moses did this in order
to impart to the nation another of Judaism's fundamental lessons. The Jewish
people were to take to heart that the success of any crop, and all of the
world's produce, is dependent solely upon the rains from Heaven, which fill
up the streams and underground waters. In other words, it is only Divine
mercy that causes the successful growth of any produce that one looks to for
either sustenance or livelihood. This feeling of dependence goes a long way
toward preventing one from becoming haughty and full of pride. It shatters
the illusion of being a "self-made man," having to rely on nothing more than
one's own intellect and abilities. There is not a society in existence that could
not benefit from a healthy injection of humility, the lofty character trait that
can better human relations and sweeten the life of the one who possesses it.

It is for this reason that there are no rivers in the land of Israel. There are
no rivers like the Nile River, whose waters are able to irrigate all the fields in
the land. There are no rivers capable of misleading an individual to mistak-

On the Sabbath add the following paragraph.

רְצֵה וְהַחֲלִיצֵנוּ יהוה אֱלֹהֵינוּ בְּמִצְוֹתֶיךָ, וּבְמִצְוַת יוֹם הַשְּׁבִיעִי הַשַּׁבָּת הַגָּדוֹל וְהַקָּדוֹשׁ הַזֶּה, כִּי יוֹם זֶה גָּדוֹל וְקָדוֹשׁ הוּא לְפָנֶיךָ, לִשְׁבָּת בּוֹ וְלָנוּחַ בּוֹ בְּאַהֲבָה כְּמִצְוַת רְצוֹנֶךָ, וּבִרְצוֹנְךָ הָנִיחַ לָנוּ יהוה אֱלֹהֵינוּ, שֶׁלֹּא תְהֵא צָרָה וְיָגוֹן וַאֲנָחָה בְּיוֹם מְנוּחָתֵנוּ, וְהַרְאֵנוּ יהוה אֱלֹהֵינוּ בְּנֶחָמַת צִיּוֹן עִירֶךָ, וּבְבִנְיַן יְרוּשָׁלַיִם עִיר קָדְשֶׁךָ, כִּי אַתָּה הוּא בַּעַל הַיְשׁוּעוֹת וּבַעַל הַנֶּחָמוֹת.

אֱלֹהֵינוּ וֵאלֹהֵי אֲבוֹתֵינוּ, יַעֲלֶה, וְיָבֹא, וְיַגִּיעַ, וְיֵרָאֶה, וְיֵרָצֶה, וְיִשָּׁמַע, וְיִפָּקֵד, וְיִזָּכֵר זִכְרוֹנֵנוּ וּפִקְדוֹנֵנוּ, וְזִכְרוֹן אֲבוֹתֵינוּ, וְזִכְרוֹן מָשִׁיחַ בֶּן דָּוִד עַבְדֶּךָ, וְזִכְרוֹן יְרוּשָׁלַיִם עִיר קָדְשֶׁךָ, וְזִכְרוֹן כָּל עַמְּךָ בֵּית יִשְׂרָאֵל לְפָנֶיךָ, לִפְלֵיטָה לְטוֹבָה לְחֵן וּלְחֶסֶד וּלְרַחֲמִים, לְחַיִּים וּלְשָׁלוֹם בְּיוֹם חַג הַמַּצוֹת הַזֶּה. זָכְרֵנוּ יהוה אֱלֹהֵינוּ בּוֹ לְטוֹבָה, וּפָקְדֵנוּ בוֹ לִבְרָכָה, וְהוֹשִׁיעֵנוּ בוֹ לְחַיִּים. וּבִדְבַר יְשׁוּעָה וְרַחֲמִים, חוּס וְחָנֵּנוּ וְרַחֵם עָלֵינוּ וְהוֹשִׁיעֵנוּ, כִּי אֵלֶיךָ עֵינֵינוּ, כִּי אֵל חַנּוּן וְרַחוּם אָתָּה.[1]

---

enly believe that it is possible to subsist in the universe without assistance from Hashem. In the case of the Nile, the Egyptians were so misguided that they actually believed the Nile to be God! The Nile of yesteryear is the dollar, oil, might, nation, and fun of today.

This is also the underlying principle in regard to the iron and copper in the land.

Iron and copper are necessary in order for man to function at a normal level in this world. It is from these metals that a man forms work tools and home appliances, both so very vital in mankind's day-to-day living. It is for this very reason that Moses specifically mentioned these metals and these

On the Sabbath add the following paragraph.

May it be Your will, HASHEM, our God, that You fortify us through Your mitzvos and through the mitzvah of the seventh day, this great and holy Shabbos. For this day is great and holy before You, to desist from work on it, and to rest on it lovingly, in accordance with the command of Your will. May it be Your will, HASHEM, our God, that You spare us any trouble, anguish, or sorrow on the day of our rest, and that You show us, HASHEM, our God, the consolation of Zion, Your city, and the reconstruction of Jerusalem, Your sacred city, for You are the Master of salvations and the Master of consolations.

Our God and the God of our fathers, may there arise, come, arrive, be seen, be accepted, be heard, be taken note of, and be remembered, a remembrance and recollection of us, and a remembrance of our ancestors, and a remembrance of Mashiach, son of David, Your servant, and a remembrance of Jerusalem, Your holy city, and a remembrance of all of Your people, the House of Israel, before You, for deliverance, for goodness, for grace, for kindness and for mercy, for life, and for peace, on this day of the Festival of Matzos. Remember us on it, HASHEM, our God, for good, take us into account for blessing, and save us so that we may live. And with a word of salvation and mercy, have pity and be gracious to us, and have mercy upon us and save us, for our eyes look to You, for You are a merciful and gracious God.[1]

_____
(1) Cf. *Nechemiah* 9:31.

---

metals alone. Silver and gold, explains the Ramban, are not basic necessities. Rather, they fall into the category of those items which can be termed luxuries. Silver vessels, gold, and expensive jewels, serve only to inflate an individual's ego, and one could hardly make a case that they fall into the category of "basic necessities." They contribute to the ever-widening social gap that places the "elite" on a pedestal while the "non-elite" — in other

וּבְנֵה יְרוּשָׁלַיִם עִיר הַקֹּדֶשׁ בִּמְהֵרָה בְיָמֵינוּ. בָּרוּךְ אַתָּה יהוה, בּוֹנֵה (בְּרַחֲמָיו) יְרוּשָׁלָיִם. אָמֵן. (אָמֵן. –Others)

בָּרוּךְ אַתָּה יהוה אֱלֹהֵינוּ מֶלֶךְ הָעוֹלָם, הָאֵל אָבִינוּ מַלְכֵּנוּ אַדִּירֵנוּ בּוֹרְאֵנוּ גּוֹאֲלֵנוּ יוֹצְרֵנוּ קְדוֹשֵׁנוּ קְדוֹשׁ יַעֲקֹב, רוֹעֵנוּ רוֹעֵה יִשְׂרָאֵל, הַמֶּלֶךְ הַטּוֹב וְהַמֵּטִיב לַכֹּל, שֶׁבְּכָל יוֹם וָיוֹם הוּא הֵטִיב, הוּא מֵטִיב, הוּא יֵיטִיב לָנוּ. הוּא גְמָלָנוּ הוּא גוֹמְלֵנוּ הוּא יִגְמְלֵנוּ לָעַד, לְחֵן וּלְחֶסֶד וּלְרַחֲמִים וּלְרֶוַח הַצָּלָה וְהַצְלָחָה, בְּרָכָה וִישׁוּעָה נֶחָמָה פַּרְנָסָה וְכַלְכָּלָה וְרַחֲמִים וְחַיִּים וְשָׁלוֹם וְכָל טוֹב, וּמִכָּל טוּב לְעוֹלָם אַל יְחַסְּרֵנוּ. (אָמֵן. –Others)

הָרַחֲמָן הוּא יִמְלוֹךְ עָלֵינוּ לְעוֹלָם וָעֶד. הָרַחֲמָן הוּא יִתְבָּרַךְ בַּשָּׁמַיִם וּבָאָרֶץ. הָרַחֲמָן הוּא יִשְׁתַּבַּח לְדוֹר דּוֹרִים, וְיִתְפָּאַר בָּנוּ לָעַד וּלְנֵצַח נְצָחִים, וְיִתְהַדַּר בָּנוּ לָעַד וּלְעוֹלְמֵי עוֹלָמִים. הָרַחֲמָן הוּא יְפַרְנְסֵנוּ בְּכָבוֹד. הָרַחֲמָן הוּא יִשְׁבּוֹר עֻלֵּנוּ מֵעַל צַוָּארֵנוּ, וְהוּא יוֹלִיכֵנוּ קוֹמְמִיּוּת לְאַרְצֵנוּ. הָרַחֲמָן הוּא יִשְׁלַח לָנוּ בְּרָכָה מְרֻבָּה

words, those who simply cannot afford to wear such jewelry — are aroused to experience feelings of jealousy that will ultimately prove to be destructive to the overall fabric of society. They also contribute greatly to the fact that man endlessly pursues luxury, all the while sacrificing his inner spirituality, which simply remains undeveloped potential. All in all, they accomplish no more than simply taking an individual one step further away from a life of true happiness and contentment.

Therefore, explain the commentators, one will be unable to find these items in the land of Israel.

And build Jerusalem, the city of sanctity, quickly in our days. Blessed are You, HASHEM, Who builds Jerusalem (in His mercy). Amen.

Blessed are You, HASHEM, our God, King of the Universe, the Powerful One, our Father, our King, our Mighty One, our Creator, our Redeemer, our Shaper, our Holy One, the Holy One of Jacob, our Shepherd, the Shepherd of Israel, the King Who is good and beneficent to all, Who in each and every day has done good, is doing good, and will do good to us. He has bestowed upon us, is bestowing upon us, and will forever bestow upon us grace, kindness, mercy, rescue, deliverance, success, blessing, salvation, consolation, livelihood, sustenance, mercy, life, peace, and all that is good. May He never let us lack for any good thing.

May the Merciful One rule over us forever. May the Merciful One be blessed in the heavens and the earth. May the Merciful One be praised for all generations, and may He take pride in us for eternity, and may we be a source of glory to Him forever and ever. May the Merciful One provide us an honorable livelihood. May the Merciful One break the yoke upon our shoulders and lead us upright to our land. May the Merciful One send us abundant blessing

---

From here, let us move to the topic of the land in which, *"you will lack nothing there"* (*Devarim* 8:9).

This, too, Moses assured the Jewish people. One of the major Torah commentators understood this to mean as follows: It is certainly foreseeable that an individual or family in the land of Israel might come upon difficult times, at times lacking the basic necessities required to live comfortably. It is possible that the land itself may experience periods of hardship, whether they are in the form of drought or famine. Yet despite the difficult periods that the inhabitants of the land may be forced to endure, there will nonetheless prevail a feeling of contentment, satiety, and happiness with all that

בַּבַּיִת הַזֶּה, וְעַל שֻׁלְחָן זֶה שֶׁאָכַלְנוּ עָלָיו. הָרַחֲמָן
הוּא יִשְׁלַח לָנוּ אֶת אֵלִיָּהוּ הַנָּבִיא זָכוּר לַטּוֹב,
וִיבַשֶּׂר לָנוּ בְּשׂוֹרוֹת טוֹבוֹת יְשׁוּעוֹת וְנֶחָמוֹת.

The following text — for a guest to recite at his host's table —
appears in *Shulchan Aruch, Orach Chaim* 201.

יְהִי רָצוֹן שֶׁלֹּא יֵבוֹשׁ וְלֹא יִכָּלֵם בַּעַל הַבַּיִת הַזֶּה,
לֹא בָעוֹלָם הַזֶּה וְלֹא בָעוֹלָם הַבָּא, וְיַצְלִיחַ
בְּכָל נְכָסָיו, וְיִהְיוּ נְכָסָיו מוּצְלָחִים וּקְרוֹבִים לָעִיר,
וְאַל יִשְׁלוֹט שָׂטָן בְּמַעֲשֵׂה יָדָיו, וְאַל יִזְדַּקֵּק לְפָנָיו שׁוּם
דְּבַר חֵטְא וְהִרְהוּר עָוֹן, מֵעַתָּה וְעַד עוֹלָם.

Those eating at their own table recite the following,
adding the appropriate parenthesized phrases:

הָרַחֲמָן הוּא יְבָרֵךְ אוֹתִי (וְאֶת אִשְׁתִּי /בַּעְלִי
וְאֶת זַרְעִי) וְאֶת כָּל אֲשֶׁר לִי.

Guests recite the following.
Children at their parents' table add the words in parentheses.

הָרַחֲמָן הוּא יְבָרֵךְ אֶת (אָבִי מוֹרִי) בַּעַל הַבַּיִת
הַזֶּה, וְאֶת (אִמִּי מוֹרָתִי) בַּעֲלַת הַבַּיִת הַזֶּה,

All guests recite the following:

אוֹתָם וְאֶת בֵּיתָם וְאֶת זַרְעָם וְאֶת כָּל אֲשֶׁר לָהֶם.

Hashem has bestowed upon each individual. Such a feeling can only be
made possible upon the realization that there exists a set of higher and loftier
values worth striving for, above and beyond the desire for any physical,
ephemeral achievement.

How can we safeguard this feeling of contentment and satisfaction, enabling us to be happy with that which we have, without having to obsess
about obtaining every luxury that this world has to offer us? What is the key
to being able to protect ourselves from getting lost in a world of materialism,
giving up any chance we may have at leading a life of tranquility and spiritual
bliss, and exchanging it for an ultimately insignificant material gain?

in this house, and upon this table at which we have eaten. May the Merciful One send us the prophet Elijah, who is remembered for the good, and may he bring us good tidings, salvations, and consolations.

The following text — for a guest to recite at his host's table — appears in *Shulchan Aruch, Orach Chaim* 201.

May it be God's will that this host not be shamed nor humiliated in This World or in the World to Come. May he be successful in all his dealings. May his dealings be successful and conveniently close at hand. May no evil impediment reign over his handiwork, and may no semblance of sin or iniquitous thought attach itself to him from this time and forever.

Those eating at their own table recite the following, adding the appropriate parenthesized phrases:

May the Merciful One bless me,

(my wife/husband and children) and all that is mine.

Guests recite the following.
Children at their parents' table add the words in parentheses.

May the Merciful One bless (my father, my teacher) the master of this house, and (my mother, my teacher) the mistress of this house

All guests recite the following:

them, their house, their family, and all that is theirs,

This is what Moses revealed to us when he taught us the verse that concludes the paragraph of praise for the land of Israel:

"And you shall eat and be satisfied and bless Hashem, your God, for the good land which He gave you" (ibid. v. 10).

The secret, as we have previously explained in our essay on Grace After Meals, lies in the recitation of blessings:

And to the extent with which the pleasantries in the life of the pious one increases, and his pleasure is multiplied, so does his requirement to recite blessings, which is the requirement to recite a blessing on all

All continue here:

אוֹתָנוּ וְאֶת כָּל אֲשֶׁר לָנוּ, כְּמוֹ שֶׁנִּתְבָּרְכוּ אֲבוֹתֵינוּ אַבְרָהָם יִצְחָק וְיַעֲקֹב בַּכֹּל מִכֹּל כֹּל,[1] כֵּן יְבָרֵךְ אוֹתָנוּ כֻּלָּנוּ יַחַד בִּבְרָכָה שְׁלֵמָה, וְנֹאמַר, אָמֵן.

בַּמָּרוֹם יְלַמְּדוּ עֲלֵיהֶם וְעָלֵינוּ זְכוּת, שֶׁתְּהֵא לְמִשְׁמֶרֶת שָׁלוֹם. וְנִשָּׂא בְרָכָה מֵאֵת יהוה, וּצְדָקָה מֵאֱלֹהֵי יִשְׁעֵנוּ, וְנִמְצָא חֵן וְשֵׂכֶל טוֹב בְּעֵינֵי אֱלֹהִים וְאָדָם.[2]

On the Sabbath add the following sentence:

הָרַחֲמָן הוּא יַנְחִילֵנוּ יוֹם שֶׁכֻּלּוֹ שַׁבָּת וּמְנוּחָה לְחַיֵּי הָעוֹלָמִים.

The words in parentheses are added on the two Seder nights
in some communities.

הָרַחֲמָן הוּא יַנְחִילֵנוּ יוֹם שֶׁכֻּלּוֹ טוֹב (יוֹם שֶׁכֻּלּוֹ אָרוּךְ, יוֹם שֶׁצַּדִּיקִים יוֹשְׁבִים וְעַטְרוֹתֵיהֶם בְּרָאשֵׁיהֶם וְנֶהֱנִים מִזִּיו הַשְּׁכִינָה, וִיהִי חֶלְקֵנוּ עִמָּהֶם).

הָרַחֲמָן הוּא יְזַכֵּנוּ לִימוֹת הַמָּשִׁיחַ וּלְחַיֵּי הָעוֹלָם הַבָּא. מִגְדּוֹל יְשׁוּעוֹת מַלְכּוֹ וְעֹשֶׂה חֶסֶד לִמְשִׁיחוֹ לְדָוִד וּלְזַרְעוֹ עַד עוֹלָם.[3] עֹשֶׂה שָׁלוֹם בִּמְרוֹמָיו, הוּא יַעֲשֶׂה שָׁלוֹם עָלֵינוּ וְעַל כָּל יִשְׂרָאֵל. וְאִמְרוּ, אָמֵן.

---

the good he encounters in the world, and all the good which encounters him (Rabbi Yehudah HaLevi, Sefer HaKuzari).

The man who recites blessings is the man who has come to the understanding that he is not entitled to every indulgence the world has to offer. He doesn't complain each time he feels a lack of one of life's luxuries. Rather,

All continue here:

ours and all that is ours — just as our forefathers Abraham, Isaac, and Jacob were blessed in everything, from everything, with blessing.[1] So may He bless us all together with a perfect blessing, and let us say: Amen.

M ay there be a favorable report of them and of us in heaven that should preserve peace. May we receive blessing from HASHEM, and charity from the God of our salvation, and may we find favor and good regard in the eyes of God and man.[2]

On the Sabbath add the following sentence:
May the Merciful One cause us to inherit the day which will be completely a Sabbath and rest day for eternal life.

The words in parentheses are added on the two Seder nights in some communities.

M ay the Merciful One grant us a day which is entirely good (that everlasting day, the day when the righteous sit with crowns on their heads, enjoying the reflection of God's majesty — and may our portion be with them)!

M ay the Merciful One make us worthy to attain the days of Mashiach and the life of the World to Come. He is a tower of salvation to His king, and does kindness to His anointed, to David and his offspring forever.[3] May He Who makes peace in His heights make peace over us and over all of Israel. Now respond: Amen.

(1) Cf. *Bereishis* 24:1; 27:33; 33:11. (2) Cf. *Mishlei* 3:4. (3) *Tehillim* 18:51.

he is grateful for that which he has, and is satisfied with his lot. The array of blessings that comprise our service of Hashem enables us to constantly absorb feelings of thankfulness and joy over Hashem's benevolence, and guarantees that we will continue to feel content and gratified all the days of our lives.

יְראוּ אֶת יהוה קְדֹשָׁיו, כִּי אֵין מַחְסוֹר לִירֵאָיו. כְּפִירִים רָשׁוּ וְרָעֵבוּ, וְדֹרְשֵׁי יהוה לֹא יַחְסְרוּ כָל טוֹב.[1] הוֹדוּ לַיהוה כִּי טוֹב, כִּי לְעוֹלָם חַסְדּוֹ.[2] פּוֹתֵחַ אֶת יָדֶךָ, וּמַשְׂבִּיעַ לְכָל חַי רָצוֹן.[3] בָּרוּךְ הַגֶּבֶר אֲשֶׁר יִבְטַח בַּיהוה, וְהָיָה יהוה מִבְטַחוֹ.[4] נַעַר הָיִיתִי גַּם זָקַנְתִּי, וְלֹא רָאִיתִי צַדִּיק נֶעֱזָב, וְזַרְעוֹ מְבַקֶּשׁ לָחֶם.[5] יהוה עֹז לְעַמּוֹ יִתֵּן, יהוה יְבָרֵךְ אֶת עַמּוֹ בַשָּׁלוֹם.[6]

Upon completion of *Bircas HaMazon* the blessing over wine is recited and the third cup is drunk while one reclines on the left side. It is preferable to drink the entire cup, but at the very least, most of the cup should be drained.

Some recite the following before the third cup:

הִנְנִי מוּכָן וּמְזוּמָּן לְקַיֵּם מִצְוַת כּוֹס שְׁלִישִׁי שֶׁל אַרְבַּע כּוֹסוֹת. לְשֵׁם יִחוּד קֻדְשָׁא בְּרִיךְ הוּא וּשְׁכִינְתֵּיהּ, עַל יְדֵי הַהוּא טָמִיר וְנֶעְלָם, בְּשֵׁם כָּל יִשְׂרָאֵל. וִיהִי נֹעַם אֲדֹנָי אֱלֹהֵינוּ עָלֵינוּ, וּמַעֲשֵׂה יָדֵינוּ כּוֹנְנָה עָלֵינוּ, וּמַעֲשֵׂה יָדֵינוּ כּוֹנְנֵהוּ:

בָּרוּךְ אַתָּה יהוה אֱלֹהֵינוּ מֶלֶךְ הָעוֹלָם, בּוֹרֵא פְּרִי הַגָּפֶן.

The fourth cup is poured. According to most customs, the Cup of Elijah is poured at this point, after which the door is opened in accordance with the verse, "It is a guarded night." Then the following paragraph is recited.

שְׁפֹךְ חֲמָתְךָ אֶל הַגּוֹיִם אֲשֶׁר לֹא יְדָעוּךָ וְעַל מַמְלָכוֹת אֲשֶׁר בְּשִׁמְךָ לֹא קָרָאוּ.

שְׁפֹךְ חֲמָתְךָ אֶל הַגּוֹיִם — Pour Your wrath upon the nations

---

⋖§ Pour Your Wrath

The great call to "Pour your wrath upon the nations" is not a request for Hashem to annihilate all the nations of the world. Rather, it is an entreaty to Hashem that he destroys the tyrants of our present day, those merciless individuals who are responsible for the spreading of anti-Semitism and who endorse the cruel treatment of the

Fear HASHEM, holy ones of His! For those who fear Him lack nothing.[1] Young lions may be poor and hungry, but those who seek HASHEM will not be in need of any good thing. Give thanks to HASHEM for He is good, for His kindness is eternal.[2] You open Your hand and satisfy the wants of every living thing.[3] Blessed is the man who trusts HASHEM; then HASHEM will be his security.[4] I was a youth and also have aged, and I have not seen a righteous man forsaken with his children begging for bread.[5] HASHEM will grant strength to His people. HASHEM will bless His people with peace.[6]

Upon completion of *Bircas HaMazon* the blessing over wine is recited and the third cup is drunk while one reclines on the left side. It is preferable to drink the entire cup, but at the very least, most of the cup should be drained.

Some recite the following before the third cup:

Behold, I am prepared and ready to fulfill the mitzvah of the third of the Four Cups. For the sake of the unification of the Holy One, Blessed is He, and His presence, through Him Who is hidden and inscrutable — [I pray] in the name of all Israel. May the pleasantness of my Lord, our God, be upon us — may He establish our handiwork for us; our handiwork may He establish.

Blessed are You, HASHEM, our God, King of the Universe, Who creates the fruit of the vine.

The fourth cup is poured. According to most customs, the Cup of Elijah is poured at this point, after which the door is opened in accordance with the verse, "It is a guarded night." Then the following paragraph is recited.

Pour Your wrath upon the nations who do not know You and upon the kingdoms who call not upon Your

---

(1) *Tehillim* 34:10-11. (2) 136:1 et al. (3) 145:16.
(4) *Yirmiyah* 17:7. (5) *Tehillim* 37:25. (6) 29:11.

Jewish nation. We therefore open wide the doors to our homes — homes that find themselves situated in a state of exile — and proclaim for all the nations to hear . . .

The prayer is one that evokes extreme curiosity among many of our people. The less knowledgeable among us might even feel that such a paragraph is slightly offensive. How did such a declaration find its way into

כִּי אָכַל אֶת יַעֲקֹב וְאֶת נָוֵהוּ הֵשַׁמּוּ.[1] שְׁפֹךְ עֲלֵיהֶם
זַעְמֶךָ וַחֲרוֹן אַפְּךָ יַשִּׂיגֵם.[2] תִּרְדֹּף בְּאַף וְתַשְׁמִידֵם
מִתַּחַת שְׁמֵי יהוה.[3]

הלל

The door is closed and the recitation of the Haggadah is continued.

לֹא לָנוּ יהוה לֹא לָנוּ, כִּי לְשִׁמְךָ תֵּן כָּבוֹד, עַל
חַסְדְּךָ עַל אֲמִתֶּךָ. לָמָּה יֹאמְרוּ הַגּוֹיִם,
אַיֵּה נָא אֱלֹהֵיהֶם. וֵאלֹהֵינוּ בַשָּׁמָיִם, כֹּל אֲשֶׁר חָפֵץ
עָשָׂה. עֲצַבֵּיהֶם כֶּסֶף וְזָהָב, מַעֲשֵׂה יְדֵי אָדָם. פֶּה
לָהֶם וְלֹא יְדַבֵּרוּ, עֵינַיִם לָהֶם וְלֹא יִרְאוּ. אָזְנַיִם
לָהֶם וְלֹא יִשְׁמָעוּ, אַף לָהֶם וְלֹא יְרִיחוּן. יְדֵיהֶם
וְלֹא יְמִישׁוּן, רַגְלֵיהֶם וְלֹא יְהַלֵּכוּ, לֹא יֶהְגּוּ
בִּגְרוֹנָם. כְּמוֹהֶם יִהְיוּ עֹשֵׂיהֶם, כֹּל אֲשֶׁר בֹּטֵחַ בָּהֶם.
יִשְׂרָאֵל בְּטַח בַּיהוה, עֶזְרָם וּמָגִנָּם הוּא. בֵּית אַהֲרֹן
בִּטְחוּ בַיהוה, עֶזְרָם וּמָגִנָּם הוּא. יִרְאֵי יהוה בִּטְחוּ
בַיהוה, עֶזְרָם וּמָגִנָּם הוּא.

---

the Haggadah? Additionally, why is it placed specifically at this point in the night's procession, immediately following the meal and right before we resume the recitation of *Hallel?* Many of these questions and feelings result from a general lack of understanding of what we are expressing when we recite it, as well as a complete misunderstanding of the words "Pour Your wrath upon the nations," words that may appear to some as racist and fanatical.

Let us attempt to arrive at a clear understanding of this paragraph, probing its depths to uncover a deeper understanding of its holy message.

It is of utmost importance to be fully aware of the backdrop upon which *Shfoch Chamascha* appears. Immediately preceding *Shfoch Chamascha* was the *Hallel.* We have just poured the fourth cup of wine, as well as "the cup of *Eliyahu HaNavi* — Elijah the Prophet," the fifth cup of

Name, for they have consumed Jacob and laid waste his dwelling.[1] Pour Your fury on them and may Your rage overtake them.[2] Pursue them with anger and obliterate them from under HASHEM's skies.[3]

HALLEL

The door is closed and the recitation of the Haggadah is continued.

Not for us, HASHEM, not for us, but for Your Name give glory, for Your kindness and Your truth. Why should the nations say: Where is their God? Our God in the heavens does whatever He desires. Their idols are silver and gold, the work of man's hands. They have a mouth, but do not speak. They have eyes, but do not see. They have ears, but do not hear. They have a nose, but do not smell. Their hands do not feel. Their feet do not walk. They do not utter sound with their throat. Their makers will be like them, all those who trust in them. Israel, trust in HASHEM — He is their help and shield. House of Aaron, trust in HASHEM — He is their help and shield. Those who fear HASHEM, trust in HASHEM — He is their help and shield.[4]

---

(1) *Tehillim* 79:6-7. (2) 69:25. (3) *Eichah* 3:66. (4) *Tehillim* 115:1-11.

---

wine that we pour during this Passover Seder. Following this, one of the family members makes his way to the front door, and opens it.

Each and every one of these actions moves us a step closer toward gaining an insight into *Shfoch Chamascha*. The time has arrived to pour the fourth cup of wine. As we are well aware, the four cups of wine drunk on the Seder night are full of deep meaning and significance. While the cups of wine are representative of redemption and freedom as far as the Jewish people are concerned, they symbolize something altogether different for the nations that have sought to destroy us from the dawn of time until our present day. For them, the cups of wine are not four cups of freedom but rather four cups of venom that hint at their eventual destruction. These four cups parallel the

יהוה זָכְרָנוּ יְבָרֵךְ, יְבָרֵךְ אֶת בֵּית יִשְׂרָאֵל, יְבָרֵךְ
אֶת בֵּית אַהֲרֹן. יְבָרֵךְ יִרְאֵי יהוה, הַקְּטַנִּים
עִם הַגְּדֹלִים. יֹסֵף יהוה עֲלֵיכֶם, עֲלֵיכֶם וְעַל בְּנֵיכֶם.
בְּרוּכִים אַתֶּם לַיהוה, עֹשֵׂה שָׁמַיִם וָאָרֶץ. הַשָּׁמַיִם
שָׁמַיִם לַיהוה, וְהָאָרֶץ נָתַן לִבְנֵי אָדָם. לֹא הַמֵּתִים
יְהַלְלוּ יָהּ, וְלֹא כָּל יֹרְדֵי דוּמָה. וַאֲנַחְנוּ נְבָרֵךְ יָהּ,
מֵעַתָּה וְעַד עוֹלָם, הַלְלוּיָהּ.[1]

---

four wicked empires that have dominated the world, each one reigning in a
different time period, and invariably responsible for endless persecution and
destruction of mass segments of the Jewish people. These are the four
empires:

1) Bavel (Babylon) — Responsible for the destruction of the first Holy
Temple.

2) Paras (Persia) — This is the Paras of Achashveirosh and Haman,
enactors of decrees that they had hoped would lead to the destruction of the
Jewish people.

3) Yavan (Greece) — Their Hellenistic culture was a major threat to the
Jewish people; its aestheticism and intellectualism were lures towards
assimilation.

4) Edom (Rome) — The Romans destroyed the second Holy Temple,
commencing *Galus Edom,* the long and painful exile in which we languish up
until our present day.

The four cups, besides stirring within us feelings of elation at having been
freed from Egyptian bondage, also serve as a reminder of our present state
of *galus,* and at the same time, embody our hopes for eventual redemption
as well as the enactment of justice upon our enemies.

The fourth cup that we drink parallels the *Galus Edom,* the *galus* that has
spared no effort at attempting to lure the Jewish nation into the clutches of
its Western culture. The pouring of this fourth cup of wine takes us back to
a different time. It reminds us of our brethren whose journeys through *galus*
led them to the European lands and the countries dominated by Islam. We
recall the tragedies that befell them, and can picture the facial expressions
that exhibited unmistakable anti-Semitism — the twisted and distorted
visages of our vile persecutors. We hear the moans that escaped the mouths
of suffering Jews, and the accusations and blood libels that were leveled

HASHEM Who has remembered, He will bless. He will bless the House of Israel. He will bless the House of Aaron. He will bless those who fear HASHEM, the small with the great. HASHEM will add upon you, upon you and your children. You are blessed of HASHEM, Maker of the heavens and the earth. The heavens are the heavens of HASHEM, but the earth He has given to man. The dead will not praise HASHEM, nor all those who descend into silence. But we will praise HASHEM forever. Halleluyah![1]

---

(1) *Tehillim* 115:12-18.

---

against them time and time again. It was during this time period that *Shfoch Chamascha* was composed and inserted into the Seder procession.

While the pouring of the fourth cup of wine evokes feelings and memories of persecution, it also awakens our hopes for imminent redemption, and our belief in the ultimate arrival of Mashiach. The arrival of Mashiach will herald the birth of the final redemption for the nation of Israel, a redemption whose harbinger — according to classical sources — will be none other than Elijah himself. It is therefore at this time that we pour an additional cup of wine in his honor. In addition, it is also the appropriate time to recite the second half of *Hallel.* We joyously sang the first half of *Hallel* before we partook of the festive meal, reciting the paragraphs *"Hallelukah hallelu avdei Hashem"* and *"B'tzais Yisrael miMitzraim."* These were paragraphs that were full of expressions of praise and adulation, thanking Hashem for redeeming us from Egypt. The second half of *Hallel,* however, deals not with our redemption from Egypt, but rather with the redemption that awaits us in the future. It deals with the major changes that will occur on the international scene in order for the redemption to spring forth, as well as the great spiritual revolution that will follow, leading to the ultimate rectification of all mankind.

It was at this very moment in course of the Seder that the hearts of our ancestors in Europe were bombarded by the many memories and feelings that the Pesach Seder can inspire. Heartened by the hope of future redemption and strengthened by unbreakable faith, the leader of the Seder decides to send his gentile neighbor — that same gentile who may presently be his daily oppressor — a message he will not soon forget. He is going to let him know that he in fact does not fear him in the least, and that deep within the chambers of his heart pumps the blood of a free man. He sends one of the

אָהַבְתִּי, כִּי יִשְׁמַע יהוה אֶת קוֹלִי, תַּחֲנוּנָי. כִּי
הִטָּה אָזְנוֹ לִי, וּבְיָמַי אֶקְרָא. אֲפָפוּנִי
חֶבְלֵי מָוֶת, וּמְצָרֵי שְׁאוֹל מְצָאוּנִי, צָרָה וְיָגוֹן
אֶמְצָא. וּבְשֵׁם יהוה אֶקְרָא, אָנָּה יהוה מַלְּטָה
נַפְשִׁי. חַנּוּן יהוה וְצַדִּיק, וֵאלֹהֵינוּ מְרַחֵם. שֹׁמֵר
פְּתָאִים יהוה, דַּלּוֹתִי וְלִי יְהוֹשִׁיעַ. שׁוּבִי נַפְשִׁי
לִמְנוּחָיְכִי, כִּי יהוה גָּמַל עָלָיְכִי. כִּי חִלַּצְתָּ נַפְשִׁי
מִמָּוֶת, אֶת עֵינִי מִן דִּמְעָה, אֶת רַגְלִי מִדֶּחִי.
אֶתְהַלֵּךְ לִפְנֵי יהוה, בְּאַרְצוֹת הַחַיִּים. הֶאֱמַנְתִּי כִּי
אֲדַבֵּר, אֲנִי עָנִיתִי מְאֹד. אֲנִי אָמַרְתִּי בְחָפְזִי, כָּל
הָאָדָם כֹּזֵב.

מָה אָשִׁיב לַיהוה, כָּל תַּגְמוּלוֹהִי עָלָי. כּוֹס
יְשׁוּעוֹת אֶשָּׂא, וּבְשֵׁם יהוה אֶקְרָא.
נְדָרַי לַיהוה אֲשַׁלֵּם, נֶגְדָה נָּא לְכָל עַמּוֹ. יָקָר בְּעֵינֵי
יהוה, הַמָּוְתָה לַחֲסִידָיו. אָנָּה יהוה כִּי אֲנִי עַבְדֶּךָ,
אֲנִי עַבְדְּךָ, בֶּן אֲמָתֶךָ, פִּתַּחְתָּ לְמוֹסֵרָי. לְךָ אֶזְבַּח
זֶבַח תּוֹדָה, וּבְשֵׁם יהוה אֶקְרָא. נְדָרַי לַיהוה
אֲשַׁלֵּם, נֶגְדָה נָּא לְכָל עַמּוֹ. בְּחַצְרוֹת בֵּית יהוה,
בְּתוֹכֵכִי יְרוּשָׁלָיִם הַלְלוּיָהּ.¹

---

family members to open wide the front door of the house, and with all the
pent-up fury, frustration, and pain — immersed in a pool of hope for a
glorious future — shouts out the plea, "Shfoch chamascha . . ."

If the gentile hears the proclamation that exits our mouths, and is aware
of the burning anger that we are sending his way, he is immediately awed by
the greatness of the Jewish spirit. Despite our pain, we raise our voices and
announce without any fear, our hopes to one day see the end of the reign of
tyrants, as we anticipate our redemption from beneath their cruel dominion.
Yet, we, the suppressed Jewish nation, despite all that we have endured,

I love Him, because HASHEM hears my voice, my supplications. For He has inclined His ear to me. In all my days I will call upon Him. Pangs of death have encompassed me, and the distress of the pit has found me. I meet with trouble and sorrow, and I call on the Name of HASHEM: Please, HASHEM, rescue my soul! Gracious is HASHEM, and righteous. Our God has mercy. HASHEM guards the simple. I was poor, and He saved me. Return, my soul, to your rest, for HASHEM has been bountiful to you. You have delivered my soul from death, my eye from tears, my foot from stumbling. I will walk before HASHEM in the lands of life. I believe that I will say: I was greatly afflicted. I said in my despondency: All men lie.

How can I repay HASHEM for all His bounties to me? I will lift up a cup of salvations, and I will call out the Name of HASHEM. My vows to HASHEM I will pay in the presence of all His people. Precious in the eyes of HASHEM is death for His pious ones. I beseech You, HASHEM, for I am Your slave. I am Your slave, the son of Your slavewoman. You have loosened my fetters. I will sacrifice to You an offering of thanksgiving, and I will call out the Name of HASHEM. I will pay my vows to HASHEM in the presence of all His people. In the courtyards of the House of HASHEM, in Your midst, Jerusalem. Halleluyah.[1]

---

(1) *Tehillim* 116.

---

do not request that Hashem annihilate all the gentiles of the world, wherever they may be. Rather, we entreat Hashem to destroy those who have laid and continue to lay the foundations of injustice and cruelty, as well as those who mercilessly attempt to destroy the Children of Israel. It is *those* individuals whose end we wish to draw near — specific individuals, yet not their entire race. Even at this moment we preserve the purity and sanctity of our prayers.

הַלְלוּ אֶת יהוה, כָּל גּוֹיִם, שַׁבְּחוּהוּ כָּל הָאֻמִּים. כִּי גָבַר עָלֵינוּ חַסְדּוֹ, וֶאֱמֶת יהוה לְעוֹלָם, הַלְלוּיָה.[1]

הוֹדוּ לַיהוה כִּי טוֹב,   כִּי לְעוֹלָם חַסְדּוֹ.
יֹאמַר נָא יִשְׂרָאֵל,   כִּי לְעוֹלָם חַסְדּוֹ.
יֹאמְרוּ נָא בֵית אַהֲרֹן,   כִּי לְעוֹלָם חַסְדּוֹ.
יֹאמְרוּ נָא יִרְאֵי יהוה,   כִּי לְעוֹלָם חַסְדּוֹ.

מִן הַמֵּצַר קָרָאתִי יָּה, עָנָנִי בַמֶּרְחָב יָהּ. יהוה לִי לֹא אִירָא, מַה יַּעֲשֶׂה לִי אָדָם. יהוה לִי בְּעֹזְרָי, וַאֲנִי אֶרְאֶה בְשֹׂנְאָי. טוֹב לַחֲסוֹת בַּיהוה, מִבְּטֹחַ בָּאָדָם. טוֹב לַחֲסוֹת בַּיהוה, מִבְּטֹחַ בִּנְדִיבִים. כָּל גּוֹיִם סְבָבוּנִי, בְּשֵׁם יהוה כִּי אֲמִילַם. סַבּוּנִי גַם סְבָבוּנִי, בְּשֵׁם יהוה כִּי אֲמִילַם. סַבּוּנִי כִדְבֹרִים דֹּעֲכוּ כְּאֵשׁ קוֹצִים, בְּשֵׁם יהוה כִּי אֲמִילַם. דָּחֹה דְחִיתַנִי לִנְפֹּל, וַיהוה עֲזָרָנִי. עָזִּי וְזִמְרָת יָהּ, וַיְהִי לִי לִישׁוּעָה. קוֹל רִנָּה וִישׁוּעָה, בְּאָהֳלֵי צַדִּיקִים, יְמִין יהוה עֹשָׂה חָיִל. יְמִין יהוה רוֹמֵמָה,

---

This, in fact, is the essence of the *Shfoch Chamascha,* which we recite on Seder night. If one examines its words closely, he will undoubtedly recognize how this prayer expresses the lofty standard of behavior and ethics of the Jewish nation, and its ability to transcend the natural feelings of hatred towards one's persecutors and oppressors.

In two verses of *Tanach* does the expression "*Shfoch chamascha*" appear. One verse is found in *Yirmiyah* (10:25), the other in *Tehillim* (79:6). Yet, we are able to detect a slight difference between the words used by Yirmiyah and those of the Psalmist. In *Tehillim* the verse states, "*Shfoch chamascha el ha'goim . . .* ," while in *Yirmiyah* the *Navi* exclaims, "*Shfoch chamascha al ha'goim . . .* " While the discrepancy between the two verses seems quite

Praise Hashem, all nations! Laud Him, all states. For His love for us is strong, and the truth of Hashem is eternal. Halleluyah![1]

Give thanks to Hashem for He is good

— for His kindness is eternal.

Let Israel say: For His kindness is eternal.

Let the House of Aaron say:

For His kindness is eternal.

Let those who fear Hashem say:

For His kindness is eternal.

Out of distress I called Yah. He responded to me expansively — Yah. Hashem is for me. I shall not fear. What can man do to me? Hashem is for me through my helpers, and I shall see the downfall of my enemies. It is better to take shelter in Hashem than to trust in man. It is better to take shelter in Hashem than to trust in those who are generous. All nations have beset me. In the Name of Hashem I cut them down. They have surrounded me and beset me. In the Name of Hashem I cut them down. They have surrounded me like bees. They were extinguished like a fire of thorns — in the Name of Hashem I cut them down. You have pushed at me and toppled me, but Hashem has assisted me. The strength and vengeance of Yah has been my salvation. There is a voice of song and salvation in the tents of the righteous. The right hand of Hashem does valiantly. The right hand of Hashem is raised high.

---

(1) *Tehillim* 117.

---

minute, it is, in fact, one of fundamental significance. The word "*el*," as opposed to the word "*al*," connotes not to place something upon something else, but rather to bring something *to* something else. In other words, David HaMelech is beseeching Hashem to "Bring Your anger to the nations of the world" — but do not pour it *upon* them. "Make aware those of the

יְמִין יהוה עֹשָׂה חָיִל. לֹא אָמוּת כִּי אֶחְיֶה, וַאֲסַפֵּר
מַעֲשֵׂי יָהּ. יַסֹּר יִסְּרַנִּי יָּהּ, וְלַמָּוֶת לֹא נְתָנָנִי. פִּתְחוּ
לִי שַׁעֲרֵי צֶדֶק, אָבֹא בָם אוֹדֶה יָהּ. זֶה הַשַּׁעַר
לַיהוה, צַדִּיקִים יָבֹאוּ בוֹ. אוֹדְךָ כִּי עֲנִיתָנִי, וַתְּהִי
לִי לִישׁוּעָה. אוֹדְךָ כִּי עֲנִיתָנִי, וַתְּהִי לִי לִישׁוּעָה.
אֶבֶן מָאֲסוּ הַבּוֹנִים, הָיְתָה לְרֹאשׁ פִּנָּה. אֶבֶן מָאֲסוּ
הַבּוֹנִים, הָיְתָה לְרֹאשׁ פִּנָּה. מֵאֵת יהוה הָיְתָה
זֹּאת, הִיא נִפְלָאת בְּעֵינֵינוּ. מֵאֵת יהוה הָיְתָה
זֹּאת, הִיא נִפְלָאת בְּעֵינֵינוּ. זֶה הַיּוֹם עָשָׂה יהוה,
נָגִילָה וְנִשְׂמְחָה בוֹ. זֶה הַיּוֹם עָשָׂה יהוה, נָגִילָה
וְנִשְׂמְחָה בוֹ.

אָנָּא יהוה הוֹשִׁיעָה נָּא.
אָנָּא יהוה הוֹשִׁיעָה נָּא.
אָנָּא יהוה הַצְלִיחָה נָּא.
אָנָּא יהוה הַצְלִיחָה נָּא.

בָּרוּךְ הַבָּא בְּשֵׁם יהוה, בֵּרַכְנוּכֶם מִבֵּית יהוה.
בָּרוּךְ הַבָּא בְּשֵׁם יהוה, בֵּרַכְנוּכֶם מִבֵּית
יהוה. אֵל יהוה וַיָּאֶר לָנוּ, אִסְרוּ חַג בַּעֲבֹתִים, עַד
קַרְנוֹת הַמִּזְבֵּחַ. אֵל יהוה וַיָּאֶר לָנוּ, אִסְרוּ חַג

---

nations of the world who do not know You and those who were unaware of
Your hand guiding them when You used them as a tool with which to afflict
the Jewish people. Let their tyrannical kingdoms be obliterated in Your fury''
(R' Samson Raphael Hirsch, *Commentary on Tehillim*). Interestingly enough,
the author of the Haggadah chose the verse from *Tehillim* to serve as the
prayer that we would recite at this point in the Seder procession. This was
done in order to reiterate the fact that we are not requesting the mass-de-
struction of the entire gentile world, but rather the elimination of a specific
segment of gentiles, those tyrants who profess wicked ideals and encourage

The right hand of HASHEM does valiantly. I shall not die, for I shall live and tell of the deeds of YAH. YAH has chastised me, but He has not let me die. Open for me the gates of righteousness; I will enter them; I will thank YAH. This is the gate of HASHEM, the righteous will enter it. I thank You, for You have answered me and become my salvation. I thank You, for You have answered me and become my salvation. The stone the builders despised has become the cornerstone. The stone the builders despised has become the cornerstone. This emanated from HASHEM; it is wondrous in our eyes. This emanated from HASHEM; it is wondrous in our eyes. This is the day HASHEM made; let us rejoice and be glad on it. This is the day HASHEM made; let us rejoice and be glad on it.

We beseech You, HASHEM, save us!
   We beseech You, HASHEM, save us!
We beseech You, HASHEM, grant us success!
   We beseech You, HASHEM, grant us success!

Blessed is he who comes in the Name of HASHEM; we bless you from the House of HASHEM. Blessed is he who comes in the Name of HASHEM; we bless you from the House of HASHEM. HASHEM is God and He will give us light. Bind the festival sacrifice with cords, leading it up to the corners of the Altar. HASHEM is God and He will give us light. Bind the festival

---

the persecution of innocent Jews. We beseech Hashem to carry out His justice in such a fashion that these tyrants should arrive at the realization that the ideals and principles upon which their lives were based were perverse and incorrect.

A classic example of the above idea, one that we witnessed in our days, is the fall of Communism. We were witnesses to the crumbling of the once mighty Communist regime, a collapse which amazingly occurred with

בַּעֲבֹתִים, עַד קַרְנוֹת הַמִּזְבֵּחַ. אֵלִי אַתָּה וְאוֹדֶךָּ,
אֱלֹהַי אֲרוֹמְמֶךָּ. אֵלִי אַתָּה וְאוֹדֶךָּ, אֱלֹהַי אֲרוֹמְמֶךָּ.
הוֹדוּ לַיהוה כִּי טוֹב, כִּי לְעוֹלָם חַסְדּוֹ. הוֹדוּ לַיהוה
כִּי טוֹב, כִּי לְעוֹלָם חַסְדּוֹ.[1]

יְהַלְלוּךָ יהוה אֱלֹהֵינוּ כָּל מַעֲשֶׂיךָ, וַחֲסִידֶיךָ
צַדִּיקִים עוֹשֵׂי רְצוֹנֶךָ, וְכָל עַמְּךָ בֵּית
יִשְׂרָאֵל בְּרִנָּה יוֹדוּ וִיבָרְכוּ וִישַׁבְּחוּ וִיפָאֲרוּ וִירוֹמְמוּ
וְיַעֲרִיצוּ וְיַקְדִּישׁוּ וְיַמְלִיכוּ אֶת שִׁמְךָ מַלְכֵּנוּ, כִּי לְךָ
טוֹב לְהוֹדוֹת וּלְשִׁמְךָ נָאֶה לְזַמֵּר, כִּי מֵעוֹלָם וְעַד
עוֹלָם אַתָּה אֵל.

הוֹדוּ לַיהוה כִּי טוֹב   כִּי לְעוֹלָם חַסְדּוֹ.
הוֹדוּ לֵאלֹהֵי הָאֱלֹהִים   כִּי לְעוֹלָם חַסְדּוֹ.
הוֹדוּ לַאֲדֹנֵי הָאֲדֹנִים   כִּי לְעוֹלָם חַסְדּוֹ.
לְעֹשֵׂה נִפְלָאוֹת גְּדֹלוֹת לְבַדּוֹ   כִּי לְעוֹלָם חַסְדּוֹ.
לְעֹשֵׂה הַשָּׁמַיִם בִּתְבוּנָה   כִּי לְעוֹלָם חַסְדּוֹ.
לְרֹקַע הָאָרֶץ עַל הַמָּיִם   כִּי לְעוֹלָם חַסְדּוֹ.
לְעֹשֵׂה אוֹרִים גְּדֹלִים   כִּי לְעוֹלָם חַסְדּוֹ.
אֶת הַשֶּׁמֶשׁ לְמֶמְשֶׁלֶת בַּיּוֹם   כִּי לְעוֹלָם חַסְדּוֹ.
אֶת הַיָּרֵחַ וְכוֹכָבִים לְמֶמְשְׁלוֹת בַּלָּיְלָה
כִּי לְעוֹלָם חַסְדּוֹ.

---

almost no bloodshed. Such a fact is truly amazing to behold. Who would
have ever believed that these once-mighty foes of Hashem would disappear
from the world without war or any major struggle? How, exactly, did this
incredible feat occur? The answer is simple in light of that which we have
just stated. The lies upon which Communism was built simply crumbled
beneath it. Its lack of truth became clear and evident in the eyes of its
previous supporters and it simply faded away. This is "el ha'goim," as

sacrifice with cords, leading it up to the corners of the Altar. You are my God and I will thank You. My God — I will exalt You. You are my God and I will thank You. My God — I will exalt You. Give thanks to HASHEM for He is good, for His kindness is eternal. Give thanks to HASHEM for He is good, for His kindness is eternal.[1]

All Your works, HASHEM, our God, will praise You, and Your pious ones, the righteous who perform Your will. And all Your people, the House of Israel, with song, will thank, bless, laud, glorify, exalt, adulate, sanctify, and acknowledge the majesty of Your Name, our King, for to You it is good to give thanks, and to Your Name it is proper to sing, because You are God for eternity. Blessed are You, HASHEM, the King Who is extolled in praises.

Give thanks to HASHEM for He is good
                    — for His kindness is eternal.
Give thanks to the God of gods
                    — for His kindness is eternal.
Give thanks to the Master of masters
                    — for His kindness is eternal.
To Him Who does great wonders alone
                    — for His kindness is eternal.
To Him Who makes the heavens with understanding
                    — for His kindness is eternal.
To Him Who stretches the earth over the water
                    — for His kindness is eternal.
To Him Who makes the great lights
                    — for His kindness is eternal.
The sun for the reign of day
                    — for His kindness is eternal.
The moon and the stars for the reign of night
                    — for His kindness is eternal.

---

(1) *Tehillim* 118.

כִּי לְעוֹלָם חַסְדּוֹ.	לְמַכֵּה מִצְרַיִם בִּבְכוֹרֵיהֶם
כִּי לְעוֹלָם חַסְדּוֹ.	וַיּוֹצֵא יִשְׂרָאֵל מִתּוֹכָם
כִּי לְעוֹלָם חַסְדּוֹ.	בְּיָד חֲזָקָה וּבִזְרוֹעַ נְטוּיָה
כִּי לְעוֹלָם חַסְדּוֹ.	לְגֹזֵר יַם סוּף לִגְזָרִים
כִּי לְעוֹלָם חַסְדּוֹ.	וְהֶעֱבִיר יִשְׂרָאֵל בְּתוֹכוֹ
כִּי לְעוֹלָם חַסְדּוֹ.	וְנִעֵר פַּרְעֹה וְחֵילוֹ בְיַם סוּף
כִּי לְעוֹלָם חַסְדּוֹ.	לְמוֹלִיךְ עַמּוֹ בַּמִּדְבָּר
כִּי לְעוֹלָם חַסְדּוֹ.	לְמַכֵּה מְלָכִים גְּדֹלִים
כִּי לְעוֹלָם חַסְדּוֹ.	וַיַּהֲרֹג מְלָכִים אַדִּירִים
כִּי לְעוֹלָם חַסְדּוֹ.	לְסִיחוֹן מֶלֶךְ הָאֱמֹרִי
כִּי לְעוֹלָם חַסְדּוֹ.	וּלְעוֹג מֶלֶךְ הַבָּשָׁן
כִּי לְעוֹלָם חַסְדּוֹ.	וְנָתַן אַרְצָם לְנַחֲלָה
כִּי לְעוֹלָם חַסְדּוֹ.	נַחֲלָה לְיִשְׂרָאֵל עַבְדּוֹ
כִּי לְעוֹלָם חַסְדּוֹ.	שֶׁבְּשִׁפְלֵנוּ זָכַר לָנוּ
כִּי לְעוֹלָם חַסְדּוֹ.	וַיִּפְרְקֵנוּ מִצָּרֵינוּ
כִּי לְעוֹלָם חַסְדּוֹ.	נֹתֵן לֶחֶם לְכָל בָּשָׂר
כִּי לְעוֹלָם חַסְדּוֹ.[1]	הוֹדוּ לְאֵל הַשָּׁמָיִם

נִשְׁמַת כָּל חַי תְּבָרֵךְ אֶת שִׁמְךָ יהוה אֱלֹהֵינוּ,
וְרוּחַ כָּל בָּשָׂר תְּפָאֵר וּתְרוֹמֵם זִכְרְךָ

---

(1) *Tehillim* 136.

---

opposed to "al ha'goim." It was a realization reached by those who had for so long denied the truth, upholding lies and supporting tyranny. Their realization made way for the end of a tyrannical movement and opened the gates of redemption to the many prisoners of Communist rule. In a similar fashion the redemption will be wrought for the Jewish people at the end of days.

This is the Jew's "Shfoch Chamascha."

To Him Who smote the firstborn of the Egyptians
— for His kindness is eternal.
And brought Israel out from among them
— for His kindness is eternal.
With a strong hand and an outstretched arm
— for His kindness is eternal.
To Him Who divided the Reed Sea into parts
— for His kindness is eternal.
And had Israel pass through it
— for His kindness is eternal.
And tossed Pharaoh and his army into the Reed Sea
— for His kindness is eternal.
To Him Who led His people through the wilderness
— for His kindness is eternal.
To Him Who smote great kings
— for His kindness is eternal.
And killed mighty kings — for His kindness is eternal.
Sichon, king of the Amorites
— for His kindness is eternal.
And Og, king of Bashan — for His kindness is eternal.
And gave their lands as an inheritance
— for His kindness is eternal.
An inheritance to Israel, His servant
— for His kindness is eternal.
Who remembered us in our lowliness
— for His kindness is eternal.
And redeemed us from our enemies
— for His kindness is eternal.
He gives food to all living creatures
— for His kindness is eternal.
Give thanks to God of the heavens
— for His kindness is eternal.[1]

The soul of every living being will bless Your Name,
HASHEM, our God, and the spirit of all flesh will
constantly glorify and exalt Your remembrance, our

מַלְכֵּנוּ תָּמִיד. מִן הָעוֹלָם וְעַד הָעוֹלָם אַתָּה אֵל,
וּמִבַּלְעָדֶיךָ אֵין לָנוּ מֶלֶךְ גּוֹאֵל וּמוֹשִׁיעַ. פּוֹדֶה וּמַצִּיל
וּמְפַרְנֵס וּמְרַחֵם בְּכָל עֵת צָרָה וְצוּקָה. אֵין לָנוּ מֶלֶךְ
אֶלָּא אָתָּה. אֱלֹהֵי הָרִאשׁוֹנִים וְהָאַחֲרוֹנִים אֱלוֹהַּ כָּל
בְּרִיּוֹת אֲדוֹן כָּל תּוֹלָדוֹת הַמְהֻלָּל בְּרֹב הַתִּשְׁבָּחוֹת
הַמְנַהֵג עוֹלָמוֹ בְּחֶסֶד וּבְרִיּוֹתָיו בְּרַחֲמִים וַיהוָה לֹא
יָנוּם וְלֹא יִישָׁן. הַמְעוֹרֵר יְשֵׁנִים וְהַמֵּקִיץ נִרְדָּמִים
וְהַמֵּשִׂיחַ אִלְּמִים וְהַמַּתִּיר אֲסוּרִים וְהַסּוֹמֵךְ נוֹפְלִים
וְהַזּוֹקֵף כְּפוּפִים לְךָ לְבַדְּךָ אֲנַחְנוּ מוֹדִים. אִלּוּ פִינוּ
מָלֵא שִׁירָה כַּיָּם וּלְשׁוֹנֵנוּ רִנָּה כַּהֲמוֹן גַּלָּיו
וְשִׂפְתוֹתֵינוּ שֶׁבַח כְּמֶרְחֲבֵי רָקִיעַ וְעֵינֵינוּ מְאִירוֹת
כַּשֶּׁמֶשׁ וְכַיָּרֵחַ וְיָדֵינוּ פְרוּשׂוֹת כְּנִשְׁרֵי שָׁמַיִם
וְרַגְלֵינוּ קַלּוֹת כָּאַיָּלוֹת, אֵין אֲנַחְנוּ מַסְפִּיקִים
לְהוֹדוֹת לְךָ יהוה אֱלֹהֵינוּ וֵאלֹהֵי אֲבוֹתֵינוּ וּלְבָרֵךְ
אֶת שְׁמֶךָ עַל אַחַת מֵאָלֶף אֶלֶף אַלְפֵי אֲלָפִים וְרִבֵּי
רְבָבוֹת פְּעָמִים הַטּוֹבוֹת שֶׁעָשִׂיתָ עִם אֲבוֹתֵינוּ
וְעִמָּנוּ. מִמִּצְרַיִם גְּאַלְתָּנוּ יהוה אֱלֹהֵינוּ וּמִבֵּית
עֲבָדִים פְּדִיתָנוּ בְּרָעָב זַנְתָּנוּ וּבְשָׂבָע כִּלְכַּלְתָּנוּ
מֵחֶרֶב הִצַּלְתָּנוּ וּמִדֶּבֶר מִלַּטְתָּנוּ וּמֵחֳלָיִם רָעִים
וְנֶאֱמָנִים דִּלִּיתָנוּ. עַד הֵנָּה עֲזָרוּנוּ רַחֲמֶיךָ וְלֹא
עֲזָבוּנוּ חֲסָדֶיךָ וְאַל תִּטְּשֵׁנוּ יהוה אֱלֹהֵינוּ לָנֶצַח.
עַל כֵּן אֵבָרִים שֶׁפִּלַּגְתָּ בָּנוּ וְרוּחַ וּנְשָׁמָה שֶׁנָּפַחְתָּ
בְּאַפֵּינוּ וְלָשׁוֹן אֲשֶׁר שַׂמְתָּ בְּפִינוּ הֵן הֵם יוֹדוּ וִיבָרְכוּ
וִישַׁבְּחוּ וִיפָאֲרוּ וִירוֹמְמוּ וְיַעֲרִיצוּ וְיַקְדִּישׁוּ וְיַמְלִיכוּ
אֶת שִׁמְךָ מַלְכֵּנוּ. כִּי כָל פֶּה לְךָ יוֹדֶה וְכָל לָשׁוֹן לְךָ
תִשָּׁבַע וְכָל בֶּרֶךְ לְךָ תִכְרַע וְכָל קוֹמָה לְפָנֶיךָ
תִשְׁתַּחֲוֶה וְכָל לְבָבוֹת יִירָאוּךָ וְכָל קֶרֶב וּכְלָיוֹת
יְזַמְּרוּ לִשְׁמֶךָ. כַּדָּבָר שֶׁכָּתוּב כָּל עַצְמֹתַי תֹּאמַרְנָה

King. You are God forever, and besides You we have no king, redeemer, savior, liberator, deliverer, supporter, or source of mercy at any time of trouble or distress. We have no God but You, God of the first and the last, God of all creatures, Master of all generations, extolled with many praises, Who conducts His world with kindness and His creatures with mercy. HASHEM does not doze or slumber. He wakes those who sleep and arouses those who slumber. He makes the mute speak. He releases the imprisoned, supports those who fall, and straightens those who are bent over. You alone we thank. Even if our mouths were as full of song as the sea, and our tongue full of joyous melody as its many waves, and our lips full of praise as the expanses of the firmament, and our eyes illuminating as the sun and the moon, and our arms spread wide as the eagles of the skies, and our feet as fleet as antelopes, we still could not sufficiently praise You or bless Your Name, HASHEM, our God and the God of our fathers, for even a thousandth or a ten-thousandth of the good that You have done for our ancestors and for us. You redeemed us from Egypt, HASHEM, our God, and delivered us from the house of bondage. You have fed us in famine and sustained us in plenty. You have saved us from the sword, rescued us from epidemic, and spared us from severe and enduring diseases. Your mercy has helped us until this time and Your kindness has not abandoned us. HASHEM, our God, do not ever desert us. Therefore the limbs which You have carved in us, the spirit and soul that You have blown into our nostrils, the tongue that You have put into our mouths — they will thank, bless, laud, glorify, exalt, adulate, sanctify, and do homage to Your Name, our King. For every mouth gives thanks to You, every tongue vows allegiance to You, every knee bends to You, every stature bows before You, every heart fears You, and all internal organs sing out to Your Name. As it is written, "All my bones say,

יהוה מִי כָמְוֹךָ מַצִּיל עָנִי מֵחָזָק מִמֶּנּוּ וְעָנִי וְאֶבְיוֹן
מִגֹּזְלוֹ.¹ מִי יִדְמֶה לָּךְ וּמִי יִשְׁוֶה לָּךְ וּמִי יַעֲרָךְ לָךְ
הָאֵל הַגָּדוֹל הַגִּבּוֹר וְהַנּוֹרָא אֵל עֶלְיוֹן קֹנֵה שָׁמַיִם
וָאָרֶץ. נְהַלֶּלְךָ וּנְשַׁבֵּחֲךָ וּנְפָאֶרְךָ וּנְבָרֵךְ אֶת שֵׁם
קָדְשֶׁךָ כָּאָמוּר לְדָוִד בָּרְכִי נַפְשִׁי אֶת יהוה וְכָל
קְרָבַי אֶת שֵׁם קָדְשׁוֹ.²

הָאֵל בְּתַעֲצֻמוֹת עֻזֶּךָ הַגָּדוֹל בִּכְבוֹד שְׁמֶךָ
הַגִּבּוֹר לָנֶצַח וְהַנּוֹרָא בְּנוֹרְאוֹתֶיךָ הַמֶּלֶךְ
הַיּוֹשֵׁב עַל כִּסֵּא רָם וְנִשָּׂא.

שׁוֹכֵן עַד מָרוֹם וְקָדוֹשׁ שְׁמוֹ. וְכָתוּב רַנְּנוּ
צַדִּיקִים בַּיהוה לַיְשָׁרִים נָאוָה
תְהִלָּה.³ בְּפִי יְשָׁרִים תִּתְהַלָּל וּבְדִבְרֵי צַדִּיקִים
תִּתְבָּרַךְ וּבִלְשׁוֹן חֲסִידִים תִּתְרוֹמָם וּבְקֶרֶב
קְדוֹשִׁים תִּתְקַדָּשׁ:

וּבְמַקְהֲלוֹת רִבְבוֹת עַמְּךָ בֵּית יִשְׂרָאֵל בְּרִנָּה
יִתְפָּאַר שִׁמְךָ מַלְכֵּנוּ בְּכָל דּוֹר
וָדוֹר שֶׁכֵּן חוֹבַת כָּל הַיְצוּרִים לְפָנֶיךָ יהוה אֱלֹהֵינוּ
וֵאלֹהֵי אֲבוֹתֵינוּ לְהוֹדוֹת לְהַלֵּל לְשַׁבֵּחַ לְפָאֵר
לְרוֹמֵם לְהַדֵּר לְבָרֵךְ לְעַלֵּה וּלְקַלֵּס עַל כָּל
דִּבְרֵי שִׁירוֹת וְתִשְׁבָּחוֹת דָּוִד בֶּן יִשַׁי עַבְדְּךָ
מְשִׁיחֶךָ.

יִשְׁתַּבַּח שִׁמְךָ לָעַד מַלְכֵּנוּ הָאֵל הַמֶּלֶךְ הַגָּדוֹל
וְהַקָּדוֹשׁ בַּשָּׁמַיִם וּבָאָרֶץ כִּי לְךָ נָאֶה
יהוה אֱלֹהֵינוּ וֵאלֹהֵי אֲבוֹתֵינוּ שִׁיר וּשְׁבָחָה
הַלֵּל וְזִמְרָה עֹז וּמֶמְשָׁלָה נֶצַח גְּדֻלָּה וּגְבוּרָה

HASHEM: Who is like You, Who saves the poor man from one stronger than he, and the poor and impoverished from the one who seeks to rob him?"[1] Who can resemble You? Who can compare to You? Who can estimate You? The great, mighty, and awesome God, the supreme God, Creator of heavens and earth. We will praise You, laud You, glorify You, and bless Your holy Name, as it says: "Of David: my soul blesses HASHEM, and all my insides bless His holy Name."[2]

O God, in the supremacies of Your might! You Who are great in the glory of Your Name, Who are mighty forever and fearful through Your awe-inspiring deeds! The King Who sits upon a high and exalted throne!

He Who dwells in eternity, high and holy is His Name. As it is written, "Let the righteous rejoice in HASHEM. It is fitting for the upright to extol."[3] By the mouth of the upright You shall be praised. And by the words of the righteous You shall be blessed. And by the tongue of the pious You shall be exalted. And amid the holy You shall be sanctified.

And in the assemblies of the myriads of Your people, the House of Israel, Your Name shall be extolled in song, our King, in each and every generation. For it is the duty of all that is created: in Your presence, HASHEM, our God and the God of our fathers, to thank, praise, laud, glorify, exalt, adorn, bless, elevate, and celebrate beyond all the songs and praises of David the son of Yishai, Your servant, Your anointed.

May Your Name be praised forever, our King, the God and King, great and holy, in the heavens and the earth. For hymn and praise befit You, HASHEM, our God and the God of our fathers — accolade and song, strength and sovereignty, eternity, greatness and might,

---

(1) *Tehillim* 35:10. (2) 103:1. (3) 33:1.

תְּהִלָּה וְתִפְאֶרֶת קְדֻשָּׁה וּמַלְכוּת בְּרָכוֹת וְהוֹדָאוֹת מֵעַתָּה וְעַד עוֹלָם: בָּרוּךְ אַתָּה יהוה אֵל מֶלֶךְ גָּדוֹל בַּתִּשְׁבָּחוֹת אֵל הַהוֹדָאוֹת אֲדוֹן הַנִּפְלָאוֹת הַבּוֹחֵר בְּשִׁירֵי זִמְרָה מֶלֶךְ אֵל חֵי הָעוֹלָמִים.

The blessing over wine is recited and the fourth cup is drunk while one reclines on the left side. It is preferable that the entire cup be drunk, but at least one should drink most of it.

Some recite the following before the fourth cup:

הִנְנִי מוּכָן וּמְזֻמָּן לְקַיֵּם מִצְוַת כּוֹס רְבִיעִי שֶׁל אַרְבַּע כּוֹסוֹת. לְשֵׁם יִחוּד קֻדְשָׁא בְּרִיךְ הוּא וּשְׁכִינְתֵּיהּ, עַל יְדֵי הַהוּא טָמִיר וְנֶעְלָם, בְּשֵׁם כָּל יִשְׂרָאֵל. וִיהִי נֹעַם אֲדֹנָי אֱלֹהֵינוּ עָלֵינוּ, וּמַעֲשֵׂה יָדֵינוּ כּוֹנְנָה עָלֵינוּ, וּמַעֲשֵׂה יָדֵינוּ כּוֹנְנֵהוּ:

בָּרוּךְ אַתָּה יהוה אֱלֹהֵינוּ מֶלֶךְ הָעוֹלָם, בּוֹרֵא פְּרִי הַגָּפֶן.

After drinking the fourth cup, the concluding blessing is recited.
On the Sabbath include the passage in parentheses.

בָּרוּךְ אַתָּה יהוה אֱלֹהֵינוּ מֶלֶךְ הָעוֹלָם, עַל הַגֶּפֶן וְעַל פְּרִי הַגֶּפֶן וְעַל תְּנוּבַת הַשָּׂדֶה וְעַל אֶרֶץ חֶמְדָּה טוֹבָה וּרְחָבָה שֶׁרָצִיתָ וְהִנְחַלְתָּ לַאֲבוֹתֵינוּ לֶאֱכוֹל מִפִּרְיָהּ וְלִשְׂבּוֹעַ מִטּוּבָהּ. רַחֵם נָא יהוה אֱלֹהֵינוּ עַל יִשְׂרָאֵל עַמֶּךָ וְעַל יְרוּשָׁלַיִם עִירֶךָ וְעַל צִיּוֹן מִשְׁכַּן כְּבוֹדֶךָ וְעַל מִזְבְּחֶךָ וְעַל הֵיכָלֶךָ. וּבְנֵה יְרוּשָׁלַיִם עִיר הַקֹּדֶשׁ בִּמְהֵרָה בְיָמֵינוּ וְהַעֲלֵנוּ לְתוֹכָהּ וְשַׂמְּחֵנוּ בְּבִנְיָנָהּ וְנֹאכַל מִפִּרְיָהּ וְנִשְׂבַּע מִטּוּבָהּ וּנְבָרֶכְךָ עָלֶיהָ בִּקְדֻשָּׁה וּבְטָהֳרָה. [וּרְצֵה וְהַחֲלִיצֵנוּ בְּיוֹם הַשַּׁבָּת הַזֶּה] וְשַׂמְּחֵנוּ בְּיוֹם חַג הַמַּצּוֹת הַזֶּה. כִּי אַתָּה יהוה טוֹב וּמֵטִיב לַכֹּל וְנוֹדֶה לְּךָ עַל הָאָרֶץ וְעַל פְּרִי הַגָּפֶן. בָּרוּךְ אַתָּה יהוה עַל הָאָרֶץ וְעַל פְּרִי הַגָּפֶן.

fame and glory, sanctity and majesty, blessing and thanksgiving, for all eternity. Blessed are You, HASHEM, God, King, great in praises, the God to Whom we owe thanks, Master of wonders, Who is pleased with melodious song — King, God, Life of the worlds.

The blessing over wine is recited and the fourth cup is drunk while one reclines on the left side. It is preferable that the entire cup be drunk, but at least one should drink most of it.

Some recite the following before the fourth cup:

Behold, I am prepared and ready to fulfill the mitzvah of the fourth of the Four Cups. For the sake of the unification of the Holy One, Blessed is He, and His Presence, through Him Who is hidden and inscrutable — [I pray] in the name of all Israel. May the pleasantness of my Lord, our God, be upon us — may He establish our handiwork for us; our handiwork may He establish.

Blessed are You, HASHEM, our God, King of the Universe, Who creates the fruit of the vine.

After drinking the fourth cup, the concluding blessing is recited.
On the Sabbath include the passage in parentheses.

Blessed are You, HASHEM, our God, King of the Universe, for the vine and the fruit of the vine, and the produce of the field, and for the precious, good, and spacious land that You willed to give as an inheritance to our ancestors, to eat of its fruit and to be sated by its goodness. Have mercy, please, HASHEM, our God, on Israel, Your people, and on Jerusalem, Your city, and on Zion, the abode of Your glory, and on Your Altar and on Your Temple. Rebuild Jerusalem, the city of sanctity, speedily in our lifetimes. Bring us up into it and let us rejoice in its reconstruction. Let us eat of its fruits and be sated by its goodness. May we bless You over it in holiness and purity (and may it be Your will to fortify us on this Sabbath day), and may You bring us joy on this day of the Festival of Matzos. For You, HASHEM, are good and do good to all, and we thank You for the land and the fruit of the vine. Blessed are You, HASHEM, for the land and the fruit of the vine.

נרצה

חֲסַל סְדוּר פֶּסַח כְּהִלְכָתוֹ. כְּכָל מִשְׁפָּטוֹ וְחֻקָתוֹ. כַּאֲשֶׁר זָכִינוּ לְסַדֵּר אוֹתוֹ. כֵּן נִזְכֶּה לַעֲשׂוֹתוֹ. זָךְ שׁוֹכֵן מְעוֹנָה. קוֹמֵם קְהַל עֲדַת מִי מָנָה. בְּקָרוֹב נַהֵל נִטְעֵי כַנָּה. פְּדוּיִם לְצִיּוֹן בְּרִנָּה.

לְשָׁנָה הַבָּאָה בִּירוּשָׁלָיִם.

On the first night recite the following. On the second night continue on page 206.

וּבְכֵן וַיְהִי בַּחֲצִי הַלַּיְלָה.

בַּלָּיְלָה.	אָז רוֹב נִסִּים הִפְלֵאתָ
הַלָּיְלָה.	בְּרֹאשׁ אַשְׁמוֹרֶת זֶה
לָיְלָה.	גֵּר צֶדֶק נִצַּחְתּוֹ כְּנֶחֱלַק לוֹ
	וַיְהִי בַּחֲצִי הַלָּיְלָה.
הַלָּיְלָה.	דַּנְתָּ מֶלֶךְ גְּרָר בַּחֲלוֹם
לָיְלָה.	הִפְחַדְתָּ אֲרַמִּי בְּאֶמֶשׁ
לָיְלָה.	וַיָּשַׂר יִשְׂרָאֵל לְמַלְאָךְ וַיּוּכַל לוֹ
	וַיְהִי בַּחֲצִי הַלָּיְלָה.
הַלָּיְלָה.	זֶרַע בְּכוֹרֵי פַתְרוֹס מָחַצְתָּ בַּחֲצִי
בַּלָּיְלָה.	חֵילָם לֹא מָצְאוּ בְּקוּמָם
לָיְלָה.	טִיסַת נְגִיד חֲרוֹשֶׁת סִלִּיתָ בְּכוֹכְבֵי
	וַיְהִי בַּחֲצִי הַלָּיְלָה.
בַּלָּיְלָה.	יָעַץ מְחָרֵף לְנוֹפֵף אִוּוּי הוֹבַשְׁתָּ פְּגָרָיו
לָיְלָה.	כָּרַע בֵּל וּמַצָּבוֹ בְּאִישׁוֹן
לָיְלָה.	לְאִישׁ חֲמוּדוֹת נִגְלָה רָז חֲזוֹת
	וַיְהִי בַּחֲצִי הַלָּיְלָה.

NIRTZAH

The order of Pesach has come to its end in accordance with its Halachah, in accordance with all of its laws and decrees. Just as we have been worthy of making the Seder this year, so may we be worthy of making it in the future. Pure One, Who dwells in His heavenly abode, raise up the countless congregation of Israel. In the near future, lead the shoots You have planted to Zion, redeemed, joyously.

Next year in Jerusalem!

On the first night recite the following. On the second night continue on page 206.

It happened at midnight.

Then You performed wondrous miracles at   night.
    At the first watch of this   night.
You brought victory to the righteous convert
    [Abraham] by dividing for him the   night.
                It happened at midnight.
You judged the king of Gerar [Abimelech]
    in a dream of the   night.
You terrified the Aramean [Laban] in the dark of   night.
And Israel [Jacob] fought with an angel
    and overcame him at   night.
                It happened at midnight.
You bruised the firstborn seed of Pasros [Egypt] at midnight.
They did not find their legions when they arose at   night.
The swift armies of the prince of Charoshes
    [Sisera] You crushed with the stars of   night.
                It happened at midnight.
The blasphemer [Sennacherib] schemed to raise
    his hand menacingly [over the precious city].
    You made his corpses rot at   night.
Bel [the Babylonian pagan deity] and his
    pedestal fell in the black of   night.
To the beloved man [Daniel] was revealed
    the secret of the visions of   night.
                It happened at midnight.

	מִשְׂתַּכֵּר בִּכְלֵי קֹדֶשׁ נֶהֱרַג בּוֹ
בַּלַּיְלָה.	
לַיְלָה.	נוֹשַׁע מִבּוֹר אֲרָיוֹת פּוֹתֵר בִּעֲתוּתֵי
בַּלַּיְלָה.	שִׂנְאָה נָטַר אֲגָגִי וְכָתַב סְפָרִים

וַיְהִי בַּחֲצִי הַלַּיְלָה.

	עוֹרַרְתָּ נִצְחֲךָ עָלָיו בְּנֶדֶד שְׁנַת
לַיְלָה.	
מִלַּיְלָה.	פּוּרָה תִדְרוֹךְ לְשׁוֹמֵר מַה
לַיְלָה.	צָרַח כַּשּׁוֹמֵר וְשָׂח אָתָא בֹקֶר וְגַם

וַיְהִי בַּחֲצִי הַלַּיְלָה.

	קָרֵב יוֹם אֲשֶׁר הוּא לֹא יוֹם וְלֹא
לַיְלָה.	
הַלַּיְלָה.	רָם הוֹדַע כִּי לְךָ הַיּוֹם אַף לְךָ
הַלַּיְלָה.	שׁוֹמְרִים הַפְקֵד לְעִירְךָ כָּל הַיּוֹם וְכָל
לַיְלָה.	תָּאִיר כְּאוֹר יוֹם חֶשְׁכַּת

וַיְהִי בַּחֲצִי הַלַּיְלָה.

On the first night continue on page 204.
On the second night recite the following.

וּבְכֵן וַאֲמַרְתֶּם זֶבַח פֶּסַח:

	אֹמֶץ גְּבוּרוֹתֶיךָ הִפְלֵאתָ
בַּפֶּסַח.	
פֶּסַח.	בְּרֹאשׁ כָּל מוֹעֲדוֹת נִשֵּׂאתָ
פֶּסַח.	גִּלִּיתָ לְאֶזְרָחִי חֲצוֹת לֵיל

וַאֲמַרְתֶּם זֶבַח פֶּסַח.

	דְּלָתָיו דָּפַקְתָּ כְּחֹם הַיּוֹם
בַּפֶּסַח.	
בַּפֶּסַח.	הִסְעִיד נוֹצְצִים עֻגוֹת מַצּוֹת
פֶּסַח.	וְאֶל הַבָּקָר רָץ זֵכֶר לְשׁוֹר עֶרֶךְ

וַאֲמַרְתֶּם זֶבַח פֶּסַח.

He who guzzled out of the sacred vessels [Belshazzar,
    king of Babylonia] was killed on that   night.
The one who was saved from the lions' den
    interpreted the terrors of the   night.
The Aggagite [Haman] nurtured hatred
    and wrote decrees at   night.
              It happened at midnight.

You initiated Your triumph against him
    by disturbing the sleep [of Ahasuerus] at   night.
You will tread a winepress [in peace after victory]
    for him who cries out [Israel]:
    Our Guardian! What will be of this   night?
Like a guardian You will call out in response:
    The morning has come, as well as the   night.
              It happened at midnight.

The day is approaching which is neither day nor night.
Most High! Make it known that Yours are
    both the day and the   night.
Appoint watchmen over Your city all day and all night.
Illuminate like the light of day the darkness of night.
              It will happen at midnight.

On the first night continue on page 204.
On the second night recite the following.

And you will say: A feast of Passover.

The power of Your mighty deeds
    You showed wondrously on   Passover.
Foremost of all festivals You exalted   Passover.
You revealed to the oriental [Abraham]
    the events of the night of   Passover.
      And you will say: A feast of Passover.

You knocked on his doors
    during the heat of the day on   Passover.
He gave bright angels a meal of cakes of
    matzah on   Passover.
He ran to fetch an ox in commemoration of
    the ox sacrificed [as the *korban chagigah* —
    the festival offering] on   Passover.
      And you will say: A feast of Passover.

זוֹעֲמוּ סְדוֹמִים וְלוֹהֲטוּ בָּאֵשׁ   בְּפֶסַח.

חֻלַּץ לוֹט מֵהֶם וּמַצּוֹת אָפָה בְּקֵץ   פֶּסַח.

טִאטֵאתָ אַדְמַת מוֹף וְנוֹף בְּעָבְרְךָ   בְּפֶסַח.

וַאֲמַרְתֶּם זֶבַח פֶּסַח.

יָהּ רֹאשׁ כָּל אוֹן מָחַצְתָּ בְּלֵיל שִׁמּוּר   פֶּסַח.

כַּבִּיר עַל בֵּן בְּכוֹר פָּסַחְתָּ בְּדַם   פֶּסַח.

לְבִלְתִּי תֵּת מַשְׁחִית לָבֹא בִּפְתָחַי   בְּפֶסַח.

וַאֲמַרְתֶּם זֶבַח פֶּסַח.

מְסֻגֶּרֶת סֻגָּרָה בְּעִתּוֹתֵי   פֶּסַח.

נִשְׁמְדָה מִדְיָן בִּצְלִיל שְׂעוֹרֵי עֹמֶר   פֶּסַח.

שֹׂרְפוּ מִשְׁמַנֵּי פּוּל וְלוּד בִּיקַד יְקֹד   פֶּסַח.

וַאֲמַרְתֶּם זֶבַח פֶּסַח.

עוֹד הַיּוֹם בְּנֹב לַעֲמוֹד עַד גָּעָה עוֹנַת   פֶּסַח.

פַּס יַד כָּתְבָה לְקַעֲקֵעַ צוּל   בְּפֶסַח.

צָפֹה הַצָּפִית עָרוֹךְ הַשֻּׁלְחָן   בְּפֶסַח.

וַאֲמַרְתֶּם זֶבַח פֶּסַח.

קָהָל כִּנְּסָה הֲדַסָּה צוֹם לְשַׁלֵּשׁ   בְּפֶסַח.

רֹאשׁ מִבֵּית רָשָׁע מָחַצְתָּ בְּעֵץ חֲמִשִּׁים   בְּפֶסַח.

שְׁתֵּי אֵלֶּה רֶגַע תָּבִיא לְעוּצִית   בְּפֶסַח.

תָּעֹז יָדְךָ וְתָרוּם יְמִינְךָ כְּלֵיל הִתְקַדֶּשׁ חַג   פֶּסַח.

וַאֲמַרְתֶּם זֶבַח פֶּסַח.

The Sodomites provoked God
    and were set ablaze on   Passover.
Lot escaped from them and baked matzos
    at the end of   Passover.
You swept clean the land of Mof and Nof
    [Egyptian cities] on   Passover.
            And you will say: A feast of Passover.

YAH, the first issue of strength You bruised
    on the watchful night of   Passover.
Mighty One, You skipped over the firstborn son
    because of the blood of   Passover,
Not to allow the destroyer to enter my doors on   Passover.
            And you will say: A feast of Passover.

The closed city [Jericho] was handed over
    [to the Jews] at the time of   Passover.
Midian was destroyed [by the Jews
    under the leadership of Gideon]
    through the merit of a cake of the *omer* on   Passover.
The mighty nobles of Pul and Lud [the Assyrians
    in the days of King Hezekiah]
    were burnt in a conflagration on   Passover.
            And you will say: A feast of Passover.

He [Sennacherib] would have stood at Nob,
    but the time of Passover arrived.
A hand wrote the decree of annihilation against Zul
    [Babylonia] on   Passover.
Their scout went to look for the enemy while their table
    was festively set on   Passover.
            And you will say: A feast of Passover.

Hadassah [Esther] gathered an assembly for
    a three-day fast on   Passover.
The head of the evil house [Haman] You killed
    on a fifty-cubit pole on   Passover.
Bring bereavement and widowhood to Utzis
    [Edom] in an instant on   Passover.
Strengthen Your hand, raise Your right hand
    as on the night that the festival of Passover was sanctified.
            And you will say: A feast of Passover.

On both nights continue here:

כִּי לוֹ נָאֶה, כִּי לוֹ יָאֶה:

אַדִּיר בִּמְלוּכָה, **בָּחוּר** כַּהֲלָכָה, גְּדוּדָיו יֹאמְרוּ
לוֹ, לְךָ וּלְךָ, לְךָ כִּי לְךָ, לְךָ אַף לְךָ, לְךָ
יהוה הַמַּמְלָכָה, כִּי לוֹ נָאֶה, כִּי לוֹ יָאֶה.

דָּגוּל בִּמְלוּכָה, **הָדוּר** כַּהֲלָכָה, וָתִיקָיו יֹאמְרוּ
לוֹ, לְךָ וּלְךָ, לְךָ כִּי לְךָ, לְךָ אַף לְךָ, לְךָ יהוה
הַמַּמְלָכָה, כִּי לוֹ נָאֶה, כִּי לוֹ יָאֶה.

זַכַּאי בִּמְלוּכָה, **חָסִין** כַּהֲלָכָה, טַפְסְרָיו יֹאמְרוּ
לוֹ, לְךָ וּלְךָ, לְךָ כִּי לְךָ, לְךָ אַף לְךָ, לְךָ יהוה
הַמַּמְלָכָה, כִּי לוֹ נָאֶה, כִּי לוֹ יָאֶה.

יָחִיד בִּמְלוּכָה, **כַּבִּיר** כַּהֲלָכָה, לִמּוּדָיו יֹאמְרוּ
לוֹ, לְךָ וּלְךָ, לְךָ כִּי לְךָ, לְךָ אַף לְךָ, לְךָ יהוה
הַמַּמְלָכָה, כִּי לוֹ נָאֶה, כִּי לוֹ יָאֶה.

מוֹשֵׁל בִּמְלוּכָה, **נוֹרָא** כַּהֲלָכָה, סְבִיבָיו יֹאמְרוּ
לוֹ, לְךָ וּלְךָ, לְךָ כִּי לְךָ, לְךָ אַף לְךָ, לְךָ יהוה
הַמַּמְלָכָה, כִּי לוֹ נָאֶה, כִּי לוֹ יָאֶה.

עָנָיו בִּמְלוּכָה, **פּוֹדֶה** כַּהֲלָכָה, צַדִּיקָיו יֹאמְרוּ
לוֹ, לְךָ וּלְךָ, לְךָ כִּי לְךָ, לְךָ אַף לְךָ, לְךָ יהוה
הַמַּמְלָכָה, כִּי לוֹ נָאֶה, כִּי לוֹ יָאֶה.

קָדוֹשׁ בִּמְלוּכָה, **רַחוּם** כַּהֲלָכָה, שִׁנְאַנָּיו יֹאמְרוּ
לוֹ, לְךָ וּלְךָ, לְךָ כִּי לְךָ, לְךָ אַף לְךָ, לְךָ יהוה
הַמַּמְלָכָה, כִּי לוֹ נָאֶה, כִּי לוֹ יָאֶה.

תַּקִּיף בִּמְלוּכָה, **תּוֹמֵךְ** כַּהֲלָכָה, תְּמִימָיו יֹאמְרוּ
לוֹ, לְךָ וּלְךָ, לְךָ כִּי לְךָ, לְךָ אַף לְךָ, לְךָ יהוה
הַמַּמְלָכָה, כִּי לוֹ נָאֶה, כִּי לוֹ יָאֶה.

To Him it is fitting. To Him it is due.

Mighty in royalty, chosen by right, His legions say to Him: Yours and only Yours; Yours, yes Yours, Yours, surely Yours; Yours, HASHEM, is the sovereignty of the world. To Him it is fitting. To Him it is due.

Distinguished in royalty, glorious of right. His faithful say to Him: Yours and only Yours; Yours, yes Yours; Yours, surely Yours; Yours, HASHEM, is the sovereignty of the world. To Him it is fitting. To Him it is due.

Pure in royalty, firm of right. His courtiers say to Him: Yours and only Yours; Yours, yes Yours; Yours, surely Yours; Yours, HASHEM, is the sovereignty of the world. To Him it is fitting. To Him it is due.

Unique in royalty, mighty of right. His disciples say to Him: Yours and only Yours; Yours, yes Yours; Yours, surely Yours; Yours, HASHEM, is the sovereignty of the world. To Him it is fitting. To Him it is due.

Ruling in royalty, feared of right. Those who surround Him say to Him: Yours and only Yours; Yours, yes Yours; Yours, surely Yours; Yours, HASHEM, is the sovereignty of the world. To Him it is fitting. To Him it is due.

Humble in royalty, redeeming by right. His righteous ones say to Him: Yours and only Yours; Yours, yes Yours; Yours, surely Yours; Yours, HASHEM, is the sovereignty of the world. To Him it is fitting. To Him it is due.

Holy in royalty, merciful of right. His angels say to Him: Yours and only Yours; Yours, yes Yours; Yours, surely Yours; Yours, HASHEM, is the sovereignty of the world. To Him it is fitting. To Him it is due.

Powerful in royalty, sustaining of right. His perfect ones say to Him: Yours and only Yours; Yours, yes Yours; Yours, surely Yours; Yours, HASHEM, is the sovereignty of the world. To Him it is fitting. To Him it is due.

אַדִּיר הוּא יִבְנֶה בֵיתוֹ בְּקָרוֹב, בִּמְהֵרָה, בִּמְהֵרָה, בְּיָמֵינוּ בְּקָרוֹב. אֵל בְּנֵה, אֵל בְּנֵה, בְּנֵה בֵיתְךָ בְּקָרוֹב.

בָּחוּר הוּא. גָּדוֹל הוּא. דָּגוּל הוּא. יִבְנֶה בֵיתוֹ בְּקָרוֹב, בִּמְהֵרָה, בִּמְהֵרָה, בְּיָמֵינוּ בְּקָרוֹב. אֵל בְּנֵה, אֵל בְּנֵה, בְּנֵה בֵיתְךָ בְּקָרוֹב.

הָדוּר הוּא. וָתִיק הוּא. זַכַּאי הוּא. חָסִיד הוּא. יִבְנֶה בֵיתוֹ בְּקָרוֹב, בִּמְהֵרָה, בִּמְהֵרָה, בְּיָמֵינוּ בְּקָרוֹב. אֵל בְּנֵה, אֵל בְּנֵה, בְּנֵה בֵיתְךָ בְּקָרוֹב.

טָהוֹר הוּא. יָחִיד הוּא. כַּבִּיר הוּא. לָמוּד הוּא. מֶלֶךְ הוּא. נוֹרָא הוּא. סַגִּיב הוּא. עִזּוּז הוּא. פּוֹדֶה הוּא. צַדִּיק הוּא. יִבְנֶה בֵיתוֹ בְּקָרוֹב, בִּמְהֵרָה, בִּמְהֵרָה, בְּיָמֵינוּ בְּקָרוֹב. אֵל בְּנֵה, אֵל בְּנֵה, בְּנֵה בֵיתְךָ בְּקָרוֹב.

קָדוֹשׁ הוּא. רַחוּם הוּא. שַׁדַּי הוּא. תַּקִּיף הוּא. יִבְנֶה בֵיתוֹ בְּקָרוֹב, בִּמְהֵרָה, בִּמְהֵרָה, בְּיָמֵינוּ בְּקָרוֹב. אֵל בְּנֵה, אֵל בְּנֵה, בְּנֵה בֵיתְךָ בְּקָרוֹב.

אֶחָד מִי יוֹדֵעַ? אֶחָד אֲנִי יוֹדֵעַ. אֶחָד אֱלֹהֵינוּ שֶׁבַּשָּׁמַיִם וּבָאָרֶץ.

אֶחָד מִי יוֹדֵעַ — **Who Knows One**

⧉ A Song at Midnight

Even after we have reached midnight of this very special night, even after we have spent hours intensively transmitting the story of the Exodus to the next generation — we do not simply turn to mundane amusements or meaningless trivia quizzes. Rather, we involve ourselves in search-

Mighty is He. May He build His House soon; quickly, quickly, in our lifetimes, soon. God, build; God, build; build Your House soon.

Exalted is He, great is He, distinguished is He. May He build His House soon; quickly, quickly, in our lifetimes, soon. God, build; God, build; build Your House soon.

Glorious is He, faithful is He, guiltless is He, righteous is He. May He build His House soon; quickly, quickly, in our lifetimes, soon. God, build; God, build; build Your House soon.

Pure is He, unique is He, powerful is He, all-wise is He, the King is He, awesome is He, sublime is He, all-powerful is He, the Redeemer is He, all-righteous is He. May He build His House soon; quickly, quickly, in our lifetimes, soon. God, build; God, build; build Your House soon.

Holy is He, compassionate is He, Almighty is He, Omnipotent is He. May He build His House soon; quickly, quickly, in our lifetimes, soon. God, rebuild; God, build; build Your House soon.

Who knows one? I know one.
One is our God in the heavens and the earth.

---

ing for the answer to a most vital "quiz" indeed: Why was it specifically the Jewish nation that was privileged to experience the Exodus, and most importantly, why will we be worthy of being redeemed once again at the End of Days? Are we truthfully of a higher caliber than all other nations?

What is the meaning of this song that we sing at midnight? Is it simply meant to be an amusing song, one that puts energy back into tired Seder participants, with its entertaining lyrics and question-and-answer format? Or perhaps the author of the Haggadah has another idea in mind, such as relaying yet another central theme of this monumental evening?

שְׁנַיִם מִי יוֹדֵעַ? שְׁנַיִם אֲנִי יוֹדֵעַ. שְׁנֵי לֻחוֹת הַבְּרִית, אֶחָד אֱלֹהֵינוּ שֶׁבַּשָּׁמַיִם וּבָאָרֶץ.

שְׁלֹשָׁה מִי יוֹדֵעַ? שְׁלֹשָׁה אֲנִי יוֹדֵעַ. שְׁלֹשָׁה אָבוֹת, שְׁנֵי לֻחוֹת הַבְּרִית, אֶחָד אֱלֹהֵינוּ שֶׁבַּשָּׁמַיִם וּבָאָרֶץ.

אַרְבַּע מִי יוֹדֵעַ? אַרְבַּע אֲנִי יוֹדֵעַ. אַרְבַּע אִמָּהוֹת, שְׁלֹשָׁה אָבוֹת, שְׁנֵי לֻחוֹת הַבְּרִית, אֶחָד אֱלֹהֵינוּ שֶׁבַּשָּׁמַיִם וּבָאָרֶץ.

חֲמִשָּׁה מִי יוֹדֵעַ? חֲמִשָּׁה אֲנִי יוֹדֵעַ. חֲמִשָּׁה חֻמְשֵׁי תוֹרָה, אַרְבַּע אִמָּהוֹת, שְׁלֹשָׁה אָבוֹת, שְׁנֵי לֻחוֹת הַבְּרִית, אֶחָד אֱלֹהֵינוּ שֶׁבַּשָּׁמַיִם וּבָאָרֶץ.

שִׁשָּׁה מִי יוֹדֵעַ? שִׁשָּׁה אֲנִי יוֹדֵעַ. שִׁשָּׁה סִדְרֵי מִשְׁנָה, חֲמִשָּׁה חֻמְשֵׁי תוֹרָה, אַרְבַּע אִמָּהוֹת, שְׁלֹשָׁה אָבוֹת, שְׁנֵי לֻחוֹת הַבְּרִית, אֶחָד אֱלֹהֵינוּ שֶׁבַּשָּׁמַיִם וּבָאָרֶץ.

שִׁבְעָה מִי יוֹדֵעַ? שִׁבְעָה אֲנִי יוֹדֵעַ. שִׁבְעָה יְמֵי שַׁבַּתָּא, שִׁשָּׁה סִדְרֵי מִשְׁנָה, חֲמִשָּׁה חֻמְשֵׁי תוֹרָה, אַרְבַּע אִמָּהוֹת, שְׁלֹשָׁה אָבוֹת, שְׁנֵי לֻחוֹת הַבְּרִית, אֶחָד אֱלֹהֵינוּ שֶׁבַּשָּׁמַיִם וּבָאָרֶץ.

Clearly, we are not about to squander even a minute of this night, a night designated for the spiritual education of our children. It is obvious that this song was composed in its trivia-style format in order to be able to clarify and best explain why the Jewish people were deemed worthy of being redeemed from Egypt.

This is indeed the question to which we must find an answer. The Midrash informs us that this was a question posed by the heavenly angels to Hashem. They asked Hashem as follows: "Why are these more deserving to be drawn close than these are? They (the Children of Israel) are idol worshipers and they (the Egyptians) are idol worshipers" (*Midrash Rabbah Shemos,* 21).

Who knows two? I know two. Two are the Tablets of the Covenant. One is our God in the heavens and the earth.

Who knows three? I know three. Three are the Patriarchs. Two are the Tablets of the Covenant. One is our God in the heavens and the earth.

Who knows four? I know four. Four are the Matriarchs. Three are the Patriarchs. Two are the Tablets of the Covenant. One is our God in the heavens and the earth.

Who knows five? I know five. Five are the Books of the Torah. Four are the Matriarchs. Three are the Patriarchs. Two are the Tablets of the Covenant. One is our God in the heavens and the earth.

Who knows six? I know six. Six are the Orders of the Mishnah. Five are the Books of the Torah. Four are the Matriarchs. Three are the Patriarchs. Two are the Tablets of the Covenant. One is our God in the heavens and the earth.

Who knows seven? I know seven. Seven are the days of the week. Six are the Orders of the Mishnah. Five are the Books of the Torah. Four are the Matriarchs. Three are the Patriarchs. Two are the Tablets of the Covenant. One is our God in the heavens and the earth.

Certainly this is an interesting question. According to the Midrash, the Jewish slaves were, in fact, no better than their Egyptian taskmasters. They were both guilty of worshiping various forms of idols. Perhaps one will suggest that the Jews were worthy of redemption on account of the many years of crushing slavery that they endured. But if this is truly the case, then why specifically were the Jewish people accorded this honor? Why did Hashem not choose another nation that was similarly afflicted and oppressed in the very same land?

The quiz which the author of the Haggadah has formulated is one which systematically adds up the different merits attributable to the nation of Israel.

שְׁמוֹנָה מִי יוֹדֵעַ? שְׁמוֹנָה אֲנִי יוֹדֵעַ. שְׁמוֹנָה יְמֵי מִילָה, שִׁבְעָה יְמֵי שַׁבַּתָּא, שִׁשָּׁה סִדְרֵי מִשְׁנָה, חֲמִשָּׁה חֻמְשֵׁי תוֹרָה, אַרְבַּע אִמָּהוֹת, שְׁלֹשָׁה אָבוֹת, שְׁנֵי לֻחוֹת הַבְּרִית, אֶחָד אֱלֹהֵינוּ שֶׁבַּשָּׁמַיִם וּבָאָרֶץ.

תִּשְׁעָה מִי יוֹדֵעַ? תִּשְׁעָה אֲנִי יוֹדֵעַ. תִּשְׁעָה יַרְחֵי לֵדָה, שְׁמוֹנָה יְמֵי מִילָה, שִׁבְעָה יְמֵי שַׁבַּתָּא, שִׁשָּׁה סִדְרֵי מִשְׁנָה, חֲמִשָּׁה חֻמְשֵׁי תוֹרָה, אַרְבַּע אִמָּהוֹת, שְׁלֹשָׁה אָבוֹת, שְׁנֵי לֻחוֹת הַבְּרִית, אֶחָד אֱלֹהֵינוּ שֶׁבַּשָּׁמַיִם וּבָאָרֶץ.

In thirteen stanzas we are presented with the various claims able to be offered by the Jewish people justifying their redemption despite the fact that they themselves were not truly worthy of it, in the fullest sense of the word.

Let us examine, one by one, each of these merits.

"Who knows one — I know one. One is our God, in the heavens and the earth."

This is our first merit: the possibility that a redemption such as this one could cause the pure belief of our forefather Abraham, the belief in one God, to once again spring forth in the hearts of the Jewish nation; the belief in the Master of the Universe, from Whom all of creation draw their life force. The extraordinary Exodus, an event that shattered all the dogmas and notions held by the world at that time, and proved beyond a shadow of a doubt how no force of nature exists independently from Hashem — was performed in order that this tenet should be ingrained in the very fibers of the Jewish people, granting them spiritual as well as physical freedom.

"Who knows two?" What is our second merit?

"I know two — two are the Tablets of the Covenant."

Once again we are shown how the Exodus was based upon the hopes of a glorious future for the Jewish people. It was performed by Hashem with the hope that the Jewish people would one day comply with all that was inscribed in the Tablets given at Mount Sinai, and that they would allow their lives to be guided by the truth contained within them. It would be a truth that the Jews would hold high and defend dearly throughout the long and winding road that is the history of mankind.

Who knows eight? I know eight. Eight are the days of circumcision. Seven are the days of the week. Six are the Orders of the Mishnah. Five are the Books of the Torah. Four are the Matriarchs. Three are the Patriarchs. Two are the Tablets of the Covenant. One is our God in the heavens and the earth.

Who knows nine? I know nine. Nine are the months of pregnancy. Eight are the days of circumcision. Seven are the days of the week. Six are the Orders of the Mishnah. Five are the Books of the Torah. Four are the Matriarchs. Three are the Patriarchs. Two are the Tablets of the Covenant. One is our God in the heavens and the earth.

The third merit — the merit of our Patriarchs.

This merit consists of the lustrous roots from which sprouted the magnificent nation of Israel. These roots are named Abraham, Isaac, and Jacob, each one a spiritual giant who forever ensured the uniqueness of the Jewish people. For even if a Jew would leave the proper path, God forbid, or even if he should worship idols and cling to the materialistic lifestyle of the Egyptians — the merit of our three forefathers would be capable of returning him to the paths traveled by our great ancestors.

This hope is further strengthened by the "four" about whom we are next to sing. Says the Haggadah: "I know four — four are the Matriarchs."

These great women, Sarah, Rivkah, Rachel, and Leah, stood by the Patriarchs' sides as they built the Jewish nation and changed the world forever. They instilled in their offspring the unbreakable faith that would carry the Jewish people throughout the generations. The strength of their faith was such that even if one of their descendants would drift from the path of righteousness, it would be no more than a temporary slip, unable to harm the roots so firmly planted by our great forebears.

This is an additional merit that justified the redemption of the Jewish people from Egypt, despite the fact that they themselves may not have been truly worthy of it at the time it occurred.

Add to the pile of merits the Five Books of the Torah that the Jews would receive over the course of their forty years of wandering in the wilderness and the six Orders of the Mishnah, ("Who knows six") the Oral Torah, which, together with the Written Torah, would shape the spiritual face of the

עֲשָׂרָה מִי יוֹדֵעַ? עֲשָׂרָה אֲנִי יוֹדֵעַ. עֲשָׂרָה דִּבְּרַיָּא, תִּשְׁעָה יַרְחֵי לֵדָה, שְׁמוֹנָה יְמֵי מִילָה, שִׁבְעָה יְמֵי שַׁבַּתָּא, שִׁשָּׁה סִדְרֵי מִשְׁנָה, חֲמִשָּׁה חֻמְשֵׁי תוֹרָה, אַרְבַּע אִמָּהוֹת, שְׁלֹשָׁה אָבוֹת, שְׁנֵי לֻחוֹת הַבְּרִית, אֶחָד אֱלֹהֵינוּ שֶׁבַּשָּׁמַיִם וּבָאָרֶץ.

אַחַד עָשָׂר מִי יוֹדֵעַ? אַחַד עָשָׂר אֲנִי יוֹדֵעַ. אַחַד עָשָׂר כּוֹכְבַיָּא, עֲשָׂרָה דִבְּרַיָּא, תִּשְׁעָה יַרְחֵי לֵדָה, שְׁמוֹנָה יְמֵי מִילָה, שִׁבְעָה יְמֵי שַׁבַּתָּא, שִׁשָּׁה סִדְרֵי מִשְׁנָה, חֲמִשָּׁה חֻמְשֵׁי תוֹרָה, אַרְבַּע אִמָּהוֹת, שְׁלֹשָׁה אָבוֹת, שְׁנֵי לֻחוֹת הַבְּרִית, אֶחָד אֱלֹהֵינוּ שֶׁבַּשָּׁמַיִם וּבָאָרֶץ.

שְׁנֵים עָשָׂר מִי יוֹדֵעַ? שְׁנֵים עָשָׂר אֲנִי יוֹדֵעַ. שְׁנֵים עָשָׂר שִׁבְטַיָּא, אַחַד עָשָׂר כּוֹכְבַיָּא, עֲשָׂרָה

Children of Israel into one that resembles a nation of the One True God. In addition to these six merits, let us be sure to count the Shabbos, that sanctified seventh day, with all of the deep spiritual significance contained within each of its precious moments. (We briefly touched on this significance above.) We mention the eight days of circumcision (dealt with at length in a previous discussion), as well as the nine months of pregnancy. For there were nine months of pregnancy that the courageous women of Israel endured despite the peril that surrounded them on all sides. This is a merit that stems from the indomitable spirit of the Jewish women who, while being subjugated beneath the cruel hand of slavery, went to any and all lengths to ensure the survival of the Jewish family. Despite the inhumane decrees of Pharaoh to murder every male child, they continued to bear children, clinging to their faith in the brilliant future that awaited the Jewish people as well as in the imminent redemption by the Hand of Hashem — without swaying in the slightest.

The Ten Commandments, with all their infinite meaning and endless significance, were also a point of merit for a Jewish nation enslaved in Egypt. The hope that the Jewish people would serve as a medium with which to spread the message of the Ten Commandments to all four corners of the

Who knows ten? I know ten. Ten are the Commandments. Nine are the months of pregnancy. Eight are the days of circumcision. Seven are the days of the week. Six are the Orders of the Mishnah. Five are the Books of the Torah. Four are the Matriarchs. Three are the Patriarchs. Two are the Tablets of the Covenant. One is our God in the heavens and the earth.

Who knows eleven? I know eleven. Eleven are the stars [of Yosef's dream]. Ten are the Commandments. Nine are the months of pregnancy. Eight are the days of circumcision. Seven are the days of the week. Six are the Orders of the Mishnah. Five are the Books of the Torah. Four are the Matriarchs. Three are the Patriarchs. Two are the Tablets of the Covenant. One is our God in the heavens and the earth.

Who knows twelve? I know twelve. Twelve are the tribes. Eleven are the stars. Ten are the Com-

---

world, was a vital justification for their being designated as a nation worthy of redemption from Egypt.

The eleven stars mentioned next refer to the eleven stars that appear in the dream of Joseph and bow down to him. The stars in Joseph's dream symbolize his brothers, the sons of our forefather Jacob. The Torah tells us that Hashem had previously compared the Jewish nation to stars, when he informed Abraham that his descendants would be as vast and as numerous as the stars which light up the heavens. In the dream of Joseph, however, we find an additional element of "bowing." On a deeper level this symbolizes yet another merit of the Jewish nation that justifies their right to redemption. "Like stars who are entirely under the control of the Master of the World, and it is He alone Who determines their time of appearance and departure, as the verse states, *"He brings forth their legions by number"* (Isaiah 40:26) — so, too, the Jewish people are entirely under the control of Hashem and His Torah," (Rabbi Lehmann, *Commentary on the Haggadah*).

"Who knows twelve" — these are the twelve tribes who together form the Jewish nation, with each tribe contributing in its own way toward our people's uniqueness. Each one stands with its feet firmly planted on the same ground, namely the ground of unyielding Jewish faith, and despite all

דְּבְּרַיָּא, תִּשְׁעָה יַרְחֵי לֵדָה, שְׁמוֹנָה יְמֵי מִילָה, שִׁבְעָה יְמֵי שַׁבַּתָּא, שִׁשָּׁה סִדְרֵי מִשְׁנָה, חֲמִשָּׁה חֻמְשֵׁי תוֹרָה, אַרְבַּע אִמָּהוֹת, שְׁלֹשָׁה אָבוֹת, שְׁנֵי לֻחוֹת הַבְּרִית, אֶחָד אֱלֹהֵינוּ שֶׁבַּשָּׁמַיִם וּבָאָרֶץ.

שְׁלֹשָׁה עָשָׂר מִי יוֹדֵעַ? שְׁלֹשָׁה עָשָׂר אֲנִי יוֹדֵעַ. שְׁלֹשָׁה עָשָׂר מִדַּיָּא, שְׁנֵים עָשָׂר שִׁבְטַיָּא, אַחַד עָשָׂר כּוֹכְבַיָּא, עֲשָׂרָה דִבְּרַיָּא, תִּשְׁעָה יַרְחֵי לֵדָה, שְׁמוֹנָה יְמֵי מִילָה, שִׁבְעָה יְמֵי שַׁבַּתָּא, שִׁשָּׁה סִדְרֵי מִשְׁנָה, חֲמִשָּׁה חֻמְשֵׁי תוֹרָה, אַרְבַּע אִמָּהוֹת, שְׁלֹשָׁה אָבוֹת, שְׁנֵי לֻחוֹת הַבְּרִית, אֶחָד אֱלֹהֵינוּ שֶׁבַּשָּׁמַיִם וּבָאָרֶץ.

חַד גַּדְיָא, חַד גַּדְיָא, דְּזַבִּין אַבָּא בִּתְרֵי זוּזֵי, חַד גַּדְיָא חַד גַּדְיָא.

וְאָתָא שׁוּנְרָא וְאָכְלָה לְגַדְיָא, דְּזַבִּין אַבָּא בִּתְרֵי זוּזֵי, חַד גַּדְיָא חַד גַּדְיָא.

וְאָתָא כַלְבָּא וְנָשַׁךְ לְשׁוּנְרָא, דְּאָכְלָה לְגַדְיָא, דְּזַבִּין אַבָּא בִּתְרֵי זוּזֵי, חַד גַּדְיָא חַד גַּדְיָא.

וְאָתָא חוּטְרָא וְהִכָּה לְכַלְבָּא, דְּנָשַׁךְ לְשׁוּנְרָא, דְּאָכְלָה לְגַדְיָא, דְּזַבִּין אַבָּא בִּתְרֵי זוּזֵי, חַד גַּדְיָא חַד גַּדְיָא.

---

those who have opposed them, on solid ground they remain.

The final merit listed is the thirteenth, which represents the Thirteen Attributes of Hashem's Mercy. It was Hashem Himself who revealed these Thirteen Attributes to Moses, and they serve as an everlasting prayer for a nation so dependent upon Divine mercy. As it states in *Masechses Rosh Hashanah*, "Any time that Israel sins — let them perform before me this procedure and I shall forgive them" (*Rosh Hashanah* 17b). Among these

mandments. Nine are the months of pregnancy. Eight are the days of circumcision. Seven are the days of the week. Six are the Orders of the Mishnah. Five are the Books of the Torah. Four are the Matriarchs. Three are the Patriarchs. Two are the Tablets of the Covenant. One is our God in the heavens and the earth.

Who knows thirteen? I know thirteen. Thirteen are the Attributes of Hashem. Twelve are the tribes. Eleven are the stars. Ten are the Commandments. Nine are the months of pregnancy. Eight are the days of circumcision. Seven are the days of the week. Six are the Orders of the Mishnah. Five are the Books of the Torah. Four are the Matriarchs. Three are the Patriarchs. Two are the Tablets of the Covenant. One is our God in the heavens and the earth.

Oㅁne kid, one kid that father bought for two *zuzim*. One kid, one kid.

And the cat came and ate the kid that father bought for two *zuzim*. One kid, one kid.

And the dog came and bit the cat that ate the kid that father bought for two *zuzim*. One kid, one kid.

And the stick came and beat the dog that bit the cat that ate the kid that father bought for two *zuzim*. One kid, one kid.

Thirteen Attributes we find the following: "Compassionate, Gracious, Slow to anger, Abundant in kindness and truth."

It is not enough to simply enunciate these Attributes when we pray to Hashem. Rather, we must strive to incorporate them into our very beings. Hashem has granted us His assurance that if we emulate these Divine Attributes, we will be worthy of forgiveness and atonement. The desire on the part of the Jewish people to make the Attributes of Kindness and Mercy manifest in their day-to-day lives was a merit worthy of earning them a most glorious redemption from the land of Egypt.

וְאָתָא **נוּרָא** וְשָׂרַף לְחוּטְרָא, דְּהִכָּה לְכַלְבָּא,
דְּנָשַׁךְ לְשׁוּנְרָא, דְּאָכְלָה לְגַדְיָא, דְּזַבִּין אַבָּא בִּתְרֵי
זוּזֵי, חַד גַּדְיָא חַד גַּדְיָא.

וְאָתָא **מַיָּא** וְכָבָה לְנוּרָא, דְּשָׂרַף לְחוּטְרָא,
דְּהִכָּה לְכַלְבָּא, דְּנָשַׁךְ לְשׁוּנְרָא, דְּאָכְלָה לְגַדְיָא,
דְּזַבִּין אַבָּא בִּתְרֵי זוּזֵי, חַד גַּדְיָא חַד גַּדְיָא.

וְאָתָא **תוֹרָא** וְשָׁתָה לְמַיָּא, דְּכָבָה לְנוּרָא,
דְּשָׂרַף לְחוּטְרָא, דְּהִכָּה לְכַלְבָּא, דְּנָשַׁךְ לְשׁוּנְרָא,
דְּאָכְלָה לְגַדְיָא, דְּזַבִּין אַבָּא בִּתְרֵי זוּזֵי, חַד גַּדְיָא
חַד גַּדְיָא.

וְאָתָא **הַשּׁוֹחֵט** וְשָׁחַט לְתוֹרָא, דְּשָׁתָא לְמַיָּא,
דְּכָבָה לְנוּרָא, דְּשָׂרַף לְחוּטְרָא, דְּהִכָּה לְכַלְבָּא,
דְּנָשַׁךְ לְשׁוּנְרָא, דְּאָכְלָה לְגַדְיָא, דְּזַבִּין אַבָּא בִּתְרֵי
זוּזֵי, חַד גַּדְיָא חַד גַּדְיָא.

וְאָתָא **מַלְאַךְ הַמָּוֶת** וְשָׁחַט לְשׁוֹחֵט, דְּשָׁחַט
לְתוֹרָא, דְּשָׁתָה לְמַיָּא, דְּכָבָה לְנוּרָא, דְּשָׂרַף
לְחוּטְרָא, דְּהִכָּה לְכַלְבָּא, דְּנָשַׁךְ לְשׁוּנְרָא, דְּאָכְלָה
לְגַדְיָא, דְּזַבִּין אַבָּא בִּתְרֵי זוּזֵי, חַד גַּדְיָא חַד גַּדְיָא.

וְאָתָא **הַקָּדוֹשׁ בָּרוּךְ הוּא** וְשָׁחַט לְמַלְאַךְ
הַמָּוֶת, דְּשָׁחַט לְשׁוֹחֵט, דְּשָׁחַט לְתוֹרָא, דְּשָׁתָה
לְמַיָּא, דְּכָבָה לְנוּרָא, דְּשָׂרַף לְחוּטְרָא, דְּהִכָּה
לְכַלְבָּא, דְּנָשַׁךְ לְשׁוּנְרָא, דְּאָכְלָה לְגַדְיָא, דְּזַבִּין
אַבָּא בִּתְרֵי זוּזֵי, חַד גַּדְיָא חַד גַּדְיָא.

Although the Haggadah formally ends at this point, one should
continue to occupy himself with the story of the Exodus and the laws
of Passover, until sleep overtakes him.

And the fire came and burned the stick that beat the dog that bit the cat that ate the kid that father bought for two *zuzim*. One kid, one kid.

And the water came and doused the fire that burned the stick that beat the dog that bit the cat that ate the kid that father bought for two *zuzim*. One kid, one kid.

And the ox came and drank the water that doused the fire that burned the stick that beat the dog that bit the cat that ate the kid that father bought for two *zuzim*. One kid, one kid.

And the slaughterer came and slaughtered the ox that drank the water that doused the fire that burned the stick that beat the dog that bit the cat that ate the kid that father bought for two *zuzim*. One kid, one kid.

And the angel of death came and slaughtered the slaughterer who slaughtered the ox that drank the water that doused the fire that burned the stick that beat the dog that bit the cat that ate the kid that father bought for two *zuzim*. One kid, one kid.

The Holy One, Blessed is He, then came and slaughtered the angel of death who slaughtered the slaughterer who slaughtered the ox that drank the water that doused the fire that burned the stick that beat the dog that bit the cat that ate the kid that father bought for two *zuzim*. One kid, one kid.

Although the Haggadah formally ends at this point, one should continue to occupy himself with the story of the Exodus and the laws of Passover, until sleep overtakes him.

This volume is part of
THE ARTSCROLL SERIES®
an ongoing project of
translations, commentaries and expositions
on Scripture, Mishnah, Talmud, Halachah,
liturgy, history, the classic Rabbinic writings,
biographies and thought.

For a brochure of current publications
visit your local Hebrew bookseller
or contact the publisher:

Mesorah Publications, ltd

4401 Second Avenue
Brooklyn, New York 11232
(718) 921-9000
www.artscroll.com